"*The Great Poems of the Bible* amply lives up to expectations. It demonstrates clearly that, like Moses of old, James Kugel's eye is very sharp, and his natural force unabated. Kugel's familiarity with and expertise in biblical Hebrew poetry are well established, and he does not disappoint in his confident, masterful handling of even the most difficult Hebrew passages. His analyses of and expansions on the text are informative and often telling, and they are gracefully woven into the commentary as a whole."

—David Noel Freedman,
General Editor of The Anchor Bible series

"James L. Kugel's splendid *The Great Poems of the Bible* is not about eighteen separate poems. It is a connected, scenic walk through Israelite life, history, and spirituality. And it's a lively, understandable trip—like a hike along a forest path with a guide who knows what to point out, and who makes the trip exciting. Each poem is the medium for shedding light on a crucial part of the Bible: God, the soul, prophecy, monarchy, wisdom, the sexes, and the afterlife. If you think this book is just about the poems, think again. The poems are doors, and Kugel opens them—wide enough to see into the biblical world."

—Richard Elliot Friedman,
Author of *The Hidden Book in the Bible*
and *Who Wrote the Bible?*

ALSO BY JAMES L. KUGEL

How to Read the Bible

The Bible As It Was

The Idea of Biblical Poetry

Traditions of the Bible

On Being a Jew

Poetry and Prophecy

In Potiphar's House

Early Biblical Interpretation

The Techniques of Strangeness

the GREAT POEMS of the BIBLE

A READER'S COMPANION WITH NEW TRANSLATIONS

JAMES L. KUGEL

FREE PRESS

New York London Toronto Sydney

FREE PRESS

A Division of Simon & Schuster, Inc.
1230 Avenue of the Americas
New York, NY 10020

This Free Press trade paperback edition October 2008

FREE PRESS and colophon are trademarks of Simon & Schuster, Inc.

For information about special discounts for bulk purchases,
please contact Simon & Schuster Special Sales at
1-800-456-6798 or business@simonandschuster.com

Designed by Maura Fadden Rosenthal/ Mspace

Manufactured in the United States of America

1   3   5   7   9   10   8   6   4   2

Library of Congress Cataloging-in-Publication Data is available.

ISBN-13: 978-1-4165-8902-0
ISBN-10:   1-4165-8902-3

For Yotam, David, Levi, and Alissa

CONTENTS

INTRODUCTION

AT FIRST, THE INVITATION to put together a selection of poems from the Bible seemed to have been addressed to the wrong person. I had actually begun writing about the Bible twenty years earlier by trying to show that the whole idea of biblical "poetry" is a bit off: biblical style is not really divided into two clearly different modes, verse and prose, so talking about the Bible's "poems" is, technically speaking, only an approximation (on this see below). What is more, I don't particularly like to talk about compositions like the psalms or prayers or prophetic speeches as poems, since this word is in any case likely to summon up a host of associations inappropriate to these texts. They are really not very much like what we think of as poetry in the mainstream Western tradition. And even the idea of making a selection—sifting through the Bible to find its high points, as it were—was bound to be somewhat repugnant to anyone who, like me, thinks of it all as sacred Scripture.

Still, there was something intriguing in the proposal. It would be a challenge to try to put together a small collection of texts that might serve as an introduction, and invitation, to the whole Hebrew Bible for those who are not familiar with its contents—not its "high points," necessarily, but a group of different compositions that together embody some of the major themes of the Hebrew Bible and present them in striking and memorable form. And as for "poetry," even if applying the categories of poetry and prose to the Bible can be somewhat misleading, it is nonetheless true that the body of texts conventionally thought of as the Bible's "poetry" shares with our own poetry a vitality and directness that prose often lacks. Perhaps as well, the conventions in both traditions allowed for a little more freedom, and a greater expansiveness, than is usual in ordinary prose.

The idea of translating the texts afresh was also intriguing. Many great translations already exist, yet I confess I was drawn to the prospect of trying to establish a somewhat different tone in my translations, one that might strike the contemporary reader's ear a bit more closely to the way, I imagined, these texts had originally sounded to their first audiences.

The publishers of the present selection also invited me to append to each translation a few words of my own, an invitation that I have willingly accepted. The brief essays that accompany these translations are hardly to be considered biblical commentary, and this for two reasons. The first is obvious: while I try in each to refer to specifics from the biblical text involved, I have refrained from writing a detailed philological or other commentary on every word. Such commentaries abound, and it would be foolish to duplicate, even if modifying here and there, their hard work. The second reason, no doubt less obvious to some, is that this book is not offered as a work of biblical criticism in the usual sense. While I hope I have said nothing here that contradicts all that has been discovered about the Bible over the last two centuries—its original historical setting, the history and culture of biblical Israel's neighbors, the stages and processes of the composition of individual books—I have not sought to make such things my central focus. At the same time, I have also shied away from a strictly literary approach, that is, from writing about the Bible the sorts of things that are written about poetry in American or European literatures. Instead, my goal throughout has been to try to concentrate on what might be called the spiritual reality addressed by different biblical texts. I admit that this is a speculative and rather risky undertaking, but I believe it is worth trying precisely because it is so often neglected. And so, in commenting on one or another topic associated with the passages selected for this book, I have tried to understand the way of seeing that underlies each passage, to enter (with, I admit, a great deal of trepidation) the spiritual world in which biblical Israelites lived. If I may be allowed the immodesty of quoting myself, a paragraph from one of the brief essays that follow really speaks for the whole undertaking:

> Perhaps it is most natural for us today to explain the differences between our view of things and those of earlier civilizations by saying that in premodern times people simply did not know this or that fact, that they were under this or that misapprehension, from which we have now happily freed ourselves. No doubt there is some truth in this proposition. But it seems to me we ought at least to be prepared to entertain the opposite hypothesis as well, that however much progress the intervening centuries may have brought in some domains, they have also led us to lose a way of seeing that existed in former times. By "way of seeing" I mean to suggest something more than simply another point of view; perhaps people were actually enabled by this way of seeing to observe things that we no longer observe nowadays. It is difficult for one who reads the Bible carefully, and takes its words seriously, not to arrive at such a conclusion: something, a certain way of perceiving, has gradually closed inside of us, so that nowadays most people simply do not register, or do not have access to, what had been visible in an earlier age. What we have—all we have—are those texts of the Bible that bear witness to that other way of seeing (and perhaps invite us, with the use of some spiritual imagination, to try to enter into it, open our eyes, and look).

THE BIBLICAL TEXTS THAT APPEAR in this volume have not been cho-
sen to answer to a single standard or criterion. Some, like Psalm
23 or Psalm 137, are simply old favorites. Others, like the Song
of Songs, or Deborah's Song, or David's Lament, have long ago
been singled out as the Bible's poetry par excellence; no book on
this topic might reasonably do without them. Still others have
been chosen partly, though not chiefly, for their representative
value, so that readers might find here a sampling of passages from
both early and late in the biblical period, as well as examples of
different sorts of elevated writings, from prophetic speeches to
songs of praise, and from the one-line poems of biblical wisdom
to the extended supplications of the Psalms. And, since this book
aims as well at providing something of an introduction to the
Bible as a whole, I have chosen one or two passages because they
raise interesting questions or shed light on topics of general inter-
est to readers of the Bible. Whatever other considerations I have
had in mind, however, I have also tried to come up with a selec-
tion that works well *as poetry*, a series of texts that can speak to
readers directly and, I hope, evocatively, movingly, in English.

Readers of some of my previous books may be puzzled by
something in the present work, namely, its steadfast insistence on
reading these texts afresh, without reference to the great interpre-
tive tradition that has accompanied the Bible through all its
meanderings. My own thoughts on the relevance of that tradition
have not changed: our Bible is inevitably the Traditional Bible,
that is, its meaning will always be mediated by the traditions of
reading and interpretation that have accompanied it from ancient
times.* But what I wanted to do here—not terribly different, in
fact, from what many a medieval Jewish interpreter of the Bible

---

*See, in particular, my book, *The Bible As It Was* (Cambridge: Harvard
University Press, 1997).

did—was to offer a kind of obiter dictum, a speculative engage-
ment with a group of biblical texts in an attempt to reveal some-
thing new about the biblical roots of our postbiblical faith,
perhaps something as well about a moment, or series of moments,
in the history of our apprehension of God, moments whose reali-
ty can sometimes slip away now that we are safely on the other
side of them.

Before turning to the texts themselves, however, there are two
topics to which I should address myself here: the choices I have
had to make in translating these biblical texts, and the nature of
biblical poetry.

Any translator faces a host of choices. There is almost always
more than one way to say something, so the translator has to
decide: Should I say it in the most elevated style available or in
some ordinary, down-to-earth sort of speech? Should I make the
text sound as if it were being uttered today, or give it the flavor of
something a little older, even out-of-date? Should I make it sound
as if it were being spoken by one of us, or try gently to remind
readers that this is still a foreign text, written in a language and
culture quite different from our own? With regard to the Bible
specifically, additional questions pose themselves. Does the
sacredness of the text mean that I should strive to translate as lit-
erally as possible, even if that means saying things that are just
not said in my own language? Or should I, on the contrary, try to
come up with something that will sound to readers nowadays
pretty much the way the biblical text must have sounded to its
original audience, even if that means translating a bit freely here
and there?

To such questions there are never hard-and-fast answers, and
biblical translations in particular run the gamut of the possibili-
ties mentioned. When the Jews of ancient Alexandria translated
the Hebrew Bible into Greek starting in the third century B.C.E.

(Before the Common Era), they produced a translation that sounded fairly natural in Greek but that here and there, quite intentionally, twists normal Greek syntax or vocabulary in order to reflect some feature of the Hebrew original. Far from being despised, these "biblicisms" came to be prized in Greek—so much so that later Greek authors, trying to give their own writings a biblical flavor, would sometimes incorporate these same strange turns of phrase or style into their own compositions. The oddness made them sound authentic, perhaps even holy. The Old Latin translation, by contrast, was a disaster. It had too many infelicities—so many that potential converts to Christianity, when first exposed to the Hebrew Bible in translation, were reported to observe that the God of the Hebrews apparently did not know Latin grammar. It was to correct this situation that Jerome, a great stylist, was commissioned to translate the Bible into Latin afresh, and he did so brilliantly. He basically used the Latin of his day, a simple but dignified idiom, though he was not innocent of an occasional evocation of the lofty Latin of Cicero or Vergil from years gone by. His translation, later known as the Vulgate, became the standard for centuries in the Christian West. But in other languages and locales translators were often stubbornly literal, sometimes going so far as to modify the syntax and even the gender of individual words in their own language in order to duplicate "exactly"—so they said—the biblical original.

In English, translators of the Bible have frequently straddled past and present, fancy and ordinary, in their choice of style. For example, many Bible translators continued to use the "Thou" form (some still do today) long after it had fallen out of use precisely because this form seems to say "lofty," "authoritative"— nay, "biblical." But others dropped it almost as soon as it became obsolete; presumably, these translators found it stilted and unnatural, hence unsuited to their goals. *Thou* was still in common use when the King James translation of the Bible was made, but its artisans were not above an occasional archaism here and there. They sometimes used the word *kine* for "cow" or "cattle," for example, even though the term had by then disappeared from ordinary speech. Yet on the whole, that translation had a refreshing newness about it—indeed, its publication was an event in the history of English literature, one that sanctified the common speech and turned a previously disdained hybrid jargon into a language in which high deeds could be recounted.

From all this it should be clear that translators of the Bible always find themselves on the same stylistic continuum, having to choose between high and low, ancient-sounding and contemporary, native and slightly foreign, slavishly literal and daringly free. In the present volume I have not set out to follow one extreme or the other, nor have I even translated in one style throughout. I have set this as my overall goal: to try to create in English the same impression that the biblical text would have made on the ears of its first audience. This in itself implies a certain flexibility of style, since the Bible is not all of a piece. The words of the prophet Amos, for example, are generally blunt, straightforward. He "tells it like it is," often (though not always) without literary embellishment. Job's book, on the other hand, is replete with fancy flourishes. His "comforters" speak in the elegant symmetries of ancient wisdom and more than once are made to sound full of high sentence and a bit obtuse. Job too speaks loftily, though sometimes, in marked contrast to them, he can also be very down-to-earth, even crass. The Song of Songs is written in a very northern, "pastoral"-sounding language designed to evoke the simple speech of countryfolk; much of it sounds utterly colloquial. How can a translator adopt a single style for such diverse material?

One thing I have definitely avoided in my translation is the attempt to "strangify" the English, to forgo the straightforward in favor of something—anything—that sounds unusual. Oddly, this has always tempted some translators of the Bible. But there is really no reason to translate the Hebrew word for "generations" as "begettings," "altar" as "slaughter-site," "offering" as "grain-gift," or "bed" as "place-of-lying," and so forth.* It may be fun for readers who don't know Hebrew to imagine that they are somehow getting closer to the original through such contortions, but actually the opposite is true. This style of translating only succeeds in making the language sound bizarre, which is certainly not how it sounded to its original audience. Such an approach is not terribly different, really, from that of those translators mentioned earlier who changed the syntax or grammatical gender of their native languages in order to "duplicate" the biblical original. Thus, there is no point in saying that what God told Abraham in Gen. 12:1 was "Go-you-forth . . . and I will make a great nation of you and will give-you-blessing" (as one recent translation does). All those hyphens do is turn a straightforward promise—"Leave your homeland . . . and I will make you a great nation and bless you"—into something more appropriate to an Indian chief in a 1950s Western. Likewise, the fact that Hebrew (but not English) employs the repetition of the verbal root for emphasis hardly justifies translating Exod. 22:22–23 as "Oh, if you afflict, afflict them... For (then) they will cry, cry out to me, and I will hearken, hearken to their cry." This may indeed duplicate repetitions in the original text, but at the expense of sounding like pidgin English or some sort of prolonged stutter. To a speaker of biblical Hebrew this sentence sounded altogether nor-

*All the examples in this paragraph are taken from Everett Fox, *The Five Books of Moses: Genesis, Exodus, Leviticus, Numbers and Deuteronomy—A New Translation* (New York: Schocken, 1995).

mal, rather like, in English, "If you indeed afflict them, then they will certainly cry out to Me, and I guarantee, I will answer them." Sometimes, such efforts only produce confusion: "Now a woman—when the flow of her blood flows for many days, when it is not the time of her being-apart, or when it flows out over-and-above her being-apart, all the days of her *tamei* flow she shall be like (during) the days of her being-apart; she is *tamei*"— wha?

It is all a bit like someone who says: "True, other people have tried to translate Balzac from French before me, but they haven't really captured what he said. When Balzac writes 's'il vous plaît,' for example, they translate this as 'please.' But the French doesn't say *please*; it says, 'if it pleases you.' So my translation will always say 'if it pleases you.' I am duplicating the French original." Is this true? Only in the most foolish, literal-minded sense. Although the French phrase "s'il vous plaît" does indeed contain the words "if," "it," "you," and "pleases," the phrase as a whole is in every way the functional equivalent of *please* in English: it is what the French say when we say "please." So to have some character in a novel say, "Pass the butter, if it pleases you" would be fundamentally to distort the sense of the original. The translation sounds stilted and arcane, whereas the original sounds natural. So too with God's assertion that "I am a delivering-shield to you" and a thousand other curiosities—these are just another form of saying "if it pleases you."

One problem that is always difficult in biblical translation concerns the name of God. There are several ways of referring to God in Hebrew, but two in particular. The first is what one might call the "generic" term for God: indeed, this Hebrew word can refer either to Israel's God or, when construed as a plural, to the gods of other nations. In that sense, "God" is no doubt the best translation, and that is how translators have rendered it in English, French, German, Yiddish, Russian, and so forth, going back to the ancient Greek translation mentioned earlier. The second term is often thought of as the "proper name" of God. It is spelled in Hebrew with the letters Y, H, W, and H (the vowels between the consonants, as in other Hebrew words, were not recorded in writing). From an early period, writing this sacred name down or speaking it aloud came to be severely restricted. In Hebrew, the word corresponding to "my lord" was often substituted for it in ordinary speech. Quite naturally, the word *kurios*, "Lord," then came to be used to substitute for this "proper name of God" in the old Greek translation, and in like fashion *Dominus* ("Lord") in Latin and "Lord" in English. To distinguish this sacred name from the ordinary word for "lord" (meaning "master" and the like)—since this word likewise appears in the Bible—translators adopted the convention of writing the sacred name in all capital letters, LORD, and the ordinary word as "lord" or "Lord." I have followed these conventions in the present work.*

---

*In modern times, some have felt even these equivalent terms to be too sacred to be used. In particular, many Jews in English-speaking countries have taken to substituting a dash for the vowels in the words mentioned, hence "G-d" and "L-rd." Others now prefer to substitute the word "Ha-shem," Hebrew for "the name," in place of the "proper name" referred to earlier. I have hesitated in regard to these questions; they do not, in English, involve issues of Jewish law per se, but are nonetheless closely connected to people's sensibilities and perceptions. It should be pointed out that the use of Ha-shem as a substitute name is probably based on a historical misunderstanding of a certain passage in the Mishnah (Yoma 6:2), though that is not my main reason for avoiding it here; its use in this volume would, quite simply, impose an unnecessary barrier between this book and much of its intended readership. The same is true, to a lesser degree, of "G-d" and "L-rd," though there is certainly much to be said for indicating in visual fashion the sanctity inherent in any such reference. If, in the end, I have decided to opt for the more common way of writing these words, it is only because it is more common; that is to say, I have done so in consideration of those same readers just mentioned, to whom in particular this book is addressed.

AND NOW TO BIBLICAL POETRY. I hesitate to say too much by way of introduction: this book as a whole is intended to serve as (among other things) an introduction to the subject, and I have specifically sought to elaborate on various aspects of it in the essays that follow (see, in particular, "A Prophet in Israel," "Where Wisdom Is Found," "Tough Women," "Solomon's Riddles," "The Fall of Jerusalem," and "For Everyone, a Season"). But a few general points ought nevertheless to be mentioned from the outset.

Poetry in many languages is written in some sort of identifiable meter; rhyme also characterizes the poetry of many different peoples. The poetry of the Bible, by contrast, has neither rhyme nor fixed meter. Instead, it is characterized by an ideal sentence form that is repeated line after line. The form might be schematized as:

$$ \underline{\hspace{5cm}} \, , \, \underline{\hspace{5cm}} \, . $$
$$ \text{A} \qquad\qquad\qquad \text{B} $$

That is to say, the sentence form consists of two parts, A and B. Each part is a short phrase or clause, usually only two, three, or four words long. The parts are separated by a brief pause (symbolized by the comma), and end in a full stop (symbolized by the period). But the contrast between this pause in the middle and the stop at the end is really a way of highlighting the relationship between the two clauses. B is always a continuation of A, related to A even though it is separated from it by the syntactic structure of the line. That is why this pause is only a pause and not a stop. By contrast, the stop at the end of B is "full" in the sense that one line does not usually carry over into the next line. The basic line of Hebrew poetry is what poets call an "end-stopped" line.

A few examples might make all this more vivid. The book of Isaiah foretells the in-gathering of Israel's exiles in these terms:

> Now I will bring your children from the east, and from the west I will gather you up.
>
> I will say to the north wind, "Come on!" and to the south wind, "Don't hold back!
>
> Give Me My sons from afar, and My daughters from the ends of the earth!"

Isa. 43:5-6

Each line, it will be observed, follows the basic sentence-form described earlier. While writing in this form may appear to be rather simple, such is not really the case (though it is certainly not as difficult as writing, say, rhymed, iambic pentameter verse in English). It is not so easy to create a Part B that is immediately recognized as both distinct from Part A yet connected to it. And so in this passage the prophet has gone out of his way to make that separate-yet-connected status clear. In the first sentence, for example, even if each clause were presented on its own as a separate sentence:

> Now I will bring your children from the east. From the west I will gather you up.

we would still have no difficulty in recognizing that they are related, coordinated utterances, since certain things in Part A are matched in Part B: "I will bring" is similar to "I will gather," "your children" is similar to "you," and "east" and "west" are commonly paired opposites. All these things help give us the feeling that Part B rounds out or finishes off Part A: I will bring your children from the east, and I will gather you up from the west. Part B is A's completion and perfect complement. As for the next two lines, it is to be noted that in both, the verb that appears in Part A is implied but not stated in Part B:

> I will say to the north wind, "Come on!" and to the south wind [*I will say*], "Don't hold back!
>
> Give Me My sons from afar, and [*give Me*] My daughters from the ends of the earth!"

Such verb ellipsis is a very common way of establishing the connectedness of A and B; B literally cannot stand without A before it. In addition, there are, in the first line, the commonly paired opposites "north wind" and "south wind" and the grammatically parallel imperatives "Come on!" and "Don't hold back!" or, in the next line, "My sons" and "My daughters" and "from afar" and "from the ends of the earth." All these things help create the feeling of a tight complementarity between Parts A and B and provide the same sort of satisfaction that rhyme sometimes creates in English verse.

Biblical critics used to refer to this Hebrew style as "parallelism," but that is not a very good name, since it focuses on what was merely one means for creating the feeling of connectedness between A and B and promotes it to the essence of the style. But verb ellipsis, for example, is just as important as parallelism as a means for creating this feeling. So is out-and-out repetition, for example:

> Vanity of vanities, says Koheleth, vanity of vanities, all is vanity.
>
> ECCLES. 1 : 2

> Until there arose a Deborah, until there arose a mother in Israel . . .
>
> Up, up, Deborah! Up, up and sing it out!
>
> JUD. 5 : 7, 12

The essence of this style is really the ideal sentence form outlined above, Part A and Part B. Now, the verses cited above from Isaiah are particularly tightly organized, and the various means by which the correspondence of Part A to Part B is expressed stand out clearly. However, this passage from Isaiah is not typical of most lines of biblical poetry; it represents the highest, most formal, use of this style. Somewhat less formal are the following lines:

> This is where birds make their nest, the stork has its home in fir-trees.
>
> High mountains are for wild goats, and crags shelter the hares.
>
> You made the moon to mark off the seasons, and You know the route of the sun.
>
> When You bring darkness nighttime descends, and all the forest creatures come out.
>
> Ps. 104:17–20

The first three lines have some of the usual sort of correspondence markers between Parts A and B ("nest" and "home," "birds" and "stork," and so on), though a bit less intensely than in the Isaiah example; but the fourth line merely presents two conjoined utterances. The word "and" in that line makes it clear that Part B is connected to Part A, but the sorts of correspondences seen elsewhere are absent here. There are a great many lines like this one in the Psalms. Consider the following:

> As a deer longs for a coursing stream, so my soul longs for You.
>
> My soul thirsts for God, the living God, for the time when I may go to see God's face.
>
> Night and day, tears have been my food, as all day long I hear, "Where is your God?"
>
> Ps. 42:2–4

While A and B in the first line constitute a straightforward comparison, "Just as . . . so . . .", in which the correspondence of the two halves is clear enough, in the second and third lines Part B is simply a continuation of Part A, another clause tacked on with scarcely any overt correspondence markers. There is certainly a feeling of some regularity, of constructedness, in these lines, a regularity that derives from the repeated sequence of partial and full stops, but the feeling of clause-for-clause correspondence is certainly less striking than in the previous examples.

Incidentally, biblical poetry was not originally written down with periods and commas of any kind, and, precisely because, in lines like those just cited, our modern standards of punctuation may require that there be other commas besides the one representing the pause between A and B, I generally prefer to indicate that medial pause by a single vertical line and the final pause by a double vertical line, thus:

> As a deer longs for a coursing stream | so my soul longs for You, God.||
>
> My soul thirsts for God, the living God | for the time when I may go and see God's face ||
>
> Night and day, tears have been my food | as all day long I hear, "Where is your God?" ||

This form of annotation tends to work better for another reason as well: sometimes in English the "final" pause might better be punctuated with a semicolon or even a comma (in other words, it is not always altogether final from the standpoint of English punctuation). Moreover, sometimes the medial pause is even less than what a comma might indicate in English; it is simply a *possible* place to pause, a syntactic opportunity. Consider these familiar lines from Psalm 23:

You set a table for me | right in the face of my enemies ||

You anoint my head with oil | my cup overflows ||

Goodness and kindness alone will pursue me | all throughout my life ||

and I will dwell in the house of the LORD | for a length of time ||

Ps. 23:5–6

Of the above lines, only the second one has a clear break between Parts A and B. The others all have a place where one *can* pause slightly, but the pause is not imposed by the syntax as in other lines.

Not only is the medial pause rather weak in these lines from Psalm 23, but the correspondence markers are almost completely absent. This psalm, in other words, is much less formal, much less structured than any of the previous examples. Was it that the psalmist somehow couldn't manage to create lines like Isaiah's? Hardly. To say that would be as foolish as to say that, for example, Walt Whitman or Wallace Stevens couldn't manage to write in rhymed couplets the way poets did in England in the eighteenth century. Styles change from time to time, and even within a particular period, very different sorts of compositions can sometimes be written by two contemporary authors, or even by a single author on two different occasions or for two different purposes. The effect of the kind of construction found in Psalm 23 or (to choose another psalm from this book) Psalm 137 is indeed less formal, less structured, than the style of Isaiah above, but each way of writing, as will be seen, is altogether appropriate to its own purpose and message.

The very looseness of their form raises an interesting question, however. How different is biblical poetry from biblical prose? The answer is what one might suppose. Sometimes the difference is very clear: there is no mistaking Isaiah's "high style" for ordinary discourse. But the line between Psalm 137 and a "prose" speech in the books of Samuel or Kings, for example, is scarcely visible; in another literature both might have been perceived as mere prose. In other words, the highly structured, ornamented style of biblical poetry at its most formal slides imperceptibly into something far less regular—the style of a great many psalms, for example—and that style in turn slides into what we call prose. There are not two ways of writing in biblical Hebrew but a continuum of styles; the extremes at either end are easily distinguished, but there is much that is located in the middle ground.

That is one reason why, as suggested earlier, talking about "poetry" and "prose" in the Bible can be misleading. Biblical Israelites had no terms corresponding to these, and there is no indication that they thought of their sacred writings as falling under one of these two general headings. If we talk about biblical "poetry," then, it must be understood that this is only an approximation, a way of referring to those prophetic speeches, psalms, songs, wise sayings, and laws that were written on the "formal" end of biblical Hebrew's stylistic continuum. At the same time, like *all* other poetry, the works presented in this book are also full of striking images and comparisons, and there is no doubt that they are often stylized and carefully crafted, so that every word counts. In this sense the label of "poetry" is altogether appropriate, as, I hope, will be seen presently.

I would like to thank those friends and colleagues who have been kind enough to read through parts of this book and/or offer suggestions concerning it, in particular: Gary Anderson, Hayyim Angel, Daniel Braunschwig, Mavis Dobbs, Roland Gill, Peter Machinist, Lawrence Rhu, and Harold Schimmel. My thanks as well to Bruce Nichols of the Free Press and Ellen Geiger of Curtis, Brown Ltd. for their help in making this book possible.

CHAPTER 1

PSALM 104

BLESS THE LORD, O MY SOUL—O LORD MY GOD,
YOU ARE VERY GREAT.

[At the creation:]

Clothed in glory and honor, You wrapped Yourself in light.

Then You put up the sky like a tent and covered it over with
water.

The clouds You took as Your chariot and rode off on the wings
of the wind.

The winds themselves You made messengers, and flames of fire
Your servants.

Once You had set the earth on its struts, so it never would
swerve or sway,

You cloaked it with water all over, water loomed over the
mountains.

How they flee at Your cry, those waters, at the sound of Your
thunder they jump back in terror,

running up mountains or down into valleys, to whatever place
You established for them.

You drew lines for them never to cross, never again will they
cover the land.

You set loose the springs that gush into rivers, cascading down between mountains,

watering all the life of the plain and slaking the animals' thirst.

Above them dwell the birds of the sky, calling out from the tops of branches.

You let water flow from Your upper abode, down the mountains to sop the earth,

Ripening grass for cattle and grains for people to harvest, bringing food from out of the dirt:

wine to gladden the hearts of men, oil to brighten their faces, and bread to fill their insides.

Let the trees of the LORD drink deep, the Lebanon cedars He planted.

This is where birds make their nest, the stork has her home in fir trees.

High mountains are for wild goats, and crags shelter the hares.

You made the moon to mark off the seasons, and You know the route of the sun.

When You bring darkness nighttime descends, and all the forest creatures come out.

Lions go roaring after their prey, seeking their food from God.

With the sun's first ray back they go, to lie down in darkened lairs.

People trudge off to work, toiling until the dusk.

How great are Your works, O LORD—

every one You made with wisdom, the world teems with what You created.

The huge, the broad-armed sea, where numberless creatures swim, tiny alongside of big—

here the ships go to and fro, and the leviathan You formed for amusement.

All of them look to You, hoping You'll give them their food in its time.

What You give them they gobble up; if You open Your hand they are fed.

But if You hide Your face, then they are dismayed.

Should You take back their spirits they perish and return to the dust of the earth.

Let loose Your spirit and their fatness comes back, the land's surface is made new again.

May the LORD's glory endure forever, let the LORD rejoice in
His creatures.

When He looks to the earth, it shudders; if He touches the
mountains they smoke.

I will sing to the LORD as I live, praise my God as long as I
breathe.

May my words be pleasing to Him, I truly rejoice in the LORD.

And let sinners be wiped from the land, let the wicked exist no
more.

Bless the LORD, O my soul, Halleluyah.

A Place in the System

By the start of the twentieth century, the previous two hundred years' accumulating doubts about the existence of God had acquired a certain swirling momentum and had begun to look to many people—even the religious folk of the American prairie—like a menacing storm, a cyclone, off in the not-too-distant plain. It might seem odd to seek to identify that cyclone with another, the famous one that sent Dorothy off on her extraordinary voyage to the Land of Oz. Nevertheless, I am always struck when I read that book (or see the movie) by its undertone of theological questioning. Certainly, *The Wonderful Wizard of Oz* is a fable about disillusionment, about discovering that the one of whom all in the Emerald City speak in hushed tones of reverence does not exist in reality but is merely a human invention. Was it not the case that Oz's author, L. Frank Baum, had in the back of his mind another sort of disillusionment, the sort that most people at the start of the twentieth century still preferred not to talk about openly?*

Dorothy and her companions—four people in difficult straits who set out on a pilgrimage in search of a miraculous cure—do not at first seem very different from the heroes of innumerable quest tales. Had this story followed the traditional scenario, it might indeed have been what Baum claimed it was in the preface to the first edition, a kind of non-frightening remake of the traditional fairy tale:

---

*Students of Oz have interpreted it in all sorts of other ways, finding in its details evocations of everything from the gold standard controversy to Freudian psychology. Underneath it all, however, the theme of religious disillusionment seems to me central.

[T]he old-time fairy-tale, having served for generations, may now be classed as "historical" in the children's library; for the time has come for a series of newer "wonder tales" in which the stereotyped genie, dwarf and fairy are eliminated, together with all the horrible and blood-curdling incident devised by their authors to point a fearsome moral to each tale. Modern education includes morality; therefore, the modern child seeks only enter-tainment in its wonder-tales and gladly dispenses with all dis-agreeable incident. Having this thought in mind, the story of "The Wonderful Wizard of Oz" was written solely to pleasure children of today.

But what was truly different about Oz was not its avoidance of the "horrible and blood-curdling" (it is still pretty frightening to most children). Rather, it was that this was a quest tale that ends with the questers' discovery that their efforts have all been in vain. The thaumaturgical Oz, it turns out, is no supernatural manipulator of reality but merely the jerry-rigged front man for an ordinary mortal, nay, a humbug, and it is this discovery that is the central movement of the book, the conclusion of the quest itself. All is not lost, of course, after the questers find out the truth; they do eventually gain some measure of satisfaction, and Dorothy even finds her way back to Kansas. But the fundamental lesson that she and the others learn is that frauds do exist, and that most of the people can indeed be fooled—are being fooled—most of the time. Even the Emerald City, it turns out, was only emerald because the Wizard had rigged up little green-tinted spectacles for all the citizens to wear. "But isn't everything here green?" Dorothy asks. "No more than any other city," Oz replies. "But when you wear green spectacles, why of course everything you see looks green to you."

Oz himself is sometimes presented in ways designed to evoke

the Almighty, albeit indirectly. "I am Oz, the Great and Terrible," he booms out to every visitor, and to readers of the Bible, the cadence of this greeting is unmistakable ("the great and terrible God" is virtually a biblical cliché, Deut. 7:21, 10:17; Dan. 9:4; Neh. 1:5, 4:8, 9:32). "Who are you," he continues, "and why do you seek me?" The word "seek" here is likewise Bible-ese and hardly standard English; indeed, now seeing Oz face to face, how could a visitor be said still to be *seeking* him at all? But "seek" in Oz's greeting is the English equivalent of the Hebrew *baqqesh* or *darosh H'*—usually mistranslated in English Bibles as "seek the LORD," but clearly intended in the sense of "seek the favor of the LORD" or "make a request of the LORD" (see Isa. 51:1, 55:6; Ezek. 20:3; Amos 5:4, 6; Ps. 40:16, 69:6, 105:3–4). To this inquiry Dorothy replies with her own pseudo-biblicism, "I am Dorothy, the Small and Meek."

Toward the end of the story, after completing their mission, Dorothy and her friends return to Oz's Throne Room only to find it empty:

> Presently, they heard a Voice, seeming to come from somewhere near the top of the great dome, and it said, solemnly,
> "I am Oz, the Great and Terrible. Why do you seek me?"
> They looked again in every part of the room, and then, seeing no one, Dorothy asked,
> "Where are you?"
> "I am everywhere," answered the Voice, "but to the eyes of common mortals I am invisible."

Oz's invisible omnipresence (however fleeting) is another feature he shares with Israel's Deity. So when it turns out that the Voice is merely that of "an old man with a bald head and wrinkled face," I suspect that, especially among Sunday School graduates of a century ago, there must have been more than one or two who in their hearts identified this moment with the other one alluded to earlier, that still-largely-unexpressed disillusionment waiting somewhere at the back of America's spiritual closet.

Nowadays, people are less reticent about their doubts. It would be so nice, they say, if there really were a God. But in their hearts they know that it cannot be so, no matter what they tell their children. There comes a time in every life when some little Toto will always knock over the screen of transmitted fantasy and reveal the Deity to be of altogether human manufacture.

WHAT IS SURPRISING is not that *The Wonderful Wizard of Oz*, along with quite a few other books of the last few centuries, have in one way or another evoked the doubts that nag at people's faith. Rather, what is remarkable is that there is not some ancient Israelite equivalent, some text somewhere in the Hebrew Bible that, even if only as indirectly as Oz, at least raises the question of God's existence or delicately, allegorically, suggests that perhaps a great fraud is being perpetrated. But there is not. Job and Ecclesiastes question God's justice, Jeremiah may wish even to take Him to court, but His existence, it seems, was simply not open to question, not even perceived as a possible subject of discourse.* The

---

*The only apparent exception is really no exception at all. Psalm 14:1 (the same verse appears in Ps. 53:2) is sometimes mistranslated, "The fool says in his heart there is no God." But the last phrase really means "God is not present," that is, He certainly exists but is somewhere else, unoccupied (for now) with this particular matter. This use of *ēn* in the sense of "not present" is common enough in biblical Hebrew (for example, Gen. 5:24, 39:11, 41:8, 42:36, 44:31). Indeed, the New Jewish Publication Society translation of the Bible goes so far as to render Psalm 14:1 "The benighted man thinks 'God does not care,'" since not caring is the apparent significance of this divine absence.

Bible does not hesitate to report blasphemous statements made about God by other nations or renegade Israelites—to the effect that some foreign deity is more powerful than Israel's God, or that God does not see the suffering of innocent people, or that God does not punish wrongdoers, or that God has abandoned Israel—but nowhere do these blasphemous statements ever include the simple assertion that God does not exist. Apparently, such a thought just never occurred to the blasphemers in question, nor to anyone else. On the contrary, God's being and fundamental nature seem everywhere simply to be assumed, a fact so well known as to require no further elaboration. For the same reason, it would seem, the Bible does not begin by defining God or demonstrating His presence in reality. There must have been no need.

Those who have sought to account for this state of affairs have sometimes chalked it up to a kind of intellectual inertia. People had always believed in "the gods," they say, so even after Israel had come along and replaced a plurality of deities with One, this alone did not necessitate a reexamination of the whole concept of divinity. God simply came to substitute for the gods without any more fundamental change. But such an answer hardly seems convincing. Inertia can carry the human spirit only so far; eventually, people do end up asking fundamental questions. Certainly life in the ancient world offered up its share of undeserved suffering; did not frequent droughts and famines, wars and natural disasters, as well as massive outbreaks of disease and an infant mortality rate that might have reached fifty percent—did not such things cause people to wonder who this God might be who was solely responsible for their fate? By what standards did He judge the world? Yet even Job's wife, seeing her husband's undeserved pains, can only say to him, "Curse your God and die." Why did she not say, "It seems you were wrong about God after all. He cannot exist if all this can happen to you"? It could hardly have been inertia that prevented one hundred percent of the people from ever considering such a possibility.

Nor, for that matter, do I think it has to do with any "primitive" state of thought that is sometimes alleged to have existed at that time. Primitive thought was left behind long before the time of biblical Israel, and there really is no indication that the ancient Israelites would have had difficulty in grasping our sort of conceptualizing or abstract thinking. People sometimes say, for example, that the argument from creation was inevitably persuasive to ancient societies: since anything like the theory of evolution was inconceivable to them, the world as it exists simply had to have a Creator somewhere minding the store. But even if such an argument is correct (and I do not believe it is), it would hardly account for the biblical evidence. After all, a divine Creator could certainly have made the world and then disappeared, ceased to exist, having set in motion the autonomous forces of the universe. In fact, this idea was advanced elsewhere in the ancient world; it was just never expressed, even by the greatest blasphemers, in the Bible.

Perhaps it is most natural for us today to explain the differences between our view of things and those of earlier civilizations by saying that in premodern times people simply did not know this or that fact, that they were under this or that misapprehension, from which we have now happily freed ourselves. No doubt there is some truth in this proposition. But it seems to me we ought at least to be prepared to entertain the opposite hypothesis as well, that however much progress the intervening centuries may have brought in some domains, they have also led us to lose a way of seeing that existed in former times. By "way of seeing" I mean to suggest something more than simply another point of view; perhaps people were actually enabled by this way of seeing to observe things that we no longer observe today. It is difficult for one who reads the Bible carefully, and takes its words seriously, not to arrive at such a conclusion: something, a certain way of perceiving, has gradually closed inside of us, so that nowadays most people simply do not register, or do not have access to, what had been visible in an earlier age. What we have—all we have—are those texts of the Bible that bear witness to that other way of seeing (and perhaps invite us, with the use of some spiritual imagination, to try to enter into it, open our eyes, and look).

One thing that is strikingly different in the biblical way of seeing—and it is certainly related to the matter at hand—has to do with the whole notion of the self that is found in the Bible and the way in which that self fits into the larger world. A human being just *is* very small, and God, as the opening line of this psalm asserts, is "very big."* In other words, it is not (or not simply) that biblical man cannot conceive of the world without God for some mechanistic reason—because, for example, the world could not *function* without God. Rather it is first and foremost that he cannot conceive of himself without God, without, that is, some notion of how he and the rest of the little creatures down here fit into the much, much larger world. This is especially true of his own capacities. They extend only so far, and if he is to be able to understand anything of the world beyond them, he needs to fit himself into the world, he needs a form of reference beyond himself.

Psalm 104, like certain other psalms, is concerned essentially with this matter of fitting into the world. Characteristically, God's greatness—the psalm's announced subject—is not expressed in His own being. Apart from a phrase here or there

---

*"You are very great" may sound a little more dignified and psalmlike, but the Hebrew literally means "very big."

("Clothed in glory and honor, You wrapped Yourself in light."), the psalm really has nothing to say about what God Himself is *like*; it all has to do with what He has done, how He has arranged the universe. This description of God's deeds has at times something oddly light-hearted or whimsical about it, for that is how this world must look from God's point of view. So it is that God has, in most homey fashion, set up the universe like a tent or hut, thatching it up on top with the waters that descend on us from time to time in the form of rain. The mighty oceans and rivers (an ancient figure of disorder and threatening chaos) here cower and jump back at God's might, their precious liquids now tamed to be part of the great food chain. Nothing here is fearsome.

> When You bring darkness nighttime descends, and all the forest creatures come out.
> Lions go roaring after their prey, seeking their food from God.
> With the sun's first ray back they go, to lie down in darkened lairs.
> People trudge off to work, toiling until the dusk.

Those lions aren't really pious; they don't *know* that they are seeking their food from God, and there is something a little whimsical about saying they do. But such is the happy world of this psalm—for indeed, it says, were it not for divine generosity, the pious lions would certainly starve. They are another, equal member in the great machinery of God. So also for the leviathan.* Its frightening, half-mythic, character may be its salient feature elsewhere in the Bible. But here, all the air has

---

* Not a whale, by the way, though what a leviathan was is far from certain: perhaps originally the term referred to some sort of crocodile, though here and elsewhere it seems to be a kind of mythological dragon or other beast of undetermined physique.

been let out of it; it is just a divine plaything, an utterly harmless curiosity in that great world that the great God has made. What is not subsumed? The roaring winds and flashing fire from heaven—these are God's angels, His own chosen messengers and intermediaries.

SINCE GOD IS VERY BIG, man is very small. To put it another way, God's space begins precisely where man's ends, so that there is no temptation for man to fill the void. Thus, when Jacob's wife Rachel finds herself unable to conceive and she begs him, "Give me children!" he quite naturally replies, "Am I in God's stead?" What lies beyond human capacity or human reckoning is not simply part of some undefined wasteland: it is all actively part of a coherent space controlled by, defined by, God. There is likewise no frontier, no outer space: "He counts off the stars by number, calls them all by name" (Ps. 147:4). That is, human ignorance in one matter or another does not mean that the thing is simply "unknown"; it is part of the coherent body of things known to God of which we humans possess only a small portion. Indeed, what is striking about the psalm from which this last line is cited—a hymn rather similar to Psalm 104—is precisely how the cosmic and the historical, society's domain and a person's inner psyche, *everything* is jumbled together, all part of God's great machine:

> The LORD rebuilds Jerusalem, gathering the scattered ones of Israel;
> He heals the broken-hearted and binds up their wounds.
> He counts off the stars by number, calls them all by name.
> Great is our Lord, and mighty, His wisdom is unfathomable.

The LORD lifts up the lowly and humbles the wicked to the ground.

Sing to the LORD with thanksgiving, make melody to our God with the harp.

He covers the skies with clouds, preparing rain for the earth; He makes the mountains green with grass.

He gives food to animals, even to the crows when they caw.

He is not swayed by the horse's pull, or the strength in the legs of a man;

the LORD delights in those who fear Him, in those who yearn for His favor.

Ps. 147:2–11

TO FEEL, IN THIS SENSE, part of God's world was the primary force that shaped the religious outlook of a great many psalms; indeed, it is found abundantly in other parts of the Bible as well. Biblical man, one might say, was *fundamentally* small, always part of a larger system. Another passage in the Psalms presents a little human hounded by God, unable to draw a breath or leave his house or even think a thought without bumping into the Impinging Deity:

O LORD, You search me out and know me.

You know when I sit around or get up, You understand my thoughts from far off.

You sift my comings and goings; You are familiar with all my ways.

There is not one thing I say that You, LORD, do not know.

In front and in back You press in on me and set Your hand upon
me.

Even things hidden from myself You know, things that are beyond
me.

Where can I go from Your spirit, or how can I get away from You?

If I could go up to the sky, there You would be, or down to Sheol,
there You are too.

If I took up the wings of a gull to settle at the far end of the sea,

even there Your hand would be leading me on, holding me in its
grip.

I might think, "At least darkness can hide me, nighttime will
conceal me."

But even darkness is not dark for You; night is as bright as the day,
and light and dark are all the same.

Ps. 139:1–12

~

AND SO, BIBLICAL MAN IS still Little Man, even if he is slightly
less little than his predecessors (see "The Death of Baal"). That is
how he is often glimpsed, from above, a little fellow who some-
times suffers from delusions of grandeur:

From the heavens the LORD looks out, seeing all of humanity.

From the place of His dwelling He looks down on all of earth's in-
habitants.

He who made the hearts of all of them [likewise] perceives their
every deed.

No king will triumph through force of arms, no mighty man
through power.

The cavalry's useless for victory—no matter its force, it will not be saved.

But the LORD's eye is turned to those who fear Him, who trust in His beneficence.

Ps. 33:13–18

This radical sense of smallness is crucial; it is, as suggested above, the very foundation of the religious consciousness of a great many psalms and other biblical compositions. Of course, to see the world in such a fashion may appear odd to some today (though it is always wise at least to consider the question of who, in any given circumstance, might be wearing the green spectacles). But it should in any case be noted that "small" is not quite all that the Psalms had to say about man's place in the universe.

The God of the Hebrew Bible is a *who*, not, even at His most remote, an unfathomably great force or a vector. Although this "who-ness" of God's has inspired some discomfort among modern theologians, it is precisely that in which biblical Israelites, and even people in more recent times, took comfort. (The French philosopher Pascal is said to have had sewn into the lining of his jacket a little scrap of writing: "God of Abraham, God of Isaac, and God of Jacob—not the God of the philosophers.") For, were it not for such a God, the "God of Abraham," there would scarcely have been any point in temples: God's grandeur might better have been grasped in sacred planetariums, and humanity's smallness a lesson drearily obvious there. But a line connected those two, God and man, a line sketched not in light-years across galaxies, but beaming into and out of the human heart. So, for all His grandeur, God did not disappear in the world of the Bible, nor did humanity, for all of its smallness:

When I see the heavens that Your fingers have fashioned, the moon and stars You have made:

What is a man that You should call him to mind, a human being that You should take note of him?

Yet You have made him almost a god, crowned him with glory and honor.

You set him over Your other creations, and put all of them at his feet.

Ps. 8:4–6

This was the perfect equilibrium to which the author of Psalm 104 likewise gave expression. Humanity is fundamentally Little Man, part of a great Breughel canvas, trudging off to work in a corner somewhere as the lions head home after their night of roaming, each comfortable with his place in the system; elsewhere, leviathan and dinky ships frolic in the sea. Yet the God whose world this is, the God who is "very big," nevertheless calls Little Man to mind, indeed exalts him above the other little things "with glory and honor." *That* was all there was to human glory; it was never in danger of filling the sky.

THE VIEW OF THINGS described above is "biblical," but it certainly lives elsewhere; indeed, anyone who has traveled in the modern Middle East will not find it altogether foreign. Something quite akin to this biblical outlook, the sense of smallness, is still there, very much the way of seeing common to most people. Actually, the religions matter little, Islam, eastern Christianity, or Judaism. Once I had the occasion to hear an Iraqi Jew describe the culture shock he experienced when, as a young man, he was forced to leave his native Baghdad to settle in the West. "In Baghdad," he said, "there were all kinds of people, some very traditional, some—like my own family—modern." (By "modern," he gave me to understand, he meant that they were not particularly punctilious about keeping the Sabbath or other religious duties.) "But all of us, modern and traditional, knew one thing: God is very big and man is very little. Once, some years after I had left Baghdad and moved to Western society, I went one evening to hear a famous theologian speak. I hoped that he would give me some piece of wisdom. But the more he spoke, the more his ideas and my own swirled around together in my head and the more upset I became. I could not get out of my mind this new thought: Man is very big, and God is very far away."

CHAPTER 2

PSALM 42

S A DEER LONGS FOR A COURSING STREAM, SO MY SOUL LONGS FOR YOU, GOD.

My soul thirsts for God, the living God, for the time when I may go and see God's face.

Night and day, tears have been my food, as all day long I hear, "Where is your God?"

But I do think of this as I pour out my soul—how I will go with a crowd, leading a throng of revelers up to the very Temple, with songs of rejoicing and praise.

So why be downcast, my soul, or murmur within me?

Trust in God, for I will yet praise Him for helping me, my God.

Whenever my soul is downcast, I call out to You—
from the Jordan headlands and Hermon, from Mount Mizar
and depth to watery depth—

calling out above the beat of Your streams, as all Your waves and breakers sweep over me,

"The Lord sends forth His protection by day, and at night it stays at my side."

A prayer to my living God:

I say to my God, my strength: Don't forget me; don't let me go humbled by hostile threats.

With death or broken bones my enemies curse me, as all day long I hear, "Where is your God?"

But why be downcast, my soul, or murmur within me?

Trust in God, for I will yet praise Him for helping me. My God.

THE DOUBLE AGENT

THE BIBLE IS FULL OF REFERENCES to a part of the human being called the "soul"—but what exactly is it? Nowadays most people tend to think of their souls (if at all) as some kind of wholly abstract, spiritual entity, one that, if it has any reality at all, certainly does not have much to do with their everyday lives. But in biblical times, the soul had an immediacy known to all. It was present in everyone, just below the surface, the great Inside that every person has. It was both mind and heart, the place of one's underlying thoughts and desires, aspirations and deepest traits. Different words were used in the Bible's Hebrew to describe this inside: *nefesh* and *neshamah*, both usually translated as "soul," as well as *ruah* ("breath, spirit"), *leb* ("heart"), *qereb* ("innards"), and others. But all these words referred to that inner reality that lies beyond—that is, underneath—a person's merely physical existence. And it was the *vital* inside. Everyone knew that if the soul ceased its activity, the person died; that is why it was associated with vital organs like the heart or vital functions like breathing. (The same is true in European languages, where words like "spirit," "psyche," and "ghost"—as well as *anima*, *pneuma*, *dusha*, *âtman*, and their offshoots—also derive from roots associated with wind or breath.)

The biblical concept of "soul" thus overlaps a great deal with our own ideas of "self," "mind," and the like. As a matter of fact, it sometimes seems to be used in the Bible merely as an indirect way of saying "I." Some modern translators render phrases like "Bless the LORD, O my soul" as "I will bless the LORD," for example.

But there is another side to the biblical soul, one that is less obvious and, as a consequence, sometimes ignored or misunderstood by readers of the Bible. For, while the soul was someone's vital inside and essential self, it was apparently not always considered to be entirely one's own possession or, consequently, completely under one's control. It was well known in the biblical world that the soul is intimately connected to God; but some biblical texts even go so far as to assert that the soul actually be-longs to God, a kind of divine island in the midst of the human body. So God "gives a soul to those upon [the earth]" (Isa. 42:5; see also Gen. 2:7) and "will gather back His soul and spirit to Him" upon a person's death (Job 34:14; see also Jon. 4:3).* Between these two events, the soul's unique state of connection to God was frequently stressed. God entered the human mind at will, speaking to the soul and from it even putting His word in a person's mouth. It is likewise the soul that "thirsts for," "desires," and "delights in" God (Pss. 35:9, 63:2; Isa. 26:9, 61:10), and the soul, or "spirit" or "heart," that addresses God in time of trouble. Such references are easily misunderstood or downplayed nowadays, precisely because the soul was indeed the great inside of every person. When some biblical figure speaks of his soul reaching out to God, does he not simply mean that he himself (or, as we might even say nowadays, his mind or heart) is reaching out? This indeed may be the case: sometimes "my soul" is no more than a synonym for "myself." But at other times—as in the psalm translated above—the soul's identity is surprisingly spoken of as an entity distinct from the "I" of the speaker.

---

*This does not necessarily assume the idea of the soul's immortality but simply its divine origin. That is, flesh can come and go, but the great inside that makes it alive is conceived to come from God and, therefore, to return to God when the body is reduced to mere (i.e., unanimated) flesh.

So why be downcast, my soul, or murmur within me?

Trust in God, for I will yet praise Him for helping me, my God.

Ps. 42:5 (SOME BIBLES, 42:6)

Gracious and righteous is the LORD, merciful is our God;

The LORD protects the defenseless—when I was brought low, He saved me.

So return, O my soul, to your place, for the LORD has been generous with you.

Ps. 116:5-7

Aloud to God I cry out, I cry out that He might hear me.

In time of trouble I seek help from my Lord: my hand is stretched out unceasingly, but my soul refuses to be comforted.

Ps. 77:2-3

Such lines suggest that simply identifying the soul with the person whose inside it inhabits may not be entirely faithful to the way the soul was perceived in biblical times.

A Jewish prayer from early postbiblical times (though it attests to a soul-body polarity not present in earlier texts) nonetheless preserves this sense of the soul's special status within a person: "The soul is Yours, and the body is Your creation." That is, while we humans are altogether God's handiwork, our souls have a different status from that of our bodies. God creates our bodies and gives them over to our management, for good or ill, but our souls are never quite our own: this most personal, inside chamber never ceases belonging to God. As other ancient Jewish texts put it, the soul is a divine "deposit" (piqqadon) given over to its human guardian for a time, but never actually the human's possession.

Certainly there was something ironic in this idea, that a person's vital center and essence is nonetheless not altogether his or her own. This circumstance threatened to make of the soul a creature of dual loyalties, indeed, a kind of double-agent in one's very midst. A biblical proverb put it well:

> A man's soul is the lamp of the LORD, who searches out his innermost parts.
>
> PROV. 20:27

The soul is God's lamp, the proverb means, in the sense that it is the soul that allows God to search through a person's innards, lighting up the most hidden recesses and chambers. So it really is something of a foreign agent at the very center of a human being, ours but not ours, whose presence there guarantees that nothing inside us can remain hidden from God.

Indeed, an ancient rabbinic commentary on this proverb used a word very much like "double-agent" to describe the soul, the word *curiosus* (which entered Hebrew from Latin at the time when the Romans controlled ancient Judea), which meant a "curious" royal detective or inquirer working for the Roman authorities:

> [With regard to the verse] "A man's soul is the lamp of the LORD, who searches out his innermost parts," Rabbi Aḥa said: Just as earthly kings have detectives (*curiosi*) who report everything that happens back to the king, so God too has detectives, and they tell Him all that a person does. . . . The matter is comparable to the case of a man who has married the king's daughter; when, after he has gotten up in the morning, he asks the king if he is well, the king tells him each day: "You did thus and so in your house, you became angry under such and such circumstances, then you beat your servants," and so on for each and every thing. Then the man

goes back and says to the members of his household, "Which of you reported that I did thus and so? How does the king know about it?" They reply: "Do not be foolish! You married his daughter and yet you ask how he knows? His own daughter tells him!" So is it with mankind: a man may do whatever he wishes, but his soul reports it back to God.

Pesiqta Rabbati 8

~

To some readers it might seem that the speaker of Psalm 42 is merely talking to himself, but the reality described by this psalm is, I think, somewhat more complex. The "soul" the psalmist addresses is distinct from himself. He, of course, has his own, very real, problems: "hostile threats," "enemies" who curse him. (If the psalmist is not still more specific about them, that is probably because this psalm, like so many, was apparently written to be recited as well by others in time of need, and so the exact sources of his distress—enemies or other dangers—are left unspecified.) But quite apart from these external circumstances is the effect they have had on the divine island in his midst. How bizarre, if we did not know about biblical souls, would the refrain of this psalm appear: "Why be downcast, my soul, or murmur within me? Trust in God, for I will yet praise Him." But in the biblical conception of things described earlier, such a refrain can indeed make sense: the soul, the inner chamber, is not "me" exactly, and I am not the one who can put it at ease again.

The word used for "soul" in this psalm, *nefesh*, has its own interesting resonance. Unlike the other terms for soul, *nefesh* sometimes refers specifically to the neck or throat. Thus, when the psalmist says elsewhere, "Save me, God, for the waters are come even unto my soul" (Ps. 69:2), he means to say, rather more concretely, that the rising waters have reached his neck and are about to drown him. Similarly, when the Israelites complain in the desert, "Our soul is dried away and there is nothing at all to eat, we have nothing but this manna" (Num. 11:6), they mean that their throats are dry with hunger and thirst. Of course, in most of the Bible, including our psalm, *nefesh* means soul; but even here, the psalmist seems to delight in evoking the word's other meaning: "My soul thirsts for God, the living God," he says, just the way another kind of *nefesh* might thirst for water; indeed, the soul on its journey to God is like a thirsty deer who smells water from a great distance and then rushes to it through the forest to slake its thirst.

In the world of the Psalms, the soul has its own needs: a sacred entity inside the human being, it needs refreshment and renewal. "God, make me a pure heart, and put a new, right spirit inside me" (Psalm 51:12). For the author of Psalm 42, such renewal is fulfilled by contact with God in the most concrete sense, "the time when I may go and see Your face." By this the psalmist alludes to the purpose of his present journey, for, in biblical times, God was thought to be present as nowhere else in His "house" or temple. This temple was not a temple or church in the modern sense, that is, not merely a place in which humans come together to pray, but a sacred structure that was deemed to be God's actual residence on earth. That is where one could be in God's very presence, "see His face" in the biblical idiom, and that is where the psalmist is headed here. This psalm is written in a northern-sounding Hebrew, and the places it evokes, the northern Hermon mountains and the Jordan headwaters with their rushing streams, seem to situate the psalmist in the far north, perhaps near the ancient sanctuary at Dan. Help is on the way, he says to his soul: you soon will be refreshed and renewed by your true Owner.

~

THIS CONCEPTION OF THE SOUL did not disappear right after the time of the Bible—far from it. Throughout late antiquity and the Middle Ages, people continued to think of their souls in this same vivid and vital fashion. The soul was that which was most oneself, yet it belonged to God; most inside oneself, it was nonetheless the only path to the Outside, to God, as it was also God's pathway into us. After a time, there was no longer any Temple in which God was deemed to be specially present, but souls still maintained their special connection to God, traveling at night, according to one common conceit, in order to be with God again while their human "hosts" slept.

One can still read medieval treatises with names like *The Healing of Souls*—for souls in those concrete days sometimes became sick and required treatment. Some of their diseases were of the sort that would nowadays be described as insanity or mental illness, a fearsome phenomenon no less in ages past than in the lives of current sufferers. But others were the sort of day-to-day occurrences that we have largely learned to ignore, the little ups-and-downs of our inner state for which we have no terminology but which, in the strict spiritual pharmacology of the Middle Ages, had identifiable causes and cures connected to the soul's intellectual and moral diet, often necessitating physical intervention (herbs, special fragrances) and a regimen of prayer and repentance for spiritual renewal.

And then, little by little, souls began to disappear from every-day discourse and ordinary life. Their disappearance is certainly connected to larger, better-known topics in the history of Western thought: the Renaissance, then the Enlightenment; the rise of modern science and the new mentality that accompanied it and made it possible; the gradual materialization and secularization of Western culture; most of all what Martin Buber called, in an apt metaphor, the "eclipse" of God in our own time. Much of the soul's former existence made sense, and drew its power, from within that old setting. Once God's light had ceased to shine unobstructed from the heavens, once the way was open and confirmed for a new way of looking at the world (and, interestingly, even before very much of this activity had actually borne fruit), the soul, with its special connection to God, began to recede into the background. Philosophers in particular found it preferable to speak about the mind, *our* mind, and other ways emerged to explain humanity's inner life. It became a strictly internal matter, and our innermost part became unreachable, inaccessible to the Outside.

To some it might thus seem that the soul, in the biblical sense, is now gone forever, its former territory having been gerrymandered into various adjoining provinces governed today by psychiatrist, physician, moral philosopher, and perhaps yet others. But certainly this is not so; however much our own times may seem to have obscured it, the fundamental duality of each person's inside cannot be altogether suppressed. For this reason more than all others, the psalmist's refrain has a special resonance, and relevance, in today's world, an insistence that, despite appearances, the soul's reality is not to be denied. "So why be downcast, my soul, or murmur within me?" Behind this question lies the double agent's paradox, the idea that that which is most inside is also the only way to the Outside, that deep within each human being is a little room, and on its far wall, a tiny door.

CHAPTER 3

PSALM 29

IVE THE LORD, O SONS OF THE MIGHTY, GIVE
THE LORD GLORY AND STRENGTH.

Give the LORD His own name's glory, bow down to the LORD in
holy splendor.

Listen! The LORD is over the waters, the glorious God has
thundered, the LORD is over the deep.

Listen! The LORD is in strength. Listen! The LORD is in splendor.

Listen! The LORD shatters cedars, how the LORD shatters cedars
of Lebanon!

He makes Lebanon skip like a calf, Sirion like a little cub.

Listen! The LORD shoots forth sparks. Listen! The LORD makes
the wilderness shake, the LORD shakes the lands of Kadesh.

Listen! The LORD makes the oak trees quiver as He strips the
forests bare,

and in His Temple, all say, "Glory!"

The LORD is enthroned above the flood, and the LORD will
continue, forever king.

May the LORD give strength to His people, may the LORD bless
His people with peace.

THE DEATH OF BAAL

IT IS STRIKING HOW LITTLE THERE IS in the Bible of what might be called "theology" proper. God is everywhere present, but not as an object of inquiry or even systematic description. Instead, He is actor, and almost all we know about Him is what He has done in intervening in human history. Of course, God is hardly said to be unknowable in biblical texts, nor yet incorporeal (that is, without a body), but somehow the text always seems to refrain from telling us, in the sense I mean, *about* Him. There is something so characteristic in the biblical account of that climactic moment when, at the great revelation at Mt. Sinai, Moses and the leaders of Israel are actually allowed to glimpse God's physical being:

> Then Moses and Aaron, Nadab and Abihu, and seventy of the elders of Israel went up [the mountain]. And they saw the God of Israel, and underneath His feet there was like a brickwork of sapphire stones, or the substance of heaven for purity.
>
> EXOD. 24:9–10

How remarkable that, at this face-to-face encounter, the narrative eye immediately drops from the sight of God Himself to the dazzling brickwork "underneath His feet," as if even this one golden opportunity to confront God head-on, so to speak, must end in an averted gaze and the elegant non sequitur, "or the substance of heaven for purity." For the same reason, apparently, when Moses asks later on to *see* God's being or bodily presence, he is told that he cannot behold God head-on, but only with a sidelong glance, from behind; and of what he saw we have not a word:

And Moses said to God, "Show me, I beg, Your glory [physical being]." And He said, "All My goodness I can cause to pass before you, and I can proclaim the name 'the LORD' before you. But I am gracious [only] to whom I choose, and I have mercy [only] on whom I choose." [Silence.] And He said, "But you cannot see My face, for no one can see Me and live." [More silence.] And the LORD said, "See, there is a place by Me to stand in the cleft of the rock. So while My glory passes by I will put you in the cleft of the rock, and I will cover you with My hand until I pass by. Then I will take My hand away, and you will be able to see Me from behind. But My face shall not be seen."

EXOD. 33:18–23

In keeping with this view-from-behind, what Moses learns on this occasion about God's nature also seems strangely inconclusive (though traditional interpretation hardly explained it as such): that God is merciful and patient and forgiving, but not unconditionally so, since He also punishes and exacts a toll (Exod. 34:6–7). More verbs, or verbs masquerading as adjectives.

As a result, what we are actually given to know about God from the Bible itself is not the sort of thing that later philosophers or modern churchmen claimed to know—no list of assertions about the nature of the Godhead, and certainly no consistent and harmonious portrait—but rather a set of often out-of-focus, and sometimes apparently contradictory, snapshots, action photos from different angles and in different lighting. What they tell us is the essential—*God was in this place*—but little more.

Psalm 29 provides one such photograph. Here God seems to move in off the "deep waters" (apparently, the Mediterranean just off the northern Israelite or Syrian shore) onto the heavily forested mainland. His arrival is heard even if He Himself is not quite seen, presumably just out of sight above the big, black, billowing clouds rolling in. The thunder and lightning that split the northern forest and send all of nature careening in terror are the hallmark of God's coming, and if this arrival is frightening, it also spells relief, perhaps even prosperity. In ancient Israel, agriculture (and hence, life itself) was wholly dependent on adequate rainfall, the blessed substance borne by those rolling clouds. This psalm, in other words, celebrates a vital, much yearned-for, event: God's bringing the life-giving rain.

But to say this is only to scratch the surface of this psalm, since the reality out of which it was uttered has scarcely been mentioned. Indeed, the greatest overall obstacle to our understanding of what the Bible does tell us about God is the gap that separates us from the mental and spiritual world of ancient Israelites. They walked about in a consciousness sometimes rather different from our own, and in no particular of this psalm is that difference so manifest as in the opening line's mention of the "sons of the mighty." For this phrase might more literally be rendered "sons of the gods," and that, quite probably, was how the phrase was understood by the psalm's earliest audience. But who were these gods, and who were their "sons"?

THROUGHOUT THE ANCIENT WORLD, the gods were the movers who made the world go. That is, the sun, the moon, the winds, and the rain did not proceed autonomously through the sky; they were *driven*, pushed by the divine beings associated with them. More generally, what happened in the world happened as a result of having been caused, ordained, and the gods were the causes. Indeed, to put things more appropriately to the spirit of the times, the gods were not so much abstract causes as personal *causers*, living, breathing entities, just out of sight or somehow present in multifarious shapes, who made things happen.

The presence of the gods was obvious enough. They were right there, in this river or in that field of grain, in nature and the concrete things of this world. As time went on and religious conceptions evolved, the being of some nature gods also migrated heavenward, to be manifest in different planets or stars, and such a move might appear inevitable. For, why were those little white dots shifting around in the sky on any dark night? Certainly some connection must exist between their movements (which varied and changed over time) and all that happened down below, down here, during the day. But whether the gods were in heaven or on earth, everything about daily life seemed to attest to their active intervention; they were always there, watching, making things go. Whatever happened, simply because it did happen, provided potential evidence of the gods' satisfaction or pique, or represented the outcome of their own internal struggles, since almost nothing in the world just happens on its own. Then how else could one explain the things that mattered most—feast or famine, pregnancy or barrenness, victory or defeat, sudden illness or recovery, life or death—if not through the gods' intervention in human affairs?

And of course they were present in more than the effects they caused. Their images were everywhere, and they themselves dwelt in special houses—temples—that dotted the ancient landscape. King and commoner spoke of them as frequently as modern people discuss the weather or movie stars (the gods had something of the quality of both!), and city-states squandered perfecty valuable, sometimes vital, resources for their worship. So bulls and bleating sheep were led to the gods' altars for slaughter, their necks sliced open and the still-warm flesh and abundant blood offered up in pious sacrifice. Sometimes the gods even demanded one's own children to be sacrificed, and so they were. Armies of priests devoted their lives to the service of the gods, poets sang of their exploits, and sages, diviners, and wizards scrutinized the gods' signs, jotting their findings onto clay tablets for future generations to ponder. Their existence, their reality, was overwhelming.

~

NO ONE KNOWS WHEN humanity first began to understand the world in terms of the gods, and of course it would be wrong to imply that there existed one single conception of the gods in any case. On the contrary, scholars of the ancient Near East and elsewhere have carefully distinguished different sorts of deities and traced the evolution of the conceptualization of the gods from earliest recorded history. But whatever their origins and development, the gods are to be apprehended first and foremost as an understanding of the world, an explanation of how it functions and why it is the way it is. An explanation, but not a "theory"—for the gods were simply an established fact, accepted by everyone without question. It has been remarked that most ordinary people nowadays have no more reason to believe in the existence of molecules and atoms than they have to believe in goblins and leprechauns, and this is true. Yet though most of our modern notion of atomic structure and its scientific application is scarcely more than a century old (as well as being quite remote from our daily experience), we do believe in it with a perfect faith. What, then, can one say of a way of understanding that had been around not for a century or two but millennia, whose veracity needed no proof in any case since it was obvious, right there in the natural order and the nighttime sky, and before which the mightiest kings and the greatest of empires stood in trembling, supplicating fealty? The gods' existence was quite axiomatic.

This axiomatic existence is presumed even by the earliest texts we have from the ancient Near East and surrounding civilizations. True, later ages sometimes did reflect on the gods' own creation, or the moment when a particular deity revealed himself or herself to humanity, but these can scarcely illuminate the process by which the *idea* of the gods' existence actually entered human consciousness for the first time. It is likewise true that anthropologists have studied primitive civilizations still in existence today, in which there is no evidence of a belief in gods, indeed, nothing corresponding to what we would call "religion" at all. But such societies cannot tell us how the transition to a belief in the gods occurred, and they are in any event exceptional; elsewhere on the globe, at least in the past and in many cases down to the present, the most varied peoples have all shared the belief that the world is ruled by gods.

Yet the genealogy of the gods is not all that obscure; they do arrive at a certain stage—importantly, not at the very beginning—of human consciousness. Rather than tie the appearance of the gods to someone called Primitive Man, we might thus do better to speak, more ambiguously, of Little Man. He is exactly as depicted in certain television documentaries: that little fellow running around naked, clucking, cheerful, afraid of some animals and hungry for others, climbing trees, eating whatever fruits and nuts and leaves and roots he can lay his hands on, by turns curious, timorous, and ferocious, screeching or strangely silent. In fact, it is probably misleading to speak of "him" at all, since he is almost never alone. It is mostly "they" that we see, ragtag little groups of hims and hers and infants, young ones of various ages, plus a strangely surviving sage or two from the previous generation, all gray and agile in old age.

What do these little people know of the world? It is everything and they are nothing, or virtually nothing. The great

Outside impinges everywhere; it shines through the thick branches at noon or hangs palpable in the darkness. If we could peer into the soul of Little Man we would find it altogether open, ready for anything: the Outside intrudes at will, making him feel this or that, *think* this or that, sending the rain and haze and sun, filling his belly, providing now a needed shelter, now a deadly pursuer, killing babies, saving babies, saving him. Everything just happens to him and to them, and so the great Outside is necessarily everything, and he and they are as nothing in its presence; indeed, they are a part of it.

Centuries, millennia pass. Seen from a distance, life seems to have changed little, yet the Little Man is different. The great Outside still impinges, but he has meanwhile been busy cataloguing things, observing the relationship between this particular rock and that kind of bird and the bend in the river. He controls very little, but the idea of control is there, or at least the idea of figuring things out with an eye to the next crisis; so he has become an observer. What fascinates him are the causes of things: this bush's leaves will make you sick, but the leaves of the one that grows near the top of the second hill are good; in fact, they stop the bleeding of a wound. The great Outside is catalogued, differentiated: this spot is special, and approaching it this way is better, safer, than approaching it from the other side. There are rules and conclusions, so everything must be studied on its own in order for its full potential to emerge, in order for its full range of effects to be understood.

Eventually, it turns out that some causes are hidden; you cannot see them doing their work but they do it anyway. This is an amazing idea but has proven itself true time and again. How else to explain the way that certain things happen, like the cycles of the moon and of the seasons? A pattern emerges. Here is not happenstance but causality, and where there are causes there are causers. In the ancient Near East, we encounter the god Dumuzi five thousand years ago, but he, and the other hidden causers, had surely been around far earlier than that. Dumuzi answers to an early god's description: "He is little more than the élan vital of new life in nature, vegetable and animal, a will and power in it that brings it about" (Thorkild Jacobsen). He, like the other ancient gods, embodies and infuses, so that the cyclical doings of his life are what bring the plants and animals into harmony, all of them led unknowingly by his unseen presence.

The very act of identifying the hidden causes represents the acquisition of an enormous measure of control. Now, no longer does the Outside loom menacingly at every turn. Behind it are actual doers whose names are known, whose lives and interactions explain what occurs. Nothing simply happens anymore. Even before the thought occurs to anyone to seek to appease them or influence their actions, the gods' very existence represents an extraordinary retreat of the Outside. Human beings have understood, and the world is a different place for it. But soon, of course, the gods will be appeased: men will mark their sacred marriage with gifts and libations or coax the earth's mother to generosity with their own, gratuitous largesse.

The connection of what is seen with what is not, of the world of the senses with that which can only be sensed, is henceforth established as a certainty. What part of the world will not now unfold its hidden workings under scrutiny? To choose an example from somewhat later on in the process of discovery: someone, at some point, comes up with the absurd notion that if you take some of the perfectly good grains that you might otherwise use to make a fine meal and, instead of eating them, stick them back into the ground, in the course of time a whole new stalk will arise in the place of each individual grain, paying you back many times over your original investment. This absurdity eventually proves to be true not only of grain but of the seeds of fruits and vegetables, and so agriculture is born—a kind of slavery, to be sure, since people will soon have to plow the earth and protect their fields, but from this slavery comes a measure of control over the food supply, and a large part of what was once the Outside's becomes ours.

It is certainly significant that one ancient text from the Near East describes the secret of agriculture as having been taught to humanity by a god who came down from the mountains. Although it might seem to us that the invention of agriculture belongs to primitive science, while a god in charge of agriculture is merely an instance of crude superstition, in ancient times the one no less than the other belonged to the realm of hidden causes; understanding either of them meant penetrating the external, superficial look of things in order to see a deeper, underlying reality. And so, if we could peer into Not-So-Little Man's soul now, we would find in it a wholly different relation to the Outside. The Outside has become, specifically, the realm of *hidden* causes. The man himself now exercises no small measure of control over his own existence, but even the territory that is not his—the hidden causes'—is divided up among known, sensed causers who can be implored by name and sometimes, apparently, placated or bought off.

But such a peep inside his soul should reveal more than that. For I have not said the essential, which is the shared existence his soul feels at this state of affairs. That is, however much charted and divided the great Outside now is, it nonetheless has a vividness that must be mentioned specifically in this day and age (since such vividness is gone from the lives of most today). The Outside is indeed there, at every turn, and it has the power to intrude where it will. Its presence is no less real for being invisible; for that reason, his life, even his inner life, is never altogether his own. Since whatever happens can have a hidden cause, he cannot dream or prosper or die without having first been touched from the Outside. Outside is thus differentiated from inside, but the passage between them is continuous, vivid, and his own soul's architecture bears witness to this state.

The journey from Little Man to Not-So-Little is enormous and quite dwarfs anything that follows; from the soul's standpoint, humanity henceforth will be essentially unchanged. How appropriate, then, that the Bible's history starts at precisely this moment in human development, when food-gatherer Adam is brought the secret of knowledge by a wise snake and so has to leave the garden where fruit is just plucked. Henceforth he will be enslaved to the plow: "By the sweat of your brow you shall eat your bread" (Gen. 3:19). That, of course, is not the whole story, for the discovery of that hidden cause was, more or less simultaneously in human history, accompanied by the revelation of another, related, truth. Women's bellies, it turns out, start to swell and then yield up babies not simply as a matter of random circumstance, but because of an act of planting that took place nine months previous, however long it might have taken for the first effects of that act to make themselves known. This implausible theory, tested repeatedly, turns out to be true, and it results in a parallel sort of slavery. That is, just as he brings forth his harvest in sweat and groaning, so fairness has dictated that she shall too: "In pain you shall bring forth children." And just as he plants seeds in ground that, if the effort is to be worth it, must be his ground, so she too (to justify the effort that follows her harvest) must now be exclusively his own: "Your urge shall be to your husband, and he shall rule over you" (Gen. 3:16). When one looked back on those who still did not know such things, were they not like children, running around naked and unashamed?

~

THE WORLD OF THE GODS was so comfortable it is an extraordinary, astonishing wonder that it ever changed. We have seen that science, discovery, had little power to undermine that conception of things. On the contrary, each new insight only bolstered the gods' hold on human existence, demonstrating anew how what we see is determined by what we do not, and that the realm of rules and knowledge is with these unseen, powerful humanoids somewhere above the clouds or beyond the horizon. Just as causes implied causers, so rules could hardly exist without rulers who made them up; the world itself was created by such rule makers, and they are patently the ones who keep it running now. So science and religion are one: a person might well understand where babies came from, but this still did not explain *how* they were created (without any actual crafting on the part of the humans involved) or why sometimes they did *not* come, not at all. That, clearly, was in the hands of the gods. So even much later, the divine was always conceived to begin precisely where human insight left off. "Just as you do not know how it is that spirit or bones [can enter] the belly of a pregnant woman, so you cannot know the work of God, who creates all" (Eccles. 11:5).

And yet, the world did change. Jewish tradition, though not the Bible itself, connects this change with the person of Abraham, a renegade son of the idol maker Terah, who somehow came to perceive the existence of the one true God through a haze of polytheistic humanoids. Later Jewish writers liked to imagine the exact circumstances under which Abraham suddenly came to see that the whole idea of the gods was folly. One attempt to reconstruct Abraham's moment of enlightenment dates from, probably, the first century of the common era:

[Abraham recalls:] When I was watching over the gods of my father Farah [Terah] and my brother Nahor, I was experimenting [to find out] which god was truly the strongest. Then, at the time when my [priestly] lot came up and I was to finish the service of my father Farah's sacrifice to his gods of wood and stone, of gold and silver and copper and iron, I, Abraham, having entered their sanctuary for the service, found a god named Marumat, which had been carved out of stone, fallen at the feet of an iron god, Nakhin. And it came to pass that, when I saw this, my heart was troubled, and I thought to myself that I, Abraham, would be unable to return it to its place all by myself, since it was heavy, [carved] out of a great stone; so I went to inform my father, and he went in with me. And as we both were moving it to return it to its place, its head fell off of it in such a way that I was left holding on to its head. And it came to pass, when my father saw that the head of his god, Marumat, had fallen off of it, he said to me, "Abraham," and I replied, "Here I am." And he said: "Bring me a chisel from the house." And I brought it. Then he carved another Marumat, without a head, out of another stone, and [placed on it] the head that had been broken off from [the first] Marumat, and then smashed that [first] Marumat. . . .

Then I said to myself, "What are these useless things that my father is doing? Is he not rather a god to his gods, since it is by virtue of his sculpting and shaping, by his skillfulness, that they come into being? It would be more fitting for them to bow down to my father, since they are his handiwork. . . ."

And I said to myself, "If it is thus, how then can my father's god Marumat, having a head made from one stone and [the rest] being made from another stone, save someone or hear a person's prayer and grant him anything?"

APOCALYPSE OF ABRAHAM, CHAPTERS 1, 3

In the same first century, a Jewish philosopher in Alexandria (Egypt), Philo, connected the tradition of Abraham's sudden enlightenment with the science of astronomy that was so zealously pursued in his homeland of Chaldea:

> The Chaldeans exercised themselves most especially with astronomy and attributed all things to the movements of the stars, believing that whatever is in the world is governed by forces encompassed in numbers and numerical proportions. They exalted the existence of what is visible, and took no thought for what is perceivable to the mind and [yet] invisible. But seeking out the numerical arrangement according to the cycles of the sun, moon, the planets and the fixed stars, as well as the changes of the yearly seasons and the overall connection of the things of heaven with what happens on earth, they supposed that the world itself was god, sacrilegiously making out that which is created to be like the One who had created it.
> He [Abraham] grew up with this idea and was a true Chaldean for some time, until, opening the soul's eye from the depth of sleep, he came to behold the pure ray in place of the deep darkness, and he followed that light and perceived what he had not seen before, One who guides and steers the world, presiding over it and managing its affairs.
>
> PHILO, ON ABRAHAM, 69–71

Such accounts notwithstanding, modern historians of religion generally view Israel's break with the world of the gods not as a one-time event, but as a gradual process. Moreover, the radical doctrine of monotheism was an understanding of things that gained acceptance only slowly and in stages. Certainly it must have been hard for people to part with an idea as deeply engrained as polytheism was. To present an analogy from our own day: even now, although the truth of the Copernican view of the solar system was demonstrated long ago and is disputed by no one, we still speak of the sun "rising" and "setting," and most people probably still *experience* sunset as if a moving, red disk were plunging below a fixed, immobile earth. Of course we know, in some intellectual fashion, that the earth is rotating on its axis, and certainly the visual phenomena that we see accord with that knowledge, yet we still have not parted from that deeply engrained, other way of understanding. How hard it must have been, then, for ancient Israelites to let go of a heaven that teemed with competing powers whose interaction, whose ups-and-downs, explained so well why the world was the way it was.

The beginnings of this process are not my focus here, but a somewhat later stage. Israel was now sworn to loyalty to its one God, yet everywhere around it—in Egypt, Mesopotamia—were nations with their own, very real, pantheons, hosts of established gods who between them divided up the things of this world. Why then this strange, Israelite exclusivism? No doubt the full consequences of abandoning polytheism for the worship of a single deity were not obvious to Israel all at once, and even when they were, some people must have been reluctant to embrace them. Indeed, to hear the Bible tell it, for a long time it was very difficult for the Israelites to give up the old, polytheistic view, and there were many moments of backsliding or hesitation.

One such moment is described in 1 Kings 18, in the famous story of Elijah and the prophets of Baal. The people of Israel knew—had been told, that is—that they were to show exclusive allegiance to their God, but they were still not sure. Baal, after all, was the old Canaanite storm god, and to the north, indeed, within the land of Israel itself, prophets of Baal urged the people to cast their lot with him. Baal had one outstanding attribute or area of specialization; ask anyone in the street what Baal does and he would say, "brings the rain." Israel's God, on the other hand, was a more elusive sort of deity, alleged to be associated with this or that function, but inscrutable. Then who do you go to when it is rain you want, rain that you need so as to have enough food to eat? And so the people hesitated, not sure what to do.

> Elijah came near to all the people and said, "How long will you keep hopping from one opinion to the other? If the LORD is God, follow Him, and if it is Baal, then follow him." But the people did not answer him a word. Then Elijah said to the people, "I am the only prophet of the LORD who is left, while Baal's prophets are four hundred and fifty. Let two bulls be given to us, and let them [the prophets of Baal] choose one bull for themselves and cut it into pieces and lay it on the wood [of the altar], but let them not put any fire to it. Meanwhile, I will slaughter the other bull and lay it on the wood, but I also will put no fire to it. Then you call on the name of your god and I will call on the name of the LORD. The god who answers by fire is indeed God."
>
> 1 KINGS 18:21–24

It is noteworthy that this challenge, which Elijah famously wins, is fought on Baal's home court—indeed, that was the whole point. For, if Baal is the storm god who brings the rain, then he logically ought to be the deity better equipped to "answer by fire," that is, to send lightning (an accoutrement of the storm god) from the sky and set the sacrificial animal ablaze. God's victory over Baal in precisely this matter is therefore decisive: when He sends down the lightning on His own offering, the people cry out, "The LORD is God, the LORD is God" (the phrase might more accurately be rendered: "The LORD is *the* God," or perhaps even better, "The LORD is the gods"), since that is the logical inference to be drawn.

However, it is not so much the outcome of this story, as its spiritual background, that is remarkable. The story bears witness to one risky moment in humanity's thinking about divinity, a moment as fraught with danger as (and in other ways as well comparable to) the one in which Nietzsche declared God to be dead. For here *Baal* is dead, and with him all the other gods; their obvious, observable activities in the natural world are henceforth to be attributed to a deity who, however much in charge of everything, is really not present in anything in nature. This point is brought home a little later on in the Elijah narrative, when the prophet goes to Mount Horeb, there to encounter God face to face:

> And behold, the LORD passed by and a great and strong wind split the mountains, and broke into pieces the rocks before the LORD. The LORD was [or "is"] not in the wind. And after the wind was an earthquake; the LORD was [or "is"] not in the earthquake. And after the earthquake was a fire; the LORD was [or "is"] not in the fire. And after the fire was the sound of the thinnest stillness. As soon as Elijah heard it, he wrapped his face in his cloak and went out and stood at the entrance of the cave. Then a voice came to him and said, "What are you doing here, Elijah?"
>
> 1 KINGS 19:11–13

God, most evidently in this passage, does not dwell in the things of this world, in natural phenomena, and so is not to be sought in any of the loud pyrotechnics that conventionally marked the gods' arrival. On the contrary, His voice comes in the tiniest little sound—that is, He seems here purposely to flaunt His *super*natural status. *

---

*"Still, small voice," the traditional rendering of the crucial phrase in this passage, is not really wrong, though "sound" rather than "voice" is what is intended. I have avoided that traditional translation here, however, because the phrase has long since ceased to mean what it meant in the original context and instead commonly designates the "voice of conscience" or the like.

Casting your lot with such a God was, is, a bold step. How much easier it was to think that He was demonstrably *some-where*, that some loud, well-known, booming sound was actually His voice. In a way, it might be said that this God was a regression to the undifferentiated Outside of an earlier consciousness; but there are no true regressions. Instead, it was the new consciousness that was now brought to conceive of divinity—"the gods"—in a new way.

"Where *is* He?" was the most obvious question for an outsider to ask an Israelite about his alleged God, and a truthful answer to that question was hardly one that would bring comfort to the answerer.

> Why should the nations say, "Where is their God?" But our God is in heaven, He does whatever He wants.
>
> Ps. 115:2-3

The God that Israel ended up embracing, while He represented a continuation of the recognition of human dependence on the divine, was nonetheless a rejection of any simple, mechanistic understanding of where the divine resides. The old, much-thumbed address book of the gods, to be consulted in time of need, was now flung into the fire, replaced by a single Name. But possessing that Name hardly meant certainty that one's request would be granted; all it meant was freedom from a previous misconception. And, precisely because of His singleness, how fearsome this deity was! (Truly, as they would only later come to appreciate, He was of an order of being altogether different from that of the mere godlings.) This was the spiritual reality of Israel during at least part of the biblical period, and it is not surprising that human beings, then as now, sometimes retreated from the disturbing ramifications that this reality seemed to impose. What Elijah demonstrated on Mt. Carmel was the pragmatic wisdom of substituting the God of Israel for Baal. But the full implications of "The LORD is the gods" were hardly spelled out on that occasion.

~

SOME BIBLICAL SCHOLARS have argued that Psalm 29 is among the most ancient compositions in the Hebrew Bible, its language in some ways reminiscent of the fourteenth century B.C.E. (or earlier) poetry of ancient Ugarit (to the north of what was to become biblical Israel). To me, however, it seems far more likely that this psalm reflects the struggles of a later period, indeed, it bespeaks the same theological hesitations that survived to the time of Elijah on Mt. Carmel and beyond.* This psalm's God, too, stands for the usurpation of Baal's powers and the beginning of the gods' twilight in the ancient Near East. Here, all those attributes formerly associated with Baal—the storm clouds, thunder and lightning—have become those of Israel's God:

> Listen! The LORD is over the waters, the glorious God has thundered, the LORD is over the deep.
>
> Listen! The LORD is in strength. Listen! The LORD is in splendor.
>
> Listen! The LORD shatters cedars, how the LORD shatters cedars of Lebanon!
>
> He makes Lebanon skip like a calf, Sirion like a little cub.
>
> Listen! The LORD shoots forth sparks. Listen! The LORD makes the wilderness shake, the LORD shakes the lands of Kadesh.

* If so, its similarity to Ugaritic poetry reflects its geographical, rather than chronological, proximity to Ugarit.

Today we seem to live in a tamer world, and one very much of human manufacture. It is difficult to image *any* event that would bring us to stand and watch in total, powerless awe, like little boys watching a mighty freight train whiz by at the crossing. But that is what is happening in these lines, and it is how they should be understood. Here comes the LORD, and no matter how many times He has come before, there is always something utterly overwhelming about His being so close at last, right there.

Along with God's Baal-like attributes here, and equally polemical, is the demotion apparently inflicted on Baal's former cohorts, the other deities. They also seem to be present here, though not quite spoken of directly but only as—strategically— the "sons of the gods." Now, "son of" in Hebrew frequently designates not actual biological filiation so much as membership in a group, so "sons of the gods" has an inherent ambiguity about it: the expression could be synonymous with "gods," or it could be something slightly less. For example, were those "sons of the gods" [or "sons of God"] mentioned in Genesis 6:2 (just before Noah's flood) actually members of the category of divinity—that is, godlings themselves—or (as ancient interpreters preferred to believe) a class of angels, divine beings of a sort but hardly gods? For that matter, what, in real terms, might such a distinction imply to an Israelite of, say, the ninth or tenth century? In any case, the divine beings addressed in Psalm 29 are told to glorify God and bow down to Him, and this is as unmistakable an assertion of their lowly status vis-à-vis Him as the "Glory" uttered at the end of the penultimate couplet. In other words, the gods may still be there in some attenuated form, but God has taken over. It is God who brings the rain, His voice *is* the thunder, and all other divine beings of heaven have been relegated to praising Him like sycophantic courtiers of a king.

It is intriguing to imagine, for just a moment, an actual

ancient Israelite, former devotee of Baal, somewhere along the coast of the eastern Mediterranean, as he grapples with all this, trying to get his mind to reckon with the reality that underlies the words of this psalm. For so many centuries the clouds had been Baal's. There was a comforting logic in that: Baal did not always come, but when he did, it was unmistakably *him*. And when he did not come, who did not rush to entreat him? The familiar pageantry, the overwhelming majesty of his temple, with its carvings and rich embroidery, and the dancing, bleeding prophets, then the stamping animals, shouts at the thud of the sacrificial carcass, the smoke and incense . . . In this ancient order lay the wisdom of the ages. But here, coming in off the waters, is this Deity who is like Baal—so like Baal that He even does the same things, is called by the same attributes—and yet who says that the very *idea* of Baal is dead. Never was a Baal. Instead, *He* was always there, "in strength" and "in splendor," but we read it wrong, we failed to see correctly. Those loud crashes, the vivid flashes, are really not any god's voice or equipment. "Listen, the LORD is over the waters!" though He is also "enthroned above the flood." What happens in this world happens before your eyes, but in a way that is deceptive.

CHAPTER 4

AMOS 4:4–5:24

 H COME TO BETHEL FOR SINS, TO GILGAL FOR
SINS GALORE!

But bring your offerings every morning, and a tithe every three
days;
send up a thanksgiving and yell "Freewill sacrifice!"—let people
know—
for such is your devotion, Israel, says the LORD God.

In return I've kept your teeth very clean, whatever your town—
nothing to eat in all your habitations—
but still you have not turned back to Me, says the LORD.

I held back the rain, with three months to go until harvest,
or I rained on this town, while on that one, no rain;
or a single field got rain, and another without it dried up.
Then two or three towns straggled over to another to drink, but
they left still parched;
and still you have not turned back to Me, says the LORD.

I struck you with blight and with mildew,
turned your gardens and vineyards to ruins,
while the locust gobbled your figs and olives,
but still you have not turned back to Me, says the LORD.

I set loose a pestilence, like that of Egypt,

killed your boys in war, let your horses be captured,

and burned your camps under your very noses,

but still you have not turned back to Me, says the LORD.

I destroyed part of you outright, like God's destruction of Sodom and Gomorrah,

so that you [who remain] are like a twig pulled out of the fire;

but still you have not turned back to Me, says the LORD.

That is why I keep doing this to you, Israel,

and since I am doing it, prepare to meet your God,

who made the mountains and created the spirit, and who tells a man what to say,

who can turn the dawn to darkness, and crush the heights with His tread—

the LORD, God of hosts, is His name.

Hear a message in the lament I sing for you, O house of Israel:

Fallen, no more to rise, is the Lady of Israel,

left alone on her land; there is no one to help her survive.

For thus says the LORD God:

The town that marched out a thousand will end up with a hundred,

and the one that marched out a hundred will be left with ten.

Yet thus says the LORD to the house of Israel: If you seek Me out, you will live.

But do not seek out Bethel, and do not go to Gilgal (or go off to Beer Sheba).

For Gilgal is going into exile, and Bethel will be turned to Beth-Sorrow.

•

"Right-thinking" people detest a rebuker, despise one who speaks the truth.

But since you crush down the poor and tax them with levies of grain,

these houses you built of hewn stone—you won't live in them,

and those charming vineyards you planted—you won't drink their wines.

For I know how many are your crimes; your sins are unbounded.

You attack the innocent for the sake of a bribe, and shove aside the poor in court.

Anyone who sees what's happening keeps quiet, for "this is an evil time."

Seek out the good and not what is evil, so that you may yet live,

and "May the Lord God of hosts be with you," as you say.

If you hate the evil and love the good, and establish justice in court,

perhaps the Lord God of hosts will take pity on the remnant of Joseph.

But thus says the Lord, the God of hosts, my Lord:

In all the squares will be cries of lament, and in all the streets, "Oh no!"

So call the farmer to mourning, and those skilled in laments to
wail. . .

•

I hate, I despise your festivals! Your assemblies give Me no
pleasure.
No matter how many your sacrifices, I will not be appeased.
The fatlings you offer to please Me I will not consider.
Take away the din of your singers, and the melody of your harps.
But let justice roll down like waters, and righteousness like a
mighty stream.

A Prophet in Israel

AMOS WAS A PROPHET who lived in the eighth century B.C.E.

This simple assertion never quite loses its shock value. Here was a man, apparently sane, who stood repeatedly before his equally sane contemporaries in Israel and said to them, "I have a message for you given to me by God; here is what He told me to tell you." And they listened; in fact, as far as we know, they generally believed what he and other prophets had to say. Modern scholars have investigated all aspects of ancient Israel—its history, religion, daily life, broader political and cultural environment—but the whole phenomenon of biblical prophecy remains in some ways baffling. Where did ancient Israelites get the idea that God speaks not just to any human beings, but to a select group of messengers, apparently chosen by God to publicize His decisions and decrees on earth?

The Bible itself seems to address this question in the context of the great revelation at Mt. Sinai, when God summons Moses up the mountain:

> When all the people saw the thundering flashes, with the sound of the trumpet and the smoldering mountain, they trembled at the sight and stood at a distance. Then they said to Moses, "You be the one to speak with us, and we will listen, but let God not speak with us, lest we die." Moses said to the people, "Do not be afraid. God has come here for the purpose of testing you, and in order that the fear of Him will always be before you, so that you not sin." But the people still stayed back, so Moses [alone] approached the thick cloud where God was.
>
> EXOD. 20:18–21

Later, reflecting on these events, Moses tells the people:

> [In the future] the LORD your God will raise up a prophet like
> me from among your brethren; listen to him. [For this is] in
> keeping with what you asked of the LORD your God at Sinai on
> the day of the assembly, saying "Let me not hear the voice of my
> LORD God [directly] any more, nor let me see this great fire any
> more, lest I die." And the LORD said to me, "They are right to
> say what they said. I will indeed raise up a prophet like you
> from the midst of their brethren, and I will put my words in his
> mouth so that he can tell them everything that I command him."
>
> DEUT. 18:15–18

Here, then, is one clear biblical answer to at least part of the
question concerning prophets. Prophets exist because ordinary
human beings cannot—or at least on one occasion could not—
stand to be in direct communication with God; some sort of spe-
cial intermediary was necessary. There was something a bit
ironic in the result. As a classical rabbinic text asks, "What is the
burden which is too heavy for 600,000 to lift up, yet one man
alone may bear it?" (Traditionally, there were 600,000 Israelites
present at the Sinai revelation.) A more modern-sounding answer
might be that only certain individuals are gifted enough to hear
God's words: in any society, the spiritual specialists are few and,
often, a bit odd.

The book of Amos addressed the same question and offered a
quite different answer. There is nothing special about me, the
prophet said, except that I happen to be the one God chose to
bring you this message.

> For the LORD God does not do a thing, unless He has revealed His
> intent to the prophets, His servants.

When a lion roars, who is not afraid?

So when the LORD God speaks, who will not be a prophet?

AMOS 3:7–8

~

Perhaps it is pointless to inquire into the prophets as human beings. Their words have been preserved for us in the Bible, is that not what matters? Yet the human side of prophecy is a subject that has, at least intermittently, occupied readers of the Bible over the ages. What did it mean to be a prophet? What would it have been like to hear and speak with the man named Amos who uttered the words above?

However prophecy first originated in Israel—this subject is most obscure—one key difference between ancient Israel and our own society has to do with people's expectations. It is striking that, after a certain point in Israel's history, prophecy seems to have become a steady, reliable presence: the "prophet in your midst" was someone whom you could count on to be there, like any other public figure. (This is the essence of what is being promised in the above-cited passage from Deuteronomy: in each age I will raise up a prophet like Moses.) If so, prophets did not have to keep on justifying their own existence or defining the institution to which they belonged; there simply were prophets, and here was another of "them." To live in such a world no doubt made it easier to be a prophet, though being a prophet was never easy.

This situation might be compared to that of the poet in Europe or America in more recent times. We do not know who the very first poet was, but after a while, there simply were poets, even inspired poets. Nobody asked, "Who made you a poet?" People simply asked, "What have you got to say?" For many centuries there were great poets and if, just now, there are not—well, perhaps that also has to do with society's expectations, or lack of them, in a world where popular singers and makers of movies or TV dramas have increasingly crowded poetry as such to the margins of our consciousness. (More about poets and prophets presently.)

In any case, the particular historical moment at which prophecy became an Israelite institution, according to the biblical narrative, came with the rise of the prophet Samuel. Before Samuel, "the word of the LORD was scarce; there was no frequent vision," whereas after his arrival, "All of Israel, from Dan to Beer-Sheba, knew that Samuel could be relied upon as a prophet of the LORD ; and the LORD continued to appear in Shiloh" (1 Sam. 3:1, 20–21). Following Samuel came a string of other great prophets. Nathan was a prophet in the court of David. The Bible never bothers to tell us why he was there. At times, as in the story of David's choice of which of his sons would succeed him, Nathan seems to function like a courtier in Elizabethan England, a participant in backroom conversations, manipulations even (1 Kings 1). Yet the same Nathan also appears elsewhere in a more classically prophetic role: he reproaches the king in the name of God. When David callously arranges the death of Uriah so that he can marry Uriah's beautiful wife Bathsheba, Nathan approaches David with what appears to be a legal query (David, as king, was also something like the Supreme Court):

And the LORD sent Nathan to David. He went to him and said: "There were two men in a certain city, the one rich and the other poor. The rich man had a great many sheep and cattle, but the poor man had only a single little ewe that he had bought, and he fed it and it grew up with him and with his sons—it would eat from their bread and drink their drink and even sleep next to him—it was like a daughter to him. But one day there came someone to visit the rich man, and he [the rich man] was reluctant to take an animal from his own flocks or herds to slaughter for the visitor['s meal], so he took the poor man's ewe and slaughtered it for the visitor." And David was very angry at the man and said to Nathan, "As the Lord lives, the man who did this thing deserves to die. Let him pay back the ewe fourfold, because he did not hesistate to do this thing." And Nathan said to David, "You are the man."

2 SAM. 12:1–10

Prophets frequently came to the king or the royal court with words of reproach, so much so that some have suggested that here is a clue to the prophet's very essence. After all, kingship did not come easy to Israel. While other nations exalted their kings to divine or quasi-divine status, Israel was heir to a different notion of things: "God is your ruler" (Judg. 8:23). Submitting to the political necessity of kingship did not sit well. To have in one's midst a man of God beholden to no one but accepted by all, a prophet who in God's name could tell the king to do this or stop doing that, was only to have surrendered part of that divine kingship. Perhaps, for the same reason, the institution of prophecy is also roughly coterminous with kingship's other end: after the return from Babylonian exile, when Jewish hopes for a restored Davidic king began to fade, so did the acceptance of prophecy.

During most of the biblical period, the "prophet in your midst" was indeed the reality that Israelites knew. The role of prophets came to particular prominence in the eighth century B.C.E., at a time when both halves of what was once David's United Monarchy (now divided into two rival kingdoms, northern Israel and southern Judah) were pursuing their own, independent courses. Early in that century, life was good, especially in the prosperous North; later on, the growing threat of the Assyrian empire darkened the horizon. No doubt both factors had something to do with the rise of the first "writing prophets," that is, those whose words have been preserved for us in collections: Amos, Hosea, Isaiah, and Micah all intoned against the corruption of their day and announced, in words that were preserved for all time, the dire fate that awaited their contemporaries.

≈

MANY PEOPLE MISCONCEIVE the function of a prophet in Israel to be that of predicting the future. But the prophets themselves, and those who heard them, saw a different function: they were essentially messengers, emissaries sent by God to announce His decisions. To be sure, here also was an element of prediction; to announce what God had decreed was usually to say what was just about to happen. But prophets were—as Nathan above—rebukers, not pundits. Their job was to tell the king, or the people as a whole, or Israel's enemies, what it was that God now wanted them to know, what He had decreed for them. Hence that most characteristic phrase of the prophet's harangue: "Thus says the LORD." This formula—precisely the same as that used by the emissary of some human potentate ("Thus says King So-and-So")—announced the prophet's actual function: to bring a message from God, a message of destruction or hope, rebuke or comfort.

But how should a prophet frame his words so that the people might absorb them? Indeed, did the prophet have any choice in the matter, or was he merely an automaton passing on God's speech? It is here that we encounter the building-block of Hebrew poetry, that standard sentence form:*

---

*For a fuller discussion of Hebrew poetic form, see "Introduction."

— — — — — — — — — —| — — — — — — — — — —||

This short, pungent, two-part sentence was the favored vehicle of prophetic announcements. In one or two lines a prophet could make clear God's will, and in a form that everyone could easily remember and repeat. Moreover, it was the elegant, precise style that characterized any "high" speech in biblical Hebrew—surely God's own messengers could hardly present their commissioned speech in any other fashion. Line after line and even page after page, these two-part utterances never lost their sharp, barbed quality; they must have seemed the only way to give the "last word" on something. And so they became, among other things, the way prophets spoke.

For example, when the prophet Jeremiah delivered to Israel a message of hope in the face of political threat, he did so in these words:

> *Thus says the* LORD:
>
> I recall to your credit your early devotion, your love as a bride—
> how you followed Me into the wilderness, in a land not sown.
> Israel is holy to the LORD, the first fruits of His harvest.
> Any who consume her will be guilty, "Evil will find them!" says
> the LORD.
>
> JER. 2:2–3

These four lines are a good example of how much a prophet could compress into a few words. In the first two lines, God refers indirectly to the beginnings of Israelite history, the time of the exodus from Egypt. You didn't need to leave Egypt, He says, and yet you did, following Me into the dry, sandy wasteland and a very uncertain future. In this you were a bit like a bride setting out with her husband (in those days, the sole provider). How did she know where her next meal would come from? All she knew was that she loved him and trusted him. And so now, years later, "I recall to your credit your early devotion," God says, and I will treat you accordingly.

The second pair of lines is even more compressed (though Jeremiah's own listeners certainly understood them right off). Long before Jeremiah's day, God had said that Israel was "holy." In Hebrew holy means "set off" and "special." The word is used both of God and of anything that belongs to God, for all that belongs to God is touched with holiness. This included, prominently, His people, "a kingdom of priests and a *holy* nation" (Exod. 19:6). But what, Jeremiah seems to ask here, does it mean in practical terms for God to have declared Israel "holy"? One well-known bit of holiness in the daily life of all ancient Israelites consisted of the first fruits of the harvest. They too were holy, since by statute they belonged to God, and so had to be carefully set aside for donation to His Temple; eating the first fruits, even the tiniest bit of them, was like stealing from God. It is in precisely that sense, Jeremiah says, that Israel is holy as well. For Israel is indeed God's first fruits among nations, the people whom He called "My firstborn son" (Exod. 4:22). Therefore "consuming" Israel—attacking her, or even taking the smallest part of her territory—is like consuming the holy first fruits that belong to God. Surely, Jeremiah says in these few words, He will not treat the former act any more lightly than the latter.

When the prophet Isaiah rebuked the people of Israel, he did so in equally compact, two-part lines:

> *Hear O heavens and hearken earth, the mouth of the LORD has spoken:*

> I brought up sons and raised them, but now they have rebelled against Me.
>
> An ox knows its owner, and an ass its master's trough.
>
> Israel does not know, my people do not begin to understand.
>
> ISA. 1 : 2 – 3

An ox is not a particularly discerning animal, certainly there are cleverer ones in the barnyard. It cannot do tricks, it doesn't come running when you whistle, but it does "know"—the word used here can also mean "be devoted to" or "obey"—its owner. Put a yoke on its neck and it will plow. An ass won't even do that. In fact, if you load it up with firewood or sacks of grain, it is just as likely as not to stop in its tracks in the middle of the market and sit down, and you can beat it and kick it, if it wants it will just stay there unmoving. But even an ass, if it does not know/obey its *owner,* at least knows "its master's trough": come dinnertime, it will stand patiently where it needs to in order to be fed. Israel, Isaiah says, is worse than either of these two. It does not obey its "owner" (and it is certainly no coincidence that Isaiah uses here a Hebrew word for "owner" that also means Creator). In fact, it does not even know where its food comes from, "its master's trough" (and it is certainly no coincidence that the word for "master" used here is also the name of the Canaanite storm god as well as, perhaps, an epithet for Israel's God). In fact, Israel "does not begin to understand," failing to obey its God or even recognize Him as the source of its own grain and sustenance. Anyone hearing these short, pungent sentences would not easily shake off the comparison.

But what can the prophets' use of this two-part sentence form, as well as their striking comparisons and vivid language, tell us about their very essence? Who *were* Israel's prophets? Two and a

half centuries ago, an English biblical scholar named Robert
Lowth proposed an answer: they were actually poets of a partic-
ular kind, the ancient Hebrew equivalent of the bards and
singers known in nations all over the world. Lowth, a professor
of poetry at Oxford, did not lightly toss off this answer. He him-
self was also a bishop in the Anglican Church and not one for
whom the Bible's sacredness was to be taken lightly. A great gap,
he felt, would always separate what he stressed was the *sacred*
poetry of the Hebrews from other, ordinary, poetry. If he never-
theless went on to assert that the prophets were fundamentally
poets, it was because he had researched for years the matter of
poetic form in the Bible and had come to the conclusion that there
was no *structural* difference between the way biblical prophets
and biblical poets expressed themselves. Both used that ever-flex-
ible, all-purpose sentence form,

— — — — — — — — — —| — — — — — — — — — —||

and both seemed to favor the striking metaphors and similes that
characterize poetry the world over. Did not all this imply some-
thing profound about the kinship between poetry and prophecy?
In a scholarly monograph originally published in 1753 in Latin
(then still the international language of scholarship), Lowth built
his argument brick by brick, describing as best he could the
workings of the two-part sentence form as well as that of biblical
metaphors and other poetic devices, and then showing their use
in different parts of the Bible: in the Psalms, in songs scattered
here and there in biblical narratives, in the Book of Job, and,
especially, in the biblical prophecies of Isaiah (whom he pro-
nounced the "most perfect model" of a prophetic poet) and
Jeremiah and Ezekiel. Indeed, these three together, Lowth said,
"as far as relates to style, may be said to hold the same rank

among the Hebrews as Homer, Simonides, and Aeschylus among
the Greeks." This conclusion, he believed, was the most far-
reaching result of his studies. Henceforth the Bible's prophetic
tirades or consolations, announcements of divine judgments or
calls for massive repentence, would have to be seen for what they
are, part of the corpus of the "sacred poetry of the Hebrews."

Lowth was certainly not the first to see behind the figure of
the biblical prophet an ancient Hebrew poet. Almost from the
start, those educated in the poetry of ancient Greece or Rome
identified the writings of biblical prophets with the barbed utter-
ances of the classical poets they had studied, and this identifica-
tion, transmitted by the Church Fathers, came to be commonplace
in medieval writings about the Bible. In some ways it was,
and still is, a natural conclusion to arrive at. Quite apart from the
matter of poetic form or stirring language, biblical prophets some-
times *behaved* like poets. For example, their words, like a poet's,
were sometimes accompanied by music; thus, a passing reference
in 1 Samuel 10:5 mentions a "band of prophets coming down
from the high place with harp, tambourine, flute and lyre, proph-
esying." Similarly, the prophet Elisha is presented in 2 Kings
3:14–16 in these terms:

> And Elisha said, "As the LORD of hosts lives, whom I serve,
> were it not that I have regard for Jehoshaphat the king of Judah,
> I would neither look at you nor see you. But now, bring me a
> musician." And when the musician played, the power of the
> LORD came upon him and he said, "Thus says the LORD."

Prophets themselves sometimes framed their words in compo-
sitions that they themselves referred to as "songs," "parables,"
"dirges," and other traditionally poetic forms. Moreover, like
certain later, European poets, biblical prophets sometimes

appeared to be insane or social outcasts. Constrained to call things as they saw them, they frequently brought upon themselves the undying enmity of the authorities. For all these and yet other reasons, even before Lowth wrote his treatise, European poets themselves had sometimes compared themselves to the biblical prophets.

But Lowth put forth his argument in the most concrete terms—as a matter of poetic form and not vague impression—and so convinced many of his readers of the objective truth of his contention. In some ways he is one of the great unappreciated figures of Western culture. For if prophets were really poets, then are not our poets at least somewhat prophetlike? In large measure as a result of his arguments, three or four generations of poets in Europe and America did indeed *become* prophetic, and the poet's inspiration came to take on much of the quality of the prophet's. Even today, prophet and poet overlap in a way that they rarely did before Lowth. More narrowly, in the world of the Bible itself, Lowth's arguments are still triumphant. Biblical scholars today still speak of biblical "poetry" as including the prophetic books of Scripture no less than the Psalms, and most modern Bibles print their translation of large chunks of the prophets in "poetic" lines rather than as straight prose.

Yet we still do not exactly think of prophets as poets, even divinely inspired poets, and it is worthwhile to consider why. To begin with, they did not say what they said, or write what they wrote, in order to find favor with this or that audience. We do not hear about people approving of a prophet's message; often, in fact, massive disapproval is what greeted him. He may have been a critic of society, but as best we can tell, not even the downtrodden greeted his words with heartfelt approval. What he had to say was news, not art (however artfully presented); so no one thought of *appreciating* a prophet's words, and if they did, the prophet himself would certainly have been vexed. In a striking passage, the people's attention to Ezekiel is compared to that paid to a popular singer—but in order to make the point that things are altogether different with a prophet:

> [God says to Ezekiel:] As for you, son of man, your countrymen like to speak about you as they stand around by the walls or in doorways; one man will talk with another, this one with that, saying, "Let us go hear what word has come from the LORD." And so they go to you the way people go, My people sit down before you and hear what you have to say, but they do not *do* it. With their lips they may do it, but their minds are only on gain. You— you are for them like a singer of lovesongs, with a beautiful voice and skilled at playing. They hear what you say, but they do not do it. When it happens, however— and it *is* happening—then they will realize that a prophet was in their midst.
>
> EZEK. 33:30–33

The prophet was not there to be found thrilling or moving; he was a messenger. And as such, he did not have an easy life. Jeremiah, in particular, details the woes of being one of God's messengers. Clearly, he would have found it easier to be something else:

> You tricked me, O LORD, and I was taken in; You got the better of me.
>
> So now I've become a joke; all day long, everyone laughs about me.
>
> Because every time I speak I end up railing; "Thieves! Robbers!" I yell.
>
> Yes, "the word of the LORD has come to me"—for shame and embarrassment all day.

But if I say "I won't mention Him, I won't speak anymore in His
name,"

then a fire burns in my heart, it rages inside my bones,

and I am too tired to hold it in, so I just can't.

JER. 20:7–9

~

AS FOR AMOS, we know little of the circumstances of his life,
but at one point he does mention his own lack of qualifications
for prophecy. After he had spoken out at the temple of Bethel—
the king's own sanctuary in the heart of the northern kingdom of
Israel—Amos was rebuked by Amaziah, the sanctuary's official
priest, who sought to banish him back to Judah. The temple offi-
cial was thus pitted against the very unofficial Amos. Amos
answered Amaziah in these words:

I am not a prophet, I am not even a prophet's son.

I am a herdsman, and a tender of sycamore trees.

But it was the LORD who took me from the flocks, and the LORD
who said to me, "Go now, be a prophet to My people Israel."

AMOS 7:14–15

There have, of course, been religious poets in every age, but
prophecy is not fundamentally a poetry of devotion. Nor is it yet a
poetry of social protest, crafted to persuade listeners of the worthi-
ness of this or that cause, although often it addresses issues of social
injustice or out-and-out politics. In the end, the prophet is some-
one who has been called, summoned, to carry a message from God.
(Some scholars have theorized that one Hebrew word for prophet,
nabi', is to be understood as "one who has been called.") He is not

free to make up what he will say, and if he is a "man of words," one who knows "the tongue of those who are learned" (Isa. 50:4), well, perhaps that is why God chose him in the first place. But the message that the prophet brings is as likely to be blunt as it is to be elegant, and, as so often in the book of Amos, it has nothing in common with the filigree and finery of his addressees:

> Seek out the good, and not what is evil, so that you may live.
>
> AMOS 5:14

The nature of human beings has long been to slide along "each in the cell of himself." It is this that Amos and the other prophets rail against. There is, as best we can tell, nothing formulaic about such denunciations of selfishness and injustice, but they are found in nearly every prophet's writings. Apparently, the prophet's gaze, once directed upward, does not return to earth to be as it was before. And so he sees the poor and the hungry, and he sees as well those who do not lift a finger to help them in their plight:

> Hear this prophecy, you Bashan cows on Samaria's hill—
> you who swindle the poor, extort the needy,
> then say to your husbands, "Honey, go get us something to drink."
>
> AMOS 4:1

> Oh you who lie down on ivory couches or sprawl on your sofas,
> who eat the fat of the flocks, or calves just whisked from their stalls,
> who strum on harps or "think up songs like David's,"
> drink wine from fancy bowls and wear the finest perfumes—
> you are troubled not at all over Joseph's downfall.
>
> AMOS 6:4–6

You trample the needy, soak even the poorest of the land.

You say, "When will New Moon day be over, so we can sell again?"

Or, "When will the sabbath be done, so we can open for grain?"

(With undersized bushels and oversized balance weights, you cheat on crooked scales.)

That's how you shake down the poor for credit, and the needy for a pair of shoes, "And let's sell the chaff for grain."

The LORD has taken an oath: "By Jacob's pride, I will never forget what they do."

•

I will turn your celebrations to mourning and all your songs into wailing.

I will put sackcloth on every hip, and baldness on every head.

I will make it like the death of an only child, and the aftermath like one bitter day.

AMOS 8:4–10

At the time that Amos spoke his words of rebuke and warning, they must have struck most of his listeners as little short of preposterous. What could ever possibly bring about such national catastrophe? Israel's northern neighbors, Assyria and Damascus, were then still relatively weak. At home, the trade economy was probably brisk and, despite the vagaries of rainfall agriculture, prosperity was in the air. Indeed, much of what Amos rails against appears to have been a massive expansion of wealth among the upper classes, built on unparalleled land expropriations and other mistreatment of the poor. The rich, at least, were doing fine, and fully expected to keep on doing so. As for

Israel's God, they seemed to believe (if they thought about Him at all) that He could be managed, bought off with abundant sacrifices. It is to such people that Amos directed the famous words of sarcasm at the beginning of our excerpt, mentioning by name two well-known places of public worship:

> Oh come to Bethel for sins, to Gilgal for sins galore!
>
> But bring your offerings every morning, and a tithe every three days;
>
> send up a thanksgiving and yell "Freewill sacrifice!"—let people know—
>
> for such is your devotion, Israel, says the LORD God.

His still more famous closing words make the same point: merely offering sacrifices, getting in with the religious authorities and the God they were there to serve, will not avert catastrophe.

> [*God says:*]
>
> I hate, I despise your festivals! Your assemblies give Me no pleasure.
>
> No matter how many your sacrifices, I will not be appeased.
>
> The fatlings you offer to please Me I will not consider.
>
> Take away the din of your singers, and the melody of your harps.
>
> But let justice roll down like waters, and righteousness like a mighty stream.

Amos's vision of divine justice must appear striking even today. No amount of external piety, he felt, could cover for unfairness. In communicating his message, he had little about him that was affable or even sociable. Certainly what he had to say made him no friends, as he himself reports:

"Right-thinking" people detest a rebuker, despise one who speaks the truth.

But since you crush down the poor and tax them with levies of grain,

these houses you built of hewn stone—you won't *live* in them,

and those charming vineyards you planted—you won't drink their wines.

For I know how many are your crimes; your sins are unbounded.

When the end came, it came swiftly. The Northern kingdom of Israel was utterly crushed in the Assyrian invasion of 722 B.C.E. The Assyrian king, starting with Tiglath Pileser III, had gradually but systematically built up their empire and turned its large standing army into a vicious fighting machine. The effects were devastat-ing. Although Amos himself did not bear direct witness to the events, his younger contemporary, the prophet Isaiah, described what the Assyrian army's onslaught was like:

Here they come in a rush—

None of them is tired, no one gives out, they don't sleep or drowse:

not a single belt is loosed, no one's boot-lace gets undone.

And their arrows are razor-sharp; their bows are drawn back all the way.

The hooves of their horses are sharp as a flint, and their chariot wheels are a whirlwind.

Their roar is like a lion's, they roar like a beast of prey,

one that growls ferociously as it grabs its food, then trots off with it; no one can stop it.

Isa. 5:26-30

The effects of the Assyrian invasion of the Northern kingdom were catastrophic both immediately and for the long term. According to the biblical account, Israelite survivors of that invasion were soon deported by the Assyrians to distant lands and replaced by foreign settlers transferred from elsewhere within the empire. The fate of the deportees, the "Ten Lost Tribes," is unknown. In any case, they never did get to return to their homes, however much their Jewish brethren in the south continued to hope for such an outcome. As Amos had said, "Fallen, no more to rise, is the Lady of Israel." Henceforth, the Southland, Judah, was the sole remnant, all that was left of a once mighty kingdom of tribes.

No one knows if Amos himself lived to see the Northerners suffer for their sins as he had predicted. But it matters little. He had said what he had to say, putting his words of rebuke in the cadenced rhythms of Hebrew's high speech:

> Hear the word that the LORD has spoken against you, O people of Israel, against the whole family that I brought up out of the land of Egypt: You are the only one I care for from among all the peoples of the land: that is why I call you to account for all of your sins. [After all,] do two go off together, unless they have both agreed to?
>
> Will a lion roar in the woods if it has no prey?
>
> Does a wild beast cry out from its cave, unless it has something trapped?
>
> Will a bird drop suddenly to the ground if it has not been snared?
>
> Does a trap snap up from the ground if something has not tripped it?
>
> Then if the alarm sounds in a town, will not the people tremble?
>
> And if evil befalls that town, will the LORD not have caused it?
>
> AMOS 3:1–6

CHAPTER 5

2 SAMUEL 1:19-27

S THE GLORY OF ISRAEL NOW A CORPSE LAID OUT UPON YOUR HIGH PLACES? OH, HOW THE MIGHTY HAVE FALLEN!

Do not tell of it in Gath, nor bring news of it to the streets of Ashkelon,
lest the Philistine women cheer, lest the heathens' daughters stamp and shout.

O mountains in Gilboa—no dew. No rain upon you, fields of Terumoth.
For there the mighty shield was profaned, the shield of Saul—the chosen king—gave way.

At the blood of the slain, or fierce soldiers' innards, Jonathan's bow did not flinch; nor did Saul's sword return from these unfulfilled.
Saul and Jonathan! Beloved and cherished in their life, in death they were not separated.
They were quicker than eagles. They were mightier than lions.

Weep for Saul, you women of Israel, who clothed you in crimson splendor and set golden ornaments upon your clothing.
O, how the mighty have fallen in the midst of battle—Jonathan, a corpse on your high places!

I grieve for you, my brother Jonathan; you were greatly beloved by me.

Your love was dearer to me than the love of women.

Oh, how the mighty have fallen, the weapons of war are now lost.

DAVID'S LAMENT

IN THE FIERCE WAR AGAINST the Philistines, Israel's first king, Saul, and three of his sons, Jonathan, Abinadab, and Malchishua, were all overtaken by Philistine forces at Mt. Gilboa. The Philistines killed Saul's sons, and the king himself, badly wounded, then took his own life. The next day, when the Philistines came to strip the soldiers of their weapons, they found Saul's body and cut off his head; then they hung his and his sons' bodies from the wall of Beth-Shan (1 Samuel 31). But a courageous Israelite raiding party managed to take down the bodies the next day and carried Saul and his sons back to Jabesh-Gilead, where the bodies were laid out and then burned, their bones buried subsequently.

David's lament tells us little about the God of Israel, or ancient Near Eastern religion, or the problem of theodicy. It is simply a lament by one of the Bible's great heroes for the dead king and his sons. According to the narrative of 1 Samuel, relations between Saul and David had hardly been cordial. The old king suffered from paranoid delusions (referred to as Saul's possession by an "evil spirit"), and David, an increasingly popular military leader, soon became the focus of those fears. Eventually, the raging monarch even sought David's life. In the meantime, however, David found himself doubly bound to the royal family, first by his marriage to Saul's daughter Michal, then by his enduring friendship with Saul's son Jonathan. Jonathan, himself a mighty warrior, was simply awed by David's courage and prowess in battle, and David was no less bound to Jonathan by admiration and friendship. As Saul's suspicions of David became more frenzied, Jonathan's friendship for David only grew stronger:

David said to Jonathan, "What did I do wrong? What sin have I committed against your father for him to want to kill me?" "Heaven forbid," he said, "you're not going to die! Look, my father doesn't do anything without telling me first. Why would my father hide such a thing from me? It can't be so!"

But David swore again and said, "Your father certainly knows that you like me. He must have said, 'Don't let Jonathan hear or he will be grieved.' But I swear by the LORD and by myself, I am just one step away from being killed."

Jonathan said to David, "Whatever you want, I will do."

David said to Jonathan, "Tomorrow is the new moon, and I am supposed to sit with the king. But let me go instead and hide in the fields until the evening of the third day. If your father notices that I'm not there, say 'David had to go to Bethlehem, his home town, to the yearly feast there for his whole family.' If he says 'Good,' then I am all right. But if he gets angry, then you can be sure that some evil had been planned against me." . . .

Jonathan said to David, "By the LORD, the God of Israel, I'll ask my father tomorrow or the next day, and if [the answer is that] he is well disposed toward David, then I'll send word to you and let you know. But if my father really does mean to harm you, then may the LORD do even worse to Jonathan if I don't tell you and send you off to safety. May the LORD be with you as once he was with my father."

. . . Then, Jonathan, out of his love for David, swore to him again, since he loved him as himself. Jonathan said to him, "Since tomorrow is the new moon [feast], you[r absence] will certainly be noticed, because your seat will be empty. So the day after tomorrow, go all the way down to the place where you hid the first time, and stay next to the Ezel stone. I'll shoot three arrows off to the side of the target, and I'll say to the boy, 'Go get those arrows.' If I then say to the boy, 'Look! The arrows are on this side of you—get them!' then you can come, you're safe and nothing is wrong, as the LORD lives. But if I say to the lad, 'The arrows are further, beyond where you are,' then leave, for the LORD has sent you away."

. . . David hid in the field. The new moon came and the king sat down to eat his meal. The king sat in his usual place, in the seat next to the wall, with Jonathan opposite him and Abner at Saul's side; David's place was empty. But Saul did not say anything on that day, for he thought, "it must be some accident—he's impure, yes, that's it, he's impure." The next day was the second of the month and David's place was again empty. Saul said to his son Jonathan, "Why didn't that son of Jesse come to the feast either yesterday or today?" Jonathan answered Saul, "David asked me if he could go to Bethlehem. He said, 'Let me go, because we have a family feast in the town and my brother told me to come. So please let me go off and visit my brother.' That's why he didn't come to the king's table."

Saul became enraged at Jonathan. "You son of a perverse, uppity woman! I know that you're siding with Jesse's son—to your eternal shame, and that of your mother too! As long as Jesse's son is alive, neither you nor your kingdom will be secure. Now go have him brought to me. He's going to die!"

"Why should he die?" Jonathan said to his father. "What has he done?"

At that, Saul threw his spear at him as if to kill him. Jonathan realized that there was no dissuading his father from killing David. So Jonathan left the table in a rage. He did not eat on the second day of the month because he was grieved about David and because his father had put him to shame. The next morning, Jonathan went out to the field to meet David, taking a young boy with him. He said to the boy, "Run ahead and fetch the arrows that I shoot." And as the boy ran, he shot the arrows so as to go beyond him. When the boy reached the spot toward which Jonathan had shot the arrows, Jonathan called to the boy, "The arrows are farther, beyond where you are." And Jonathan called to the boy, "Hurry up, don't just stand there!" Then

Jonathan's boy gathered up the arrows and brought them to his master.

1 SAM. 20:1–38

So it was that Jonathan saved David from the king's anger. When, long afterward, Saul and Jonathan were themselves killed in battle, the way stood open for David to become king. Yet David hardly greeted this event with gladness. As the biblical narrative makes clear, David's respect for the office of king was undiminished despite Saul's insane persecution of him; after receiving news of Saul's death, David—ever the military man—was moved to mention only Saul's resolve and personal daring on the battlefield. As for the loss of his friend Jonathan, David's feelings were altogether unambiguous, for here was his truest friend and ally, dead with half his life unlived.

It is doubtless to show David's nobility of spirit on this occasion that the biblical narrative has preserved this moving elegy. In simple words, David takes leave of the two men who had so dominated his life in recent years. His words have a restrained, understated quality that goes counter to the usually emotional language of mourning, but well befits one who had already seen many friends cut down in battle. What David says is so straightforward, and the movement from one theme to the next so direct and guileless, that readers for centuries have felt the depth of David's loss in their own hearts.

In biblical Hebrew, it was customary to mark a lament with a question or exclamation beginning with the word "How" (*eikh* or *eikhah*), an expression of the dismay felt upon great loss. Thus, various laments over the fall of Jerusalem to the Babylonians, collected in the book of Lamentations, begin "How . . ." (Lam. 1:1, 2:1, 4:1, etc.), and the mourning Temple singers, now captives in Babylon, similarly ask, "How can we sing a song of the

LORD" (Ps. 137:4). David's repeated "How. . ." comes in this poem's refrain line, "O, how the mighty are fallen." It aptly says what is in his heart at the sudden disappearance of these two looming figures.

CHAPTER 6

JOB 28

HERE IS A MINE FOR SILVER, AND A PLACE FROM WHICH GOLD IS EXTRACTED.

Iron is taken out of the earth, and copper is smelted from rocks.

Men probe the bounds of darkness, for the ore of deep shadow and gloom.

Far below the passerby's tread, in foresaken tunnels, they dig.

From the earth itself comes food, but underneath is molten fire,

whose stones are the source of sapphire, and the place of particle gold.

This pathway no eagle has known, nor the falcon's eye surveyed.

Panthers do not range this far, and the serpent won't chance upon it.

Here men work flint with their hands and root out the bottoms of mountains,

split open channels in granite, so their eyes will miss no treasure.

They muzzle the raging streams, bringing hidden things up to light.

But where can wisdom be found? And what is the place of understanding?

No one can name its worth; it is not in the world of the living.

The ocean says, "It is not in me," and the sea says, "Not here."

Bars of gold cannot buy it, its price is not measured in silver.

It cannot be weighed against gold of Ophir, or onyx or sparkling sapphire.

Gilded glass will not match it, nor can it be swapped for jewels.

Let no one speak of coral or crystal—the price of wisdom is dearer than pearls.

Ethiopian topaz does not compare, it outweighs the purest gold.

But where does wisdom come from? And what is the place of understanding?

It is hidden from the eyes of the living, unseen by the birds of the air.

The underworld and death say, "With our ears we have heard it spoken of."

But God knows its path; it is He who knows its place.

For He looks to the ends of the earth, sees all that is under the heavens,

weighing the wind in a balance, and measuring out the waters.

He determined the portions of rain, decided the flashes of thunder.

That was when He saw and surveyed it [wisdom], He established and searched it throughout.

But to man He said,

"The fear of the LORD—that is wisdom, and to turn from evil is understanding."

Where Wisdom Is Found

THE STORY OF THE BOOK OF JOB is well known. Job, a prosperous man in the land of Uz, suddenly loses everything: his wealth and livelihood, his children, and even his own health. Downcast and afflicted with sores all over his body, he tries to accept his fate but cannot. No matter how hard his "comforters"—sage advisers schooled in the ways of wisdom—urge him to accept God's justice, Job finds himself unwilling: there must be some mistake, he says, or our understanding of the world must be wrong. Finally, God Himself addresses Job, and after indicting his ignorance and shortsightedness, restores Job's health and good fortune as before.

In the midst of the protracted give-and-take between Job and his comforters comes an extended hymn to wisdom (Job 28). To understand it is to understand the basic assumptions of the Book of Job as well as the significance of God's final answer to Job's suffering. It all has to do with wisdom as it existed in the ancient Near East.

THE WORD WISDOM in Hebrew does not generally refer to a person's ability to understand things, though it can sometimes be used in that sense. On the whole, however, "wisdom" designates a specific body of knowledge. So, for example, the Bible's assertion that Solomon's wisdom "was greater than the wisdom of the people of the east, and all the wisdom of Egypt" (1 Kings 5:10 [some books, 4:30]) does not seek to compare his power of understanding with that of the sages of other nations, but refers to the greater body of learning that he had acquired. (For this reason, indeed, the text goes on to specify what that learning consisted of: three thousand proverbs, a thousand and five songs, plus a knowledge of plants, animals, birds, reptiles, and fish [1 Kings 5:12–13].) So similarly, when Ecclesiastes speaks of *acquiring* wisdom, it is clear that he does not mean increasing his potential for understanding, but coming to possess some actual body of learning: "I had gotten more and greater wisdom than all who ever ruled before me over Jerusalem, and my mind had come to know much wisdom and knowledge" (Eccles. 1:16). Wisdom usually meant things known, a body of individual insights.

Those insights, however, were neither infinite nor random. For, in the ancient world, knowledge was conceived to be an altogether static thing. What a person might come to know about the world was never new. It was inevitably part (although only a small part) of a definite, already existing body of knowledge. It was the totality of this finite body that "wisdom" signified.

Wisdom, in this sense, was deemed to play a special role in the world. Wisdom's insights included the very rules by which the world was governed, both the natural world and human society. In biblical Israel, as indeed elsewhere in the ancient Near East, this meant that wisdom had a divine character. The word wisdom thus designated, among other things, the set of plans with which God had created and continued to run the world:

> By wisdom the LORD founded the earth, by understanding He established the heavens.
>
> PROV. 3:19

> How great are your works, O LORD—every one you made with wisdom, the world teams with Your creations.
>
> PS. 104:24

How great are Your works, O LORD, deep indeed are Your plans.

One who is a fool cannot know this, nor a boor understand it.

Ps. 92:6–7

In modern times, we think of the world's rules as autonomous: there just is something called gravity or the first law of thermodynamics. But in the biblical world of God's presence, it was God who established the rules. Some of the rules were obvious enough: the sun will always rise in the east and set in the west, metals are extracted from rocks by heating them, storks roost in fir trees, and so on. But other parts of the divine plan—most of it, in fact—were hidden. However finite, the totality of wisdom was somehow beyond the grasp of any human being.

In alluding to this circumstance the Bible offers various explanations for it. One, certainly, was that God had intentionally hidden the rules by which the world worked, leaving it up to this or that sage to discover individual pieces of the puzzle:

It is the glory of God to conceal things, and the glory of kings to find them out.

PROV. 25:2

If only God would speak, if only He would open His lips to you, then He would tell you the secrets of wisdom, [reveal] understanding twice over;

yea, God would make you forget your suffering!

But can you grasp God's insights? Can you probe to the Almighty's limit?

JOB 11:5–7

This theme of concealed wisdom underlies the hymn translated above. "Where is wisdom to be found?" Job asks, and in formulating his answer he mentions some of the bits of wisdom that human beings *have* managed to figure out: how to mine silver and gold or smelt iron and copper, where to dig out precious stones from beneath the earth or gather coral and pearls from the sea. But all these images of digging deep and coming back with a prize are meant to point to that huge, underlying plan that is still largely beyond a man's reach, the great set of rules that is "deep, deep, who can grasp it?" (Eccles. 7:24).

A second reason is frequently mentioned for humanity's inability to understand the way the world works, and that is the brevity of human life. How could a human being even hope to discover any significant part of wisdom in the paltry number of years that are allotted to him?

> Since his [mankind's] time is apportioned, numbered by You down to the months, who have set his portion irrevocably,
>
> leave him alone, desist, and let him finish out his day like a hired hand.
>
> JOB 14:5

> The time of our lives is but seventy years, or if mightily [doled out], then eighty, and most of them are [consumed in] toil and fatigue . . .
>
> PS. 90:10

It is only toward the very end of life that human beings can begin to grasp God's ways:

> Wisdom is with the aged, and understanding in length of days.
>
> With [God] are wisdom and might; He has counsel and understanding.
>
> JOB 12:12–13

And so, finite though it might be, the corpus of knowledge underlying the world could hardly be mastered in a single human lifetime.

> For we are from yesterday, and [therefore] *know nothing*, our time on earth is a fleeting shadow.
>
> JOB 8:9

Indeed, sometimes the two motifs—God's hiding of wisdom and man's brevity on earth—were combined to explain human ignorance:

> [God] creates everyone nicely in his time, but He puts something hidden in their hearts, so that man cannot find out what God has created from beginning to end.
>
> ECCLES. 2:11

Given these fundamental circumstances, what could a human being hope to discover of the great rules governing life on earth?

~

BUT SOME THINGS *can* be found out; individual parts of the great divine plan were at times discovered by human contemplation. The very sages who bemoaned life's brevity and man's inability to uncover what God has hidden were also engaged in a centuries-long effort to pass on the individual insights that had been arrived at here and there. Already mentioned were those elements of the natural world—such as sunrise and sunset, the phases of the moon and movements of the stars, plus the ways of animals and birds and plants—that could be understood through careful observation. Such "scientific" matters certainly formed part of the theoretical corpus of wisdom known to biblical sages, as the above-mentioned passage detailing Solomon's wisdom (1 Kings 5:10 ff) attests on one end of the biblical time line. On the other, there is the figure of the biblical sage Enoch, to whom are attributed, in a section of the relatively late (third century B.C.E. and later) book bearing his name, observations about the length of the solar year as opposed to the lunar year and other complex astronomical and meteorological calculations (1 Enoch 72–82). So what we think of as science was certainly part of the ancient sage's domain. But it was only part; the other part had to do with human affairs, with how people behaved with one another and how God (sometimes in consequence) treated human beings. Indeed, it is a striking fact that the wisdom found within the Bible itself is generally not so much after scientific as *moral* truths, those great (or sometimes folksy) verities about the ways of God and man. For, no less than science, such things were deemed to be part of the great divine plan, indeed, an extremely vital part for human beings to know.

The sages who transmitted ancient wisdom might have described their undertaking as follows: The great divine plan that underlies all of reality is like a detailed design drawn on graph paper. Since the graph is basically hidden, no one can ever hope to survey its entirety. But here and there, individual sages have caught a glimpse of one little part of it, one little square on the graph paper, and if we can preserve their insights one by one and eventually put them together, then we will nonetheless have something, some individual parts of the divine plan. Perhaps we may even get some feeling for what the whole plan is like.

But how could these diverse insights into the divine plan be preserved and transmitted from generation to generation? It is here that we return to that building block of biblical poetry, the ideal sentence form,

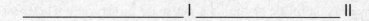

Ancient Near Eastern sages did not write philosophical treatises. They did not aim, as the ancient Greeks did, to unfold their thinking in long, discursive analyses. Instead, they cherished each and every insight on its own and sought to package each in that modular, highly transportable sentence form that was, at the same time, easily remembered yet extraordinarily flexible and subtle. So it was that the *mashal*—the Hebrew word refers to any proverb written in this two-part sentence form—became the basic unit of wisdom, not only in Israel but throughout the ancient Near East. Collections of hundreds of these "one-line poems" are among the oldest texts we have and bear witness to a protracted, collective effort to preserve each of the known coordinates of the divine plan.

The two-part construction of this poetic line (see Introduction) is hardly an incidental detail: it is the very genius of the form. Thus, the relationship between Part A and Part B is often quite subtle. A good example might be a biblical *mashal* whose subject is, as a matter of fact, *meshalim* (that is, the plural of *mashal*):

> A thistle got stuck in a drunkard's hand, and a proverb in the mouth of a fool.
>
> PROV: 26:9

Drunkards in the Bible are not known particularly for their boisterousness or meanness or insensitivity to pain, but for their lack of balance: they are often depicted as "staggering" and falling to the ground (Isa. 19:14, 24:20; Ps. 107:27; Job 12:25). So, apparently, the drunkard in this proverb. He must have fallen to the ground and, in groping around, thrust his hand into some sort of thornbush or briar and so gained possession, as it were, of a thistle or thorn: it got stuck in his hand. The event described in part B, the proverb asserts, is of a similar character. A fool may quote proverbs, but this does not mean that he has purposely set about learning them, nor that he truly understands or lives by their wisdom. Like the drunkard's thorn, the fool's proverb has been acquired quite by accident. Part B, as is usually the case, is thus the whole point of the *mashal* here, and part A, as frequently, is an image or specific case to which B is being compared. But of course to say only that is to pass over the little details, the poetry, of the comparison. For, certainly, it is important that the fool of part B is being compared to an utterly senseless drunk in part A, and still more that the proverb mentioned in part B is implicitly compared to something sharp and prickly in part A—since, in the biblical world, proverbs were *proverbially* sharp (they are "goads" and "nails" in Eccles. 12:11; see also Deut. 28:37, 1 Kings 9:7). The aptness, the associatedness, of likeness and likened in both cases seems to confirm the truth of the *mashal* well beyond the matter of accidental acquisition which is its overt common term. And so, yes, a proverb in a fool's mouth is indeed just like a thistle in a drunkard's hand, paining him rather than goading others—isn't it obvious once you think about it?

Proverbs like these were certainly pondered and studied. Some, like the above, were fairly straightforward and down-to-earth. But others required a sage's sustained contemplation in order for him to get the point:

A name is better than scented oil, and the day of death than the day of one's birth.

ECCLES. 7:1

The north wind gives birth to rain, and secret speech to an angry face.

PROV. 25:23

One who grabs a dog by the ears, a passerby who meddles in a dispute not his own.

PROV. 26:17

A good man's name [zekher] is a blessing, but the name [shem] of wicked men rots.

PROV. 10:7

Like the sound of thorns under a pot, so is the laughter of fools.

ECCLES. 7:4

There is no delegation in time of war, and evil will not protect those who do it.

ECCLES. 8:8

If a tree falls to the south or to the north, wherever it falls, there it is.

ECCLES. 11:3

(For an explanation of these and other *meshalim*, see "Solomon's Riddles.")

~

IT IS IN THIS SAME POETIC "wisdom style" that Job and his comforters speak throughout the book—and no wonder, since they are all wisdom sages. Now, wisdom in the ancient Near East was not a particularly Israelite preserve. It was found as well in ancient Egypt and in Mesopotamia; in fact, those places were deemed to be centers of wisdom, while Israel stood at the periphery. Solomon's exceptional wisdom is thus said to have "surpassed the wisdom of all the people of the east and all the wisdom of Egypt" (1 Kings 4:30 [or, 5:10]) precisely because those lands were where wisdom was championed. And it is certainly no accident that Job is from the land of Uz and no Israelite, nor are his comforters. Although the Book of Job is written in Hebrew, it was important to establish that the people in it are all representatives of wisdom as it was pursued in its purest form, in the famous academies far to the east or south of the land of Israel (which is also why the book's Hebrew is peppered with what are presumably Edomite and other foreign-sounding roots).

~

JOB, LIKE HIS COMFORTERS, has been trained not only in individual *meshalim*, but in the overall worldview of wisdom. It might seem surprising to think that wisdom *could* have a worldview, a philosophy. Was it not just a collection of individual insights? Nonetheless, wisdom sages did espouse a certain outlook on life. Wisdom's pursuit had always been more than a dry, intellectual exercise, more than just the search for individual pieces of the divine puzzle. In fact, when we encounter it in the Bible, wisdom is truly a way of life. Considered together, the individual insights of ancient sages had a certain consistency to them, and anyone who wished to pursue wisdom intellectually was likewise committed to living in accordance with its results, walking, as the sages put it, on the path of wisdom.

The first of these great themes has already been mentioned. Those who pursued wisdom believed first and foremost in the existence of a great divine plan or pattern underlying all of reality. This notion goes well beyond the more common idea that God controls all of life. It is not God's *control* that is involved here, but the existence of the great, preestablished pattern. That pattern is what Job's hymn is talking about: "Where can wisdom be found?" does not simply mean (as one might otherwise suppose), "Where can I find some wisdom and so become wiser?" Rather it means something more like: "I see the world and all that goes on in it, but where is the set of rules that is responsible for what I see? That set of rules must exist, since there is an apparent pattern underlying things; but then, why is it so precious, so deeply hidden, that no one seems able to put his hands on it?" No one, that is, but God. And even God himself, in a sense, is subject to that pattern (though He is, of course, frequently presented as its author),* since everything that He does or will do must obey its general stipulations.

Other themes flow naturally from this one. For example, ancient sages frequently assert that the divine plan is predicated

---

* It is interesting that our hymn does not quite say that God created wisdom, as does, for example, Proverb 8:22. It says that God *discovered* it: "That was when He saw and surveyed it, He established and searched it thoroughly." It is almost as if Job would agree with those ancient (and some modern) philosophers who believe in the eternity of the universe: it, and its rules, were always there.

on justice and right. Accordingly, the world has been arranged so that those who do good are rewarded and those who do not are punished. One could scarcely imagine that things could be any other way in a set of plans designed by God; the principle of divine reward and punishment is thus one of the crucial items of belief in the sage's world. Sometimes this principle was stated flat out:

> What the wicked man fears he ends up with, but the wish of the righteous is granted.
>
> PROV. 10:24

> No harm befalls the righteous, but the wicked are full of misfortune.
>
> PROV. 12:21

Other times, the same message was stated with a more poetic flair:

> One who goes straight goes safely, but he who makes his path crooked will be found out.
>
> PROV. 10:9

> When the whirlwind has passed the evil man is gone, but the righteous man is the world's foundation.
>
> PROV. 10:25

People sometimes have a tendency to sell biblical wisdom short. This is especially true in our own age, because the very nature of wisdom is misunderstood. It was not given principally as an explanation of how things work. It was fundamentally an attempt to impart an outlook and an instruction; like all such things,

it is necessarily abstract and schematic. "No harm befalls the right-
eous, but the wicked are full of misfortune"—is that truly the way
the world works? Certainly anyone in biblical times knew that
this often appeared not to be the case, knew incidents from his
own or other people's lives that tragically, horrendously, seemed
to impart just the opposite lesson. And how nice it would be if the
wickedness that human beings create were indeed like a passing
whirlwind that never outlived its wicked perpetrators! But his-
tory, and even personal memory, suggest that some evil lives long
after its devisers have perished, as no doubt ancient Israelites also
knew. But the world of wisdom is one of *nevertheless*. It lives in the
soul, a place of inside essences. However reality might appear in
the sunlight of everyday perception, in the realm of spiritual ab-
solutes, reality takes on another aspect. There the spirit rules, and
what *really* is, is not always what the eye sees.

Indeed, it is this same otherworldly, abstract sense of things
that causes wisdom writings to divide all of humanity into the two
groups mentioned in the proverbs cited above (and almost every-
where else in wisdom writings): the "righteous" and the
"wicked"—although "good" and "bad" might be a better trans-
lation, providing at least a feel for how these paired opposites usu-
ally function. Now, anyone who inhabits terra firma knows full
well that few human beings belong entirely to one category or an-
other. Why, then, do wisdom writings insist on assigning all of us
to one of these two groups? It is because in that severe eternity,
there really is no room for—no point in—nuance and shadow: the
great choices are made in the depths of the human soul, far from the
sunlight. In this sense the world of biblical wisdom is very much
akin to that of medieval European painting or medieval and Re-
naissance allegory: there is no attempt to render realistically the
human form or the ordinary events of this world, since that reality
is in any case trivial. What counts is what is underneath, the true

significance of ordinary things, and so everything turns into her-aldry and symbolism. Ordinary movement breaks down into dis-crete, significant cameos; life seems to take place in slow-motion.

For the same reason, the message of biblical wisdom could never be translated into ordinary cinema; but animated car-toons—*there* is a medium suitable for its spirituality. In that domain of primary colors, there are no shadows, and if the sun is seen at all, it is as a big yellow circle with squiggly rays shooting out of it. Only such a medium can capture the inside events of the soul, such as the time when the (wicked) cat, out to trick the (righteous) mouse, quickly sketches a picture of a tunnel and tacks it up onto a brick wall. Along comes the mouse on his motorcycle, heads straight for the picture—and drives on through it. It is a tunnel! Then the cat, in hot pursuit, heads his motorcycle toward the same spot, but craaash! It is back to being a picture of a tunnel tacked to a brick wall.

This is wisdom's world as well, in which the testimony of the senses is by definition suspect, treacherous, and everything that happens obeys a set of higher moral laws. If biblical man is fundamentally small, that smallness is, in wisdom writings, an expression of human inadequacy, even pathos. Here Little Man is indeed cartoonlike, pursuing his sometimes pathetic little plans from frame to frame:

> For at the window of my house, through my lattice, I looked down.
>
> There, among the foolish ones, I glimpsed amidst the boys a senseless lad,
>
> passing in the street next to her corner, now striding up toward her house;
>
> it is dusk, as day turns dark; nighttime comes with its shadows.
>
> And here comes the woman out to meet him, dressed as a harlot, but secretly planning.

She is loud and she is wayward, her feet will not let her stay home.

A step in the street, a step in the market, she lies in wait at every corner.

Now she seizes him and kisses him, then with impudent face she says,

"The larder's full of food—I had to pay my [sacrificial] vows today.

That's why I came out to meet you, looking all around—and now I've found you!

Well . . . my couch is spread with coverings, colored weaves of Egyptian linen.

The bed's perfumed with spices, myrrh and aloe and cinnamon.

Come, let's take our fill until daybreak and delight ourselves with love.

My husband? He isn't here! Gone off on some long trip,

with a bag of money in his hand—he won't be back till mid-month."

So she leads him astray with her talk, with smooth words she overcomes him.

He goes off with her right away, like a bull about to be slaughtered.

PROV. 7:6–22

Just as Little Man is as nothing before God, so his little plans are meaningless in the presence of the Great Plan, the underlying wisdom that guides all the world's affairs.

The LORD overthrows the nations' plans, undoes the peoples' designs.

The LORD'S plan stands forever, the designs of His heart for every age.

PS. 33:10–11

The LORD knows human designs—that they are a breath [i.e., passing, futile].

PS. 94:10

To humans belong the plans of the mind, but from the LORD comes the spoken reply.

PROV. 16:1

A man's mind may plan his path, but it is the LORD who will determine his steps.

PROV. 16:9

Many are the designs in a man's mind, but the LORD'S plan—that is what will stand.

PROV. 19:21

The divine plan is, not, however, indifferent to Little Man for all his smallness. On the contrary, what happens in human affairs, no less than the great cataclysms of nature, is determined by God's underlying set of rules. So the theme of reward and punishment is a crucial one in wisdom literature. The righteous are inevitably rewarded for their goodness, while the wicked are just as inevitably punished, and it could scarcely be otherwise. Since the world is fundamentally divided into the righteous and the wicked, there can be no doubt that their Maker will, in the course of events, apportion to each group its just desserts.

JOB'S EXPERIENCE, however, seems to teach otherwise. He knows, or thinks he knows, that his sufferings are undeserved. How then can this wisdom sage, an apostle of the wisdom outlook, face such apparent injustice? He has lost everything—children, wealth, well-being; now God, as Job sees it, is slowly torturing him until he dies. Certainly his experience was not altogether unique. Other sages must have also suffered, or at least observed undeserved suffering firsthand.* But Job's downfall is outstanding by its suddenness and severity. What is one to do? What should a person think? In the *nevertheless* world of wisdom, even such a life as Job's must be held to conform to the preordained ideal.

So it is that patience is another, crucial part of the wisdom outlook. Patience is the cardinal virtue of the sage. Since he knows that all happens according to the divine plan, the apparent triumph of the wicked, or suffering of the righteous, must be only temporary. In the end, he believes, right will win out, so in the meantime one must simply wait. What one waits for is not the world to come or a reward after death, but something in *this* world: eventually, right here on earth, the wicked of each generation will get what is coming to them, and so will the just. One must not only wait for the divine equilibrium to be established, but wait *patiently*:

> Better is the end of a thing than its beginning; better is patience than a haughty spirit.
>
> ECCLES. 7:8

---

*The author of Ecclesiastes similarly observed that "sometimes the righteous receive what befits the deeds of the wicked, while the wicked sometimes receive what befits the deeds of the righteous" (Eccles. 8:14).

Once again, a mashal's coordinated assertions really stand in the relation of "Just as A, So B," or "You agree with A, now therefore admit B." The wisdom of A here is indeed undeniable. Anyone would concur that something completed is far better than something that is merely in the planning stage, its final outcome far from certain; the difference is that between unarguable fact and laudable intentions. By just the same proportion, says the sage, so is patience, a willingness to take the long view, better than haughtiness. For if you are not willing to hold off until the thing is completed, your "I will not allow this to happen" or even "How can this happen to me?" will always be off the mark, a reaction to something-in-potential rather than something that really is.

Only one of Israel's ancestors is described as "wise," and that is Joseph (Gen. 41:39). Not only is he so described, but he does precisely those things—interpreting dreams, advising the king—that were typical of the ancient Near Eastern sage. So it is hardly surprising that the cardinal virtue of patience characterizes this wise hero's action at every turn. Sold as a slave by his brothers, he does not despair but soon rises to the top of Potiphar's household staff. Even his next reversal, when he is cast down into a dreary dungeon because of a false accusation by his master's wife, does not break Joseph, because, like any sage, he knows that righteousness in the end will win out. And so it does: he becomes, through a series of divinely manipulated events, viceroy of Egypt. The divine plan is thus not only something Joseph believes in, it is something that his whole life story demonstrates. Everything had been plotted in advance; the seven years of plenty are followed by the seven years of famine. God communicates this plan to Joseph, using Pharaoh as a mere conduit to the true sage's powers of understanding. Then, set in his justly deserved place of honor, Joseph never seeks to repay his brothers the ill that they caused him, since, in any case, all has happened according to the Great Plan. As Joseph himself tells them, "You are not the ones who sent me down here, but God" (Gen. 44:8), and later, "As for you, you planned evil against me, but God planned it for the good, so as to keep alive a mass of people, as indeed has happened" (Gen. 50:20).

Being patient is related, in Hebrew as in Latin,* to bearing and suffering. The ancient Near Eastern sage's patience included, prominently, his ability to suffer, to take it, knowing as he knew that his pains were either the just punishment for some sin he had committed, or part of some divinely instituted test. In either case, if the divine plan means that the righteous will ultimately be rewarded, what harm could there be in a few bumps along the way? "Are your sufferings pleasing to you?" asks one exponent of rabbinic Judaism—the most direct heir of the biblical wisdom tradition in post-biblical times—to another (Babylonian Talmud, *Berakhot* 5b). It is a reasonable question if you believe, as he did, that human suffering is ultimately a way of setting things aright again between the sufferer and God, indeed, a down payment for future rewards. And so even Job, at the height of his questioning, knows what is expected of him.

∼

SOMETIMES, ESPECIALLY IN TIME of suffering, what one fervently believes is as real as a glass of water. Doubled over on a bed of pain, the other "realities" of the world begin to fade and then depart entirely, and one finds oneself in a room where everything is strange and new, a world of the most touching pastels and little issues of

---

*Those people sitting in the doctor's office are called "patients" not because they are waiting but because they are sufferers, *patientes*.

inexplicably overwhelming importance. Weakened, one is over-
whelmed; a dull throbbing becomes one's intimate acquaintance,
and the events of the soul are measured on the evanescent mountain
ranges of the hospital's monitoring devices. Now nothing is halfway
or subtle, mere existence becomes engrossing. So is it for Job:

> But now, my soul is exhausted, as my suffering tightens its grip.
>
> Nighttime snatches my strength away, but my sweats do not let up.
>
> With great effort I loosen my clothes, or pull on my tunic's collar.
>
> I've been thrown down to the mud; yes indeed, I am "dirt and
> ashes."*
>
> If I bow to You, You don't answer; if I stand, You pay me no
> mind.**
>
> You've become my tormentor; You hound me with all Your force.
>
> You whisk me up with the wind, until even common sense fails.
>
> Oh, I know that death awaits me; there's one meeting place for all
> life.
>
> But one can't be required to be injured! Must one cry out in pain to
> perish?
>
> And have I not wept at my hardship, vexing my soul at my down-
> fall?
>
> I cried aloud—but evil came back; though I yearned for the light,
> there was blackness.
>
> Now my insides are never at peace; my final pains have come look-
> ing for me.

JOB 30:16–27

---

*A proverbial expression of human insignificance (see Gen. 18:27; "I am but
dirt and ashes"). But Job uses the expression ironically: someone who is in the
mud is indeed like dirt and ashes.

**Bowing down and standing up (with arms held upward) were both biblical
postures of prayer.

Job knows just how far his arm extends, even as he composes his words of bitter reproach. What God tells him at the end of the book is nothing he had not already heard, but it was important in ancient Israel for God to have said it anyway, important that it be the last word. You *don't* know, you are a mere human being.

> Who's this that impoverishes insight with words that lack understanding?
>
> Stand on your feet like a man! Now *I'll* ask, and you give the answers:
>
> Where were *you* when I set earth's foundations? Tell me if you're so clever.
>
> Who fixed its size—you must know—or measured it out with a cord?
>
> Into what were its bases sunk, or who put its cornerstone down,
>
> as the morning stars droned in chorus, and the sons of God all sang?

•

> Have you surveyed the whole earth? Tell Me, if you have mastered it.
>
> What is the path to where light is, and where is the wellspring of darkness?
>
> Can you take it back to its homeland, or survey the route to its palace?
>
> You must know—you were born back then! Your life has gone on for *so* long.

•

> Can you reverse My verdict? Declare Me guilty, so your side wins?
>
> Is your arm as strong as God's, or can you shout as loud as the thunder?

•

Who is it who stands to confront Me? Who lent Me cash and now wants it back?

Everything under the heavens belongs to Me.

> JOB 38:2-7, 18-21; 40:8-9; 41:2-3

⁓

THE VERY END OF THE HYMN to wisdom in chapter 28 of Job might appear puzzling:

> He determined the portions of rain, decided the flashes of thunder.
>
> That was when He saw and surveyed it [wisdom], He established and searched it throughout.
>
> But to man He said,
>
> "The fear of the Lord—that is wisdom, and to turn from evil is understanding."

Many translators of the last line have rendered its first word as "And" rather than "But." Either rendering is certainly possible; it seems to me, however, that "but" is what the Book of Job had in mind. For if God indeed knows all of wisdom, it seems to ask, then why should He not disclose it to mankind, or at least to his chosen sages? But, like it or not, He does not. What the hymn says, what the Book of Job itself seeks to say, is that humanity has been given only a very minor, albeit divinely granted, consolation prize: the hope, sometimes as fervent as fever, that the first step toward a state of understanding in which suffering makes sense is "the fear of the Lord"—rooted in a respect for the great gap between God and man—and that for mere mortals, departing from evil is at least a start, perhaps *the* start, the "beginning of understanding."

CHAPTER 7

JUDGES 5

 HEN REVENGE WAS SWEET IN ISRAEL, AND THE ARMIES WENT OUT WITH NOBLE HEART— BLESS THE LORD!

Listen, you kings! Hear me, O princes!

I will sing, I will sing of the LORD, I will praise the LORD the God of Israel.

O LORD, when You left Seir, when You came up from Edom's plain,

the whole land trembled, the heavens poured out—clouds poured out their waters.

The mountains quivered before the LORD of Sinai, the LORD God of Israel.

But in the days of Shamgar ben Anath, in the days of Yael, the caravans stopped.

Travelers kept to roundabout paths as the highwaymen grew fat in Israel, the highwaymen grew fat with spoils.

Until a Deborah arose, until there arose a mother in Israel:

"Let God choose armed men, let the armed men of the cities go forth."

Not a shield or spear was to be seen, among forty thousand in Israel.

My thoughts are to the fighters of Israel, the noblest of the people—bless the LORD!

O you who ride the tawny donkeys, who dwell by Madon and travel through the underbrush, the sound of trumpeters is at the watering places!

From there they will win the LORD's victory, victory over the highwaymen in Israel—that is when the army of the LORD will go down to the gates.

Up, up, Deborah! Up, up and sing it out!

"Arise Barak, take your prisoners, son of Abinoam!"

Then the mighty ones came down to Sarid, the army of the LORD came down for Him against the warriors.

From Ephraim, the greatest part were in the valley; afterward [came] Benjamin against the armies.

From Makhir came down the commanders, and from Zebulon, those who bear the the leader's staff, along with the princes of Issachar.

With Deborah and Issachar Barak stood ready, sent into the valley with his foot soldiers.

But in the legions of Reuben, great were the searchings of heart.

Why is it you sit among the sheepfolds, listening to the lowing of the flocks?

In the legions of Reuben, great were the searchings of heart.

Gilead dwells on the far side of the Jordan, and Dan—why does he stay in ships?

Asher crowds the seashore, hunkered down along the docks.

But Zebulon—an army scornful of death, while Naphtali climbs the heights of the plain.

When the kings came they fought, the kings of Canaan fought, at
Taanakh by Megiddo's waters; they took no silver spoils.

From out of the heavens the stars fought, from out of their orbits,
fought against Sisera's forces.

The river Kishon swept them away—Kishon River went out to
greet them—

march ahead mightily, O my soul.

Then the horses' hooves came pounding—with the gallop, the
galloping horses.

"Curse Meroz," said the LORD's messenger, "let its people be
cursed,

since they did not come to help the LORD, to help the LORD
against the warriors."

The greatest of women is Yael, wife of Heber the Kenite, the
greatest of women in tents.

He asked for water, she gave him milk, in a lordly bowl she offered
him drink.

But her hand she slipped to a stick, her right hand to a workman's
club,

then she clubbed Sisera and crushed his skull, she split and broke
open his temple.

He went down between her feet, fell down, splayed out;

between her feet down he went, fallen; and where he went down,
that's where he stayed fallen, the oppressor.

Through the window she peered, Sisera's mother, muttering
through the lattice,

"Why is his chariot so long in coming? Why are his chariot's hoofbeats so late?"

Let her smartest handmaiden answer—in fact, let her answer herself!

"It must be that they're dividing the spoils they've grabbed, yes—

'One or two women for every soldier, and this specially dyed cloth for Sisera,

specially dyed and embroidered, a dyed embroidery to wear on my neck.'"

So may all the LORD's enemies perish; but let those who are devoted to Him be like the sunrise in its strength!

TOUGH WOMEN

THE PRECISE EVENTS behind Deborah's victory song are difficult to reconstruct on their own. Some sort of domestic enemy—"highwaymen" is only an educated guess for this curious Hebrew collective, *perazon*—now held the people in thrall. The caravans on which commercial life depended had ceased; the caravaneers were afraid to take to the regular roads. According to the chapter that precedes this song, the Canaanite king, Jabin, and his general, Sisera, were then oppressing the people; somehow they and the song's "highwaymen" are to be connected with each other, perhaps as allies.

Into this breach step not one but two heroic women, and they save the day. The first is "Deborah."* According to the book of Judges, she exercised an important leadership role: seated at the Soothsayer's Palm Tree,** she rendered legal decisions (Judg. 4:5).

---

*If I put her in quotation marks it is only because of a long-held hunch that later tradition has actually turned what was once an ordinary common noun into a proper one. That is, the same letters that spell the name Deborah could just as well be spelling out a female agentive form of the regular Hebrew verb for *speak*: the word taken as "Deborah" could thus originally have referred to an anonymous female speaker or soothsayer (*dābôrāh*) in this song. It is noteworthy that chapter 4 of Judges likewise asserts that she was a kind of speaker, that is, a prophetess from the tribe of Ephraim (Judg. 4:4); perhaps this also reflects a tradition based on the original sense of "Deborah."

**That is, "[the] Deborah's Palm Tree," apparently similar to the "Teacher's [or: "Oracle-Giver's"] Oak Tree" in Genesis 12:6 and the "Diviner's Oak Tree" in Judges 9:37. The fact that the latter two trees are connected with common nouns—indeed, with words for two other kinds of speakers—may be another indication that "Deborah" is simply a common noun meaning "female soothsayer." Note also the tree mentioned in Genesis 34:8, the "Oak of Weeping." It is connected to an entirely different (and otherwise unknown) Deborah, Rebekah's nurse. Is this Deborah mentioned by name (although her name is quite irrelevant to the story) as a hint that the "Oak of Weeping" was also known as "[the] Deborah's Oak"?

As a divine messenger, she might also be expected to do what she actually does in the song (and what many of the other judges of her time did), indicate the precise moment when God will support a military attack: "Arise Barak, take your prisoners, son of Abinoam!"

The moment must have hardly seemed an auspicious one for such a fight. The potential forces were in sorry shape, with nary "a shield or a spear to be seen, among forty thousand in Israel." Moreover, the disunity of the tribes—some did eventually send troops, but others (Reuben, Gilead, Dan, and Asher are here singled out with bitter scorn) dithered and dallied—could hardly have seemed to foretell victory. Yet in an extraordinary battle, in which the stars or planets themselves seem to have taken up the cause of Israel, the Canaanite armies were defeated and Sisera, the Canaanite general, was forced to flee the battlefield for his life.

At this point the camera jumps to that other heroine, Yael (some Bibles: Jael), the wife of Heber the Kenite. The fleeing Sisera comes to her tent, apparently seeking refuge, and she offers it willingly. In fact, she generously ups his modest request for a drink of water. But as he drinks his "milk" (more likely, that watery yogurt drink still consumed in parts of the modern Middle East), apparently distracted and off guard, she approaches and smashes him mightily with a club. He falls at once at her feet, where he dies: "So may perish all the LORD's enemies."

THE FORM ITSELF of the song deserves some comment. Here one does not find line after line of orderly, two-part sentences as in the clas-sical Hebrew high style. Instead, the song is composed in that choppy, resumptive way of writing known here and there in the

Bible's songs and attested abundantly in the ancient Canaanite po-
etry of nearby Ugarit, such as this:

> Dan'el investigates, goes around the parched land, he sees a plant
> in the parched land, he sees a plant in the scrub.
>
> He embraces the plant and kisses [it], "Ah me, for the plant.
>
> May the plant flourish in the parched land, may the herb flourish
> in the scrub,
>
> may the hand of the hero Aqhat gather you, may it put you in the
> granary."
>
> Dan'el investigates, goes around the consumed land, sees a grain-
> ear in the consumed land, a grain-ear he sees in the blasted land.

   Ugaritic poetry and ancient songs like Deborah's seem to
suggest that the classical, two-part sentence form emerged from
with in an originally looser, "seconding" style, in which two-,
three-, or four-word phrases were simply strung together in
sequence by means of frequent repetition or restatement. Thus,
while some lines in Deborah's song do indeed fit the classic pattern:

_____ I _____ II

many others look more like:

_____ I _____ I _____ II

or even:

____ I _____ I _____ I _____ II

wherein a single phrase is repeated twice or even three times in
the same line with only minor variation. This "two steps for-

ward, one step back" way of writing sounded, precisely because of its stops and starts, like a highly ornamented way of speaking, elevated above ordinary discourse:

> I will sing, I will sing of the LORD, I will praise the LORD the God of Israel.
>
> O LORD, when You left Seir, when You came up from Edom's plain,
>
> the whole land trembled, the heavens poured forth—clouds poured forth their waters.
>
> Then she clubbed Sisera and crushed his skull, she split and broke open his temple.
>
> He went down between her feet, fell down, splayed out;
>
> between her feet down he went, fallen; and where he went down, that's where he stayed fallen, the oppressor.

It is easy to feel the power of the original Hebrew, its choppy ferocity. Even today, the text has not lost much of the wild thrill it must have conveyed when it was first uttered—the fear and privation of Israel's tribes under oppression; Deborah's unexpected, hope-bringing oracle; tension and frustration at the lack of volunteers for muster; but then, miraculous victory nonetheless, and sweet revenge. Against all odds, justice has been done, and with what flair!

Scholars have long noticed a few discrepancies between this song and the chapter that precedes it, Judges 4. That chapter relates basically the same story as the song, but in narrative prose. Here again are Deborah, Barak, Sisera, and Yael. Deborah gives her battle oracle (Judg. 4:14) and Barak attacks; Sisera flees and is later killed by Yael. But there are disagreements on other details. In the "prose" account the battle occurs at Mt. Tabor, in the song at Taanakh, near Megiddo. In prose Deborah is from the hill country of Ephraim, in the song she seems to come from, or at least be with, the tribe of Issachar. The number and identity of the partic-ipating tribes are different as well. All this has suggested to some that two different accounts had been preserved when the book of Judges was compiled and that each has been given its place.

There is one telltale item, however, that indicates that the prose account of chapter 4 may itself ultimately derive from a song, one similar to the song of Deborah as preserved in chapter 5 although differing in the details mentioned (Mt. Tabor, Deborah's tribe, and so forth). The telltale item is the manner of Sisera's death. According to chapter 5 (the song), as Sisera downs his drink in Yael's tent, she clubs him in the head. It seems clear from the context that Sisera is standing when this happens: he *falls down* between her feet—the implication is certainly that he had previously been standing. But there is always an ambiguity inherent in the sentence form

_____ | _____ ||

Sometimes the two parts can set forth two *different* (albeit related) items or ideas, as, for example:

Sing to the LORD a new song | play sweetly with exultation||

but at other times the two parts seem almost synonymous, describing a single item or action in different words:

I will sing to the LORD as I live | I will make melody to my God while I yet am ||

The difference between these two examples is not absolute. Even though, in the first example, no one would dispute that the second part of the line says something different from the first, the two halves are both talking about the same act of singing/playing. Likewise, in the second example, although the two halves are clearly talking about the same act, the very fact that each uses different words means that, strictly speaking, they are *not* saying exactly the "same thing." (That is, "sing" is not necessarily the same as "make melody," to refer to the Deity as "the LORD" is not the same as calling Him "God," and so forth.) Because such coordinated, separate-yet-related clauses are simply a given of Hebrew poetic form, there are bound to be cases where the precise meaning is unclear. Is the poet really referring to two different things, or is he simply freely rewording a single thing twice? Thus a line from ancient Ugaritic poetry:

> He took a lamb as a sacrifice in his hand | a kid in two hands ||

If "lamb" and "kid" are being used synonymously—that is, the poet is saying that he took a "sacrificial animal, it really doesn't matter what kind"—then both halves of the verse describe a single gesture. But it is equally possible that there are two actions here: first he took a lamb, then he took a kid. A similar ambiguity is found in certain biblical verses that contain numbers:

> There are three things too wondrous for me, four that I do not know.
>
> PROV. 30:18

> For three sins of Damascus, and for four, I will not revoke it [the punishment].
>
> AMOS 1:3

In the case of Proverbs 30:18, the text goes on to name four wondrous things, so "three, nay, four" seems to be the meaning. But

Amos goes on to mention only *one* sin of Damascus, so the alternation of "three . . . four . . ." seems to be altogether stylized; "three, four, a lot—it really doesn't matter."

Most of the time such ambiguity was not troubling. Indeed, sometimes biblical authors exploited this potential vagueness for its poetic possibilities. But the ambiguity in one line from the Song of Deborah turned out to be crucial:

> But her hand she slipped to a stick | her right hand to a workman's
> club ||

Are there two actions here or one, two implements or one? The word translated as "stick" has a variety of meanings in the Bible. It often means specifically a tent peg, but it can also mean some sort of digging stick (Deut. 23:13) and possibly other sorts of sticks as well. As for "workman's club," this is an altogether unique phrase. The word translated "club" appears nowhere else in the Bible; since it comes from a verb that means to strike or hit, "club" is probably as good a translation as any. Even the "workman's" part is somewhat interpretive—"toiling club" might be more accurate.*

So what really happened? Since Sisera *falls at her feet* in the song, it seems most likely that Yael did whatever she did with a

---

*The traditional Hebrew text of this line contains the particle *waw* (or *vav*), which often means "and." Thus, the line might be translated, "But her hand she slipped to a stick, *and* her right hand to a workman's club," implying that two implements were used. But this is hardly conclusive. The particle *waw* is often used emphatically, or to indicate that there is an ellipsis (as here, of the verb "slipped"); it may not mean "and" at all. What is more, the version of the Hebrew text used by the ancient Greek translators of the Bible apparently had no *waw*, since the Greek translation ("Septuagint") has no word "and" here. Thus, the question of how many things Yael seized remains unresolved.

single blow delivered from a single implement: she smashed him and he fell. Indeed, the song is most emphatic about this fall:

> He went down between her feet, fell down, splayed out;
>
> between her feet down he went, fallen; and where he went down, that's where he stayed fallen, the oppressor.

But because of the ambiguity of the line cited, another interpretation was possible. Suppose the first "stick" referred to was indeed a tent peg and the second was a different implement, a workman's *hammer*. Then it would seem that Yael might actually have driven a stake into Sisera's head—*that* is how she shattered his temple. But for such a thing to have taken place, it is doubtful that the two of them could have been standing; she certainly would not come up to Sisera holding both implements and say to him, "Hold still a minute while I line up this tent peg with your temple—there!" Such a thing would only be possible if he were completely offguard, say, asleep. Indeed, Yael could have offered him the "milk" in order to make him doze off after his flight from battle; then, as he lay unconscious, she could have come up to him in all safety and smashed the tent peg into his head. If he then "went down between her feet," perhaps he simply rolled (or was pulled) off the bed after the initial blow.

Such is precisely the scenario envisaged by the "prose" account of Judges chapter 4:

> And Yael went out to meet Sisera and she said to him, "Over here, my lord, come over here to me, don't worry." So he went over to her tent and she covered him with a blanket. He said to her, "I'm thirsty—give me a bit of water to drink." So she opened up a skin of milk and gave it to him to drink and then covered him again. Then he said to her, "Stand by the door of

the tent, and if anyone comes and asks if there's a man in here, say no." But Yael, the wife of Heber, took the peg of a tent [two words: literally, "the tent peg (or "stick") of a tent"] and put the hammer [a different, less ambiguous, word than the "club" of the song] in her hand, and she went up softly to him and sank the tent peg into his temple, and he flopped down onto the ground—he had been tired and dozed off—and he died. In the meantime, Barak came in pursuit of Sisera. Yael went out to meet him and she said to him, "Come and let me show you the man you're looking for." He went into her tent and there was Sisera, fallen down dead with a tent peg in his temple.

JUDG. 4:18–22

It seems as if the author of this account had read, or heard, the "song" version, but had interpreted its crucial line as

But her [left] hand she slipped to a tent peg | and her right hand to a workman's hammer ||

—two quite separate actions with two different implements. If that was indeed what happened, then she must have used them to finish Sisera off while he was lying unconscious, perhaps indeed put to sleep by the generous drink of milk mentioned in the song. Only in that manner would Yael have had the opportunity to kill him with *two* implements, using the hammer to drive a tent peg into his skull.

~

IT WILL NOT HAVE ESCAPED the alert reader that Yael is a bit more ladylike—for a killer—in chapter 4 than in chapter 5. It is one thing to confront one's victim standing and finish him off with a powerful, if unexpected, smash of a club. It is quite another to cover him with blankets, put him to sleep with a drink of milk, then come up on him as he dozes and drive the ancient Semitic equivalent of an ice pick through his brain. This notwithstanding, even the more "feminine" Yael does end up killing the bad guy, thus performing successfully the hard job that Barak had set out but failed to accomplish. So whether one reads chapter 4 or 5, one might well ask: Were women just *tougher* back then? For that matter, what is one to make of "Deborah" (or the anonymous soothsayer)? The same chapter 4 that somewhat feminizes Yael nonetheless presents a Deborah who barks out orders like a general (albeit in the name of God):

> She sent a message calling to Barak, son of Abinoam from Kedesh (Naphtali), in which she said: "The LORD, the God of Israel, orders that you proceed to Mt. Tabor, taking ten thousand troops with you from the tribes of Naphtali and Zebulon. Then I [God] will draw Sisera, Jabin's general, to you at the river Kishon, along with his chariotry and his troops; and I will give him over to your power." But Barak said to her, "If you come with me, then I will go, but if you won't come with me, I will not go." And she said, "I will indeed go with you."
>
> JUDG. 4:6–8

Here is a professional soldier who apparently will not go off to battle unless this strong woman—the appropriately described "mother in Israel"—holds his hand all the way! Are these tough biblical women there to teach a lesson about how men and women *really* used to be?

One should be careful not to conclude too much. Barak probably wants Deborah to accompany him not for comfort but precisely because she is God's messenger: her presence would not only bring divine protection but, in concrete terms, would allow him to know just the right moment for battle. (This is what other "judges" announce: Ehud [Judg. 3:28], Gideon [Judg. 7:15].) Moreover, if Deborah is a *judge* (in this period of biblical history, the term might better be translated simply as "leader") well, the Book of Judges seems repeatedly to delight in God's surprising choice of divinely inspired leaders: the hoodlum son of a prostitute (Jephthah), a somewhat overzealous womanizer (Samson), or someone from the "weakest clan in Manasseh" who is also "the least in my family" (Gideon) are similarly unlikely choices. Thus, it would probably be unwise to base a conclusion about the general status of women from Deborah's high office. As for Yael's killing of Sisera, her being a woman was the whole point: to be killed by a woman was an ignominious death, one in which the victim's enemies, male and female, would exult precisely because of the eternal shame it conferred. This is made clear by the continuation of the above-cited passage:

> But Barak said to her, "If you come with me, then I will go, but if you won't come with me, I will not go." And she said, "I will indeed go with you. But there will not be any glory for you on the journey on which you are embarking, for the LORD will *sell out Sisera by the hand of a woman*." And Deborah went off with Barak to Kedesh.
>
> JUDG. 4:8–9

The point is that Sisera is denied a warrior's death: he is "sold out."

Of course, some of what the Bible says about women has long been misinterpreted in the opposite direction. For example, even today most readers (and translators) fail to understand what God says in the book of Genesis before He creates Eve. In the story,

Adam already exists but is alone. "It is not good for the man to be alone," God declares, "I will make a help for him"* (Gen. 2:18). He then searches among all the various animals and brings them to Adam, apparently in an attempt to find him this "help." But scholars have long wondered why the more common word for "help," the feminine noun *ezrah*, does not appear here, but rather the masculine form *ezer*. (If ever there was a circumstance in which the feminine form was warranted, it was here!) What is more, the phrase "help *for him*" is, in Hebrew, something more like "help *corresponding to him*." Why should Eve be described as a (masculine) help corresponding to Adam?

Some time ago a Jewish biblical scholar suggested—the idea has strangely not been taken up—that *ezer* here is to be identified as the Hebrew equivalent of a word found in Arabic (*'adhrā'*), a feminine noun that means "virgin" or "young woman." If this Arabic root also existed in Hebrew, *ezer* is indeed what it would look like. So the argument seems altogether persuasive. What God proposed to create was not a "help" at all but a "young woman corresponding to [that is, belonging to the same species as] Adam." It was precisely because a survey of the existing animals failed to yield a female corresponding to Adam (Gen. 2:19–20) that God has to create one out of Adam's own side or "rib."

If, thus, woman was not created to wait on man hand and foot, men and women nevertheless had quite different roles in the Bible, and this was clearly not a case of "separate but equal." The story of Adam and Eve concludes with God telling Eve that Adam will now "rule over" her, paradigmatically, so it seems (Gen. 3:16). The situation of women was, in any case, quite dif-

* Many translations read "help-mate," but there is no "mate" in the Hebrew text.

ferent in the ancient world from what it is in modern society. Parents contracted marriages for their children at an early age, and this was a straightforward financial transaction, like buying a car or a house; the young (often, very young) bride then went off into the possession of her husband.

Woman's domain was very much inside the village, indeed, inside the home. She had, or aspired to have, many children, life's greatest blessing for both man and woman. It was quite literally a *blessing*: "Be fruitful and multiply!" are God's repeated words of blessing to humanity in general as well as to a single individual (Gen. 1:22, 28; 9:1, 7; 28:4; 35:11); the same idea appears elsewhere in a longer formulation: "May the LORD increase you with the likes of you a thousandfold and [so] bless you as He said to you" (Deut. 1:11). Of course, "home" itself was somewhat different in those days. Three generations might regularly populate that space, and the dense pattern of village housing, and dense network of overlapping blood ties therein, meant in any case that many other women (sisters, sisters-in-law, aunts, cousins, and so forth) were, quite literally, across the room or at least within shouting distance. But this was so in part because the world outside the town—the "field"—was potentially dangerous. It is stated in biblical law that if a woman claimed to have been raped within the confines of a town, both she and the rapist were to be killed, because if she had "cried out" she surely would have been heard—and saved. But if she claimed that the rape took place "in the field," then he alone was to be killed and nothing was done against her, because in the open field no one could have heard her (Deut. 22:23–24). Out in the open was not, in any case, a place where a woman might normally be found. The proud boast of a certain Cilician king of the eighth century B.C.E. was that "in my days, a woman might go alone [in "dangerous" places] with her spindles, thanks to Baal and the gods," that is, she could actually walk about anywhere in broad daylight unescorted without having to worry about being raped or kidnaped or killed.* This, alas, was apparently not the day-to-day reality of most women in the ancient Near East. Even the murderous Yael is "the greatest of women in tents."**

All this must be taken into account in an understanding of the place of women in the Bible, including the stories of Deborah and Yael. But another difference should also be part of any assessment of the ultimate significance of the heroism of these two women. In biblical times (and even in our own day, elsewhere on the globe) enemies were principally external; the main fight was people's daily fight to survive and thrive as best they might, to protect themselves against attack and to increase their numbers. In those days, a woman who delivered a war oracle or killed an enemy general, by whatever means, was celebrated, but not particularly because of her sex; she was simply a hero. Just now, however, in modern society's "gender wars," the perceived enemy is necessarily internal. In this grim, zero-sum game, tough women have taken on an entirely new significance.

---

*This is from the bilingual (Phoenician and Luwian) Karatepe inscription, column 2, 4–5. A similar boast is found in a bilingual tablet of royal correspondence unearthed at Susa, "A man walks to where his heart desires, and [even] a woman with her spindle and distaff." The closeness of the two formulations may indicate that this was the somewhat standardized boast of a monarch, a boast whose actual relation to reality remains to be otherwise attested.

**Some translations of this verse read, "more blessed than women in tents." But this apparent "comparative" is really here (as often in Hebrew) a superlative. The point is certainly not to imply that Yael is something other than a "woman in tents," since that clearly is what she is in the story.

PSALM 51

E GENEROUS, GOD, IN YOUR KINDNESS; IN YOUR GREAT MERCY, ERASE WHAT I DID.

Wash me clean of my misdeed, purify me of my sin.

For I know that I did wrong. My sin is always on my mind.

You are the one I offended; I did what is evil in Your sight.

You always are fair in Your sentence, impartial in what You decree.

But consider, I was born to transgression, conceived by my mother in sin.

Secretly You love faithfulness; so in secret help me grow wise.

Clean me with hyssop till I am pure, wash me till I'm whiter than snow.

Let me have gladness and joy once again, let the bones that You struck rejoice.

Turn away from my sin, and blot out all my offenses.

God, make me a pure heart, put a new, right spirit inside me.

Please, don't send me away; don't take Your holy spirit from me.

Give me back the joy of Your help, hold me up with a kindly spirit.

Let me teach sinners Your ways, so offenders may turn back to You.

God, my salvation, save me from death, so I can celebrate Your kindness.

Open my lips, O LORD, and my mouth will declare Your praise.

You don't want any sacrifice I could give; You have no desire for offerings.

God's sacrifices are a chastened spirit; a chastened, broken heart God will not reject.

And in Your favor be good to Zion, rebuild Jerusalem's walls.

Then true sacrifices will be Your delight, whole and burnt offerings; then let the sacrificial animals go up to Your altars.

A PURE HEART

ONE OF THE CRUCIAL CONCEPTS of biblical religion is almost altogether absent from modern life. The whole of the biblical world was divided into two great domains, the holy and the profane. (It would not be terribly misleading to think of these two terms as somewhat parallel to "special" and "ordinary" in our own world.) In the category of the holy was, first, God Himself, and then anything that was closely attached to or associated with God: His Temple and all the accoutrements thereof, the first fruits of the harvest and firstborn of the flocks (since these belonged to God), the sabbath day, the priests who served in the Temple, and so forth. Whatever was not holy was just ordinary, everyday, usual.

Anything that was holy had to be treated with care. As God says to Moses in their first encounter at the burning bush, "Take your shoes from off your feet, for the place that you are standing on is holy ground" (Exod. 3:5). Holy space was different from ordinary space, and you could not just barge into it as if it were ordinary. In almost exactly the same terms, Joshua is later told, "'Take your shoes from off your feet, for the ground that you are standing on is holy'; and so Joshua did" (Josh. 5:15). With the holy you had to watch your step, literally. Ecclesiastes says, "Guard your step as you walk to the house of God" (Eccles. 4:17). When the Book of Isaiah seeks to caution about strict observance of the sabbath, it uses a similar image: "If you keep your foot back from the sabbath, from pursuing your affairs on my holy day . . ." (Isa. 58:13). Whatever was holy was approached with caution; this imposed a whole new way of walking. There was nothing abstract about this; by "walking" is meant actual walking.

The reason has to do with a second polar opposition, the "pure" and the "impure." The impure was the enemy of the holy. As a consequence, anyone who wished to enter God's house, His Temple, had to be pure, that is, cleansed of all impurity. Now, impurity is not exactly synonymous with "uncleanness," although the concepts are in some ways analogous. But ordinary dirt, for example, is not "impure," and so getting dirty did not in itself make a person unfit to approach the holy. Someone became impure by coming into contact with a person or substance that gave off impurity. Touching a dead body, for example, made one impure. Certain bodily functions created impurity. A man became impure through the emission of semen; a woman became impure through childbirth or menstruation. Those with a certain unidentified skin disease (usually mistranslated as "leprosy") were impure. The Bible lists a whole host of animals, birds, and fish that are impure and thus may not be eaten, while other animals, birds, and fish may. What the common denominator of all these kinds of impurity was is a question that continues to challenge biblical scholars; equally challenging are the actual laws and procedures for purification, since different kinds or degrees of impurity required different sorts of cleansing. But one thing is clear. Purity was a concern for all those who wished to go before God. They had to be constantly vigilant beforehand so as not to enter a house, for example, that had become impure, or to sit on a chair that had been made impure. On their way to the Temple itself, they had to walk with great caution lest they accidentally brush up against someone or something that would render them impure. Should they become impure, repurification required, in most circumstances, a certain waiting period and one or more immersions in a stream or specially prepared bath, depending on the sort of impurity.

Thus far one might think that purity was an entirely physical concept. Whatever the precise rationale for this or that thing imparting impurity, it was a matter of the body, of physical contact or presence, and the means to purification were similarly physical. Yet purity and impurity were not only physical. The language of impurity was also used—and there is no reason to think of this as a mere figure of speech—to describe intangible, nonphysical things. For example, God makes people "pure" from their sins on the Day of Atonement: "For on that day atonement will be made for you, to purify you from all your sins; you shall be purified before the LORD" (Lev. 16:30). The reason is that sin, in the Bible, is often *almost* physical. Sin stinks. It has a way of adhering to a person like physical impurity, and so it must be removed, taken care of. It will not go away on its own.

So, for example, when a single person, Achan the son of Carmi, failed to obey God's decree and looted goods that were to be burned, the Israelite troops were routed. Joshua protested to God, but God answered him:

> "Get yourself up! Why should you prostrate yourself? Israel has sinned and broken my covenant . . . Get up and clean [literally, "make holy"] the people, tell them 'Clean yourselves for tomorrow. For thus says the LORD, the God of Israel: something forbidden is in your midst, O Israel.'"
>
> JOSH. 7:10–12

The "something forbidden" are the looted goods. So long as they are not destroyed they are a source of corruption that adheres to all the people and from which they need to be cleansed.

One of the most remarkable passages in this connection is the prophet Isaiah's own account of how he became a prophet:

> In the year that King Uzziah died, I saw my LORD seated high up on a lofty throne whose skirts filled the Temple. Seraphim

hovered above Him. Each had six wings: with two of them each would cover his face, with two others his feet, and with the two others he would fly. And each one would call to the other and say, "Holy, holy, holy is the LORD of Hosts; His glory fills the whole earth." The supports of the threshold began to shake from the sound of the calling, and the Temple began to fill with smoke. And I said, "Woe is me! I am as good as dead. For I have impure lips, and I live among a people of impure lips—yet my eyes behold the king, the LORD of Hosts." But then one of the seraphim flew toward me carrying a coal which he had picked up with tongs from off of the altar, and he touched it to my mouth and said, "Now that this has touched your lips, your sin is gone and your wrongdoing has been done away with." Then I heard my LORD's voice saying, "Who can I send? Who will go for us?" And I said, "I am here. Send me."

ISA. 6:1–8

There is no such concept as "impure of lips" in the Bible's laws of purity. But it seems clear what Isaiah meant: I have spoken in a way analogous to that careless, ordinary way of walking that can lead to physical impurity; indeed, I live among a people who are, in this sense, impure of lips, and I have been in contact with them. By what right can I now behold God's very being? In saying this, Isaiah was not showing some sort of false modesty. He felt he was in mortal danger, and the danger would not go away just by his standing there. He needed to be purified, and so he was. What the seraphim—usually understood as some sort of angel, but the word literally seems to mean "burners," "burning ones"—did was to cleanse his lips with a burning coal. Once so purified, he could go on and stand before God, indeed, bear God's message on his own lips.

~

THE HUMAN NEED to be purified, made fresh again, can be grasped today, even though we no longer live in the biblical polarities of "holy-ordinary" and "pure-impure" by which this need was once easily apprehended. But no less nowadays than of old, human beings still stumble into this or that error as they walk sloppily along in life. In fact, sometimes they don't stumble, they jump willingly. And even today, people still have what T. S. Eliot called a "sense of sin," a feeling for sin as a contaminating substance and an enduring source of impurity. To be sure, not everyone seems to have it to the same degree, but for those who feel it keenly, this "sense of sin" carries its own imperative. It can (as in Eliot's play *The Cocktail Party*) make them do strange things, send them off on the longest journeys.

Psalm 51 is about this "sense of sin," the feeling of being stained with an impurity that will not go away and that now threatens everything. The desperation is palpable. "Wash me clean of my misdeed, purify me of my sin. . . Cleanse me with hyssop till I am pure, wash me till I'm whiter than snow. . .Turn away from my sin, and blot out all my offenses." Unless one knows about that other kind of impurity, the kind contracted by physically touching a dead body or some other impure thing, these words lose much of their significance. What the psalmist says in the plainest terms here is that he feels the contact of his sin on himself. It follows him wherever he goes. He wants to wash it away but ordinary washing won't get rid of it. What he needs, what he asks for, is a fresh start.

> God, make me a pure heart, put a new, right spirit inside me.
>
> Please, don't send me away; don't take Your holy spirit from me.

The need to be pure again is not merely a matter of internal satis-faction or well-being. "Don't take Your holy spirit from me" probably means here, "Don't kill me."* Death is, in any case, on the speaker's mind, as the psalm makes explicit later on; in his present, stained state, he does not feel that he can last long. He asks to be made pure, new again, so that he can begin life com-pletely afresh as one who walks carefully in the mandorla of purity, like someone forever on his way to the Temple.

But how does one become "purified" from sin? The procedure for other kinds of impurity, those acquired through physical con-tact, was straightforward enough, but what about sin? Of course, in the days of temple worship, certain sacrifices were prescribed for certain sins. Yet it is clear that, for the speaker of this psalm, no such procedure is in itself sufficient ("You don't want any sacrifice that I could give; You have no desire for offerings").** Something else has to take place. So all the speaker can do is make his request in words spoken directly to God. As another psalm reports:

> As long as I kept my silence, my bones wasted away, and I wailed all day long.
>
> Day and night Your hand would be heavy upon me; my strength oozed away in the summer dry spell.
>
> But when I told You of my sin and did not hide my wrongdoing,

---

*Why should God withdraw His "holy spirit"—the speaker's soul, that is—from him? Precisely because it is holy; holiness cannot dwell in the midst of impurity.

**Some have suggested, in view of the closing lines of this psalm, that it was actually composed in the period after the destruction of the Jerusalem Temple by the Babylonians in 587–6 B.C.E., but that, even if true, seems hardly the whole point. Others maintain that the last two lines are a later addition to this psalm.

when I said, "I will confess my sins to the LORD"—then You forgave my sinful wrongdoing.

Ps. 32:3–5

The Jewish *viddui* and the Christian confessional attest to the ongoing need for something to take place, for some words to be said, in order for purification to occur. (Along with those words, people sometimes fasted for forgiveness or otherwise afflicted themselves.) Psalm 51 itself, in fact, has played such a role. Over the centuries both Jews and Christians have found in the mere recital of its words the needed act. Eventually this psalm became one of the seven "penitential psalms" that many recited by heart to atone for their sin.*

~

One who covers up his sins will not prosper, but he who acknowledges and abandons them will find mercy.

Prov. 28:13

This *mashal*, like so many, contains a little surprise. The phrase "will not prosper" does indeed mean that, on the first or even second hearing. But the same Hebrew verb also means "to cause to prosper," and combined with the direct object "his/her way," or even with that object only implied, it can mean "to succeed." That is the less obvious message of the first part of this proverb: one who tries to hide his sins not only will not prosper in general, he will not even succeed at hiding his sins. The only alternative, then, is found in Part B, acknowledging and abandoning them. These two became the canonical elements of penitence: speaking words of confession and abandoning the sin.

---

*The others were Pss. 6, 32, 38, 102, 130, and 143

In later times as well, the connection between purification from some physical contaminant and purification from sin was strong. Ben Sira, the second-century B.C.E. author of Ecclesiasticus (some Bibles: "Sirach"), evoked it directly:

> One who touches a dead body, bathes [in order to remove the impurity] and then touches it again, what good will his washing have done him?
>
> Such is a person who fasts for his sins and then goes and does them again.
>
> SIR. 34:25–26

Similarly,

> So long as a person holds a source of impurity in his hand, then even if he washes in the Siloam or in all the waters of Creation, he can never be purified. But if he casts the impurity from his hand, a bath of minimum measure is enough to purify him. So does it say, "He who confesses and abandons [his sins] will gain mercy" [Prov. 28:13].
>
> TOSEFTA, Ta'aniyot 1 : 8

⁓

IN THE WORLD OF THE HEBREW BIBLE, there was nothing automatic about God's forgiveness. All the human being could do was ask for it and hope that his request would be granted.

Psalm 51 has been connected* with a specific sin, one re-

---

* The Bible precedes Psalm 51 with the heading, "For the leader, a psalm of David. When Nathan the prophet went to him after he had gone in to Bathsheba." Some modern scholars believe that headings like this one were added to the psalms at a later stage of editing—that, in this case, an anonymous editor reading this psalm came to the conclusion that David must have composed it in his most desperate hour.

counted in the life of David (2 Sam. 11). According to the biblical narrative, David fell in love with a woman who was already married; Bathsheba was the wife of Uriah the Hittite. David was in a position, however, to take care of that inconvenience. As commander of the army, he ordered that Uriah be sent to the front lines and that, once he was in place, the troops around him suddenly be pulled back, exposing Uriah to mortal danger. So it came to pass: Uriah died in battle, and Bathsheba became David's wife. But David did not get away with it. The prophet Nathan came to deliver God's rebuke to David (see "A Prophet in Israel") and to announce his punishment: the newborn child that David had conceived with Bathsheba would die.

David became frantic. He knew that he had done wrong. He begged God to spare the baby's life, he fasted and he cried, he lay on the ground and would not move, but nothing availed. After seven days of illness the child died.

> David got up from the ground and put on anointing oil and changed his clothes and went into the house of the LORD and prostrated himself. Then he went home and, at his request, they brought him food and he ate. His servants said to him, "What is this that you are doing? When the baby was still alive you fasted and wept. Now that the baby is dead you get up and eat food?" He answered, "While the baby was alive I fasted and wept because I thought, 'Perhaps the LORD will take pity on me and let the baby live.' But now that it is dead, why should I fast? Can I bring it back to life? I will go to [join] it—it will not come back to me." And David comforted his wife Bathsheba and he went to her and lay with her and she gave birth to a son. He called his name Solomon, and this one the LORD loved [that is, spared].
>
> 2 SAM. 12:20–24

There is a limit to what one can do, the narrative seems to say; an ancient Israelite might try to set things aright, but in the end the verdict was God's alone to decide. As a consequence, biblical piety had little traffic in prolonged self-absorption or self-contemplation, as Psalm 51 itself attests. The polarities of holy and ordinary, pure and impure, were a way of understanding the world and understanding oneself, but purification was not an aim in itself. It was a necessary step to allow one to go before God or to return to Him after impurity. The psalmist asks that such purification be permitted to him so that he, in turn, can instruct others:

> Let me teach sinners Your ways, so offenders may turn back to You.
>
> God, my salvation, save me from death, so I can celebrate Your kindness.
>
> Open my lips, O LORD, and my mouth will declare Your praise.

CHAPTER 9

THE ONE-LINE POEM

(CHOSEN FROM PROVERBS AND ECCLESIASTES)

 name is better than scented oil, and the day of death than the day of one's birth.

ECCLES. 7:1

The north wind gives birth to rain, and secret speech to an angry face.

PROV. 25:23

One who grabs a dog by the ears, a passerby who meddles in a dispute not his own.

PROV. 26:17

A good man's name [zekher] is a blessing, but the name [shem] of wicked men rots.

PROV. 10:7

Like the sound of thorns under a pot, so is the laughter of fools.

ECCLES. 7:4

If a tree falls to the south or to the north, wherever it falls, there it is.

ECCLES. 11:3

SOLOMON'S RIDDLES

DAVID, ACCORDING TO THE BIBLICAL ACCOUNT, was a youthful shepherd, musician, and sometime war lord who rose to prominence in the court of Israel's first king, Saul. Through his military prowess, personal flair, and diplomatic savvy, David not only ended up succeeding Saul as king but cobbled together a new nation that united North and South and outlying areas into a single, powerful entity. Almost overnight, what had once been a collection of independent and disunified tribes was now a regional powerhouse, threatened by no one and, on the contrary, inspiring fear in the hearts of its immediate neighbors. David's reign of nearly half a century was not untroubled, and more than once internal enemies nearly toppled him from the throne. But he survived to old age intact and left all that he had created to the next king, his son Solomon.

Solomon is presented in 1 Kings as a champion of wisdom, that worldview/ philosophy/ way of life that existed within and outside Israel in ancient times:

> And God gave Solomon very great wisdom and understanding, and breadth of mind like the sand on the shore, so that Solomon's wisdom surpassed the wisdom of all the peoples of the east and all the wisdom of Egypt. He was wiser than any man, more than Ethan the Ezrahite, and Heman, Calcol, and Darda, the sons of Mahol, and his fame spread to all the nations roundabout. He could speak three thousand proverbs, and his songs were a thousand and five. He could speak about trees, from the cedar that is in Lebanon to the hyssop that grows out of the wall; and he could speak about animals and birds, reptiles

and fish. People would come from every nation to hear the wisdom of Solomon as well as all the kings of the earth, for they had heard of his wisdom.

1 KINGS 5:9–14 (SOME BIBLES: 4:29–34)

Certainly part of Solomon's association with wisdom had to do with the trajectory of the kingdom he ruled. David had presided over the nation's rise; it was Solomon's lot to equip it with all the splendor that such a kingdom deserved. He built, according to 1 Kings 6, the magnificent Jerusalem Temple, an undertaking that required seven years to complete. The same narrative also mentions an apparently still more elaborate, thirteen-year building project, the construction of Solomon's royal palace. Israel was now, suddenly, an international power to be reckoned with, and a new, cosmopolitan air hovered over the capital city. Kings in the ancient Near East had always liked to gather professional sages and wise men to their courts as advisers and administrators; trained in the ancient wisdom tradition, such men knew the virtues of patient restraint and how to consider a matter from all angles before acting. Solomon doubtless had such advisers and so became a patron and champion of the wisdom of the ages.

The most famous story of Solomon's wisdom no doubt puzzles many modern readers. The Bible recounts that two prostitutes who lived together in the same house gave birth at the same time. One night, while they slept, one of the babies died. Each mother claimed that the surviving baby was hers. The case came before Solomon who, as king, also functioned as the supreme judiciary.

Then the king said, "This one says, 'It is my son that is alive,' and that one says, 'No, the dead son is yours and it is mine that is alive.'" So the king said, "Bring me a sword," and a sword was brought to the king. And the king said, "Divide the child in two, and give half to the one and half to the other." Then the woman whose son was the living one said to the king—for she was moved by great pity for her child—"Please, my lord, give the living child to her, but whatever you do, don't kill it!" Meanwhile the other one said, "Neither of us should have it. Divide it." The king said, "Give the child to her [the first woman] and do not kill it, for she is the mother." And all Israel heard of the ruling that the king made and they were in awe of the king, for they saw that the wisdom of God was in his heart to have ruled so.

1 KINGS 3:23–28

The story sounds absurd on the face of it, unless one assumes the existence of a law that the narrative omits to mention: disputed property whose true ownership could not be established by witnesses was indeed to be divided. Such a legal principle is known from elsewhere, though the "property" in question was of course never a living human body; the law applied to a piece of real estate or gold or some similarly divisible good.* But in saying "Divide the child in two," Solomon was apparently evoking a principle that was widespread enough, and well-known enough, to fool both mothers into thinking it might apply in their case as well. Moreover, it may well be that the two mothers' response to Solomon's intended imposition of this principle was not really a sure-fire indication of who the true, biological mother was. In ancient Israel as in more modern times, people were not always sane and certainly did not always react logically in stressful circumstances. No doubt it would have taken considerably more investigation to determine with certainty who the true mother

---

*Or even, to judge by the (considerably later) rabbinic form of this law, a disputed garment. See Mishnah, *Baba Meṣi'a* 1:1. The garment might also be sold and the profits divided by the disputants.

really was. But it did not matter. Solomon does not say, "She is the *true* mother," only "She is the mother," that is, whatever the biological relationship, this woman is the only one of the two fit to be given responsibility for the child henceforth.

Another narrative in 1 Kings likewise refers to Solomon's wisdom:

> The queen of Sheba, hearing of Solomon's reputation, came to test him with riddles. She arrived in Jerusalem with a great retinue, camels loaded down with spices and a large quantity of gold as well as precious stones. When she met with Solomon she spoke to him concerning everything that she was interested in, and Solomon answered her concerning each thing; there was nothing that the king did not know or could not tell her. And when the queen of Sheba saw all of Solomon's wisdom, as well as the palace that he had built, and the food of his table, with his courtiers sitting about and his servants standing in attendance in their finery, and moreover the wine that he served and the sacrifices that he would offer in the house of the LORD, she was left nearly speechless. She said to the king, "So it is true what I heard in my own land concerning you and your wisdom. I did not believe what I heard until I came and saw with my own eyes. Now I see that not the half of it was told to me. You have acquired even more wisdom and wealth than what I had heard. Fortunate indeed are these men, your courtiers, since, standing ever in attendance before you, they can hear of your wisdom."

> 1 KINGS 10:1–8

The happy overlap of intellectual and material success attested in this passage would certainly give the lie to the American jibe, "If you're so smart how come you're not rich?" (Perhaps the queen of Sheba was legitimately impressed by both, or perhaps she was simply shrewdly assessing the fabric of which the king's self-esteem was woven.) In any case, the word "riddles" in the first sentence is of great interest here. Later tradition has embellished this encounter between King Solomon and the queen of Sheba and supplied the "riddles" mentioned in the text. For example, one ancient source* has her pose these riddles:

> "It came out as dust from the ground, and its food was dust from the earth; poured out like water, it lights up the house." (The answer: naphtha.)

> "When a breeze blows hard over everyone's head, this one cries out with a bitter cry and bends itself over like a reed; it's good for the rich but bad for the poor; fine on the dead but not on the living; it makes the birds glad and the fishes sad." (Answer: flax.)**

Interestingly, other traditions have her ask not riddles but serious matters of science, theology, or natural lore:

> "How does the sphere of heaven move, to the right or to the left? And in its rotation does it make a complete circle or not?"***

---

* Second Targum to Esther.

**The flax in the first part is probably a boat's sail, which whistles in the wind and bends; the rich turn flax into fine cloth, but in its rough form it is worn by the poor as rags; for the same reason linen shrouds are all right for the dead (they don't mind the feel), but not for the living. Birds eat flax seed, but fish are caught in nets made of flax.

***From the Armenian "Questions Addressed by the Queen and Answers Given by Solomon, son of David" in J. Issaverdens, *The Uncanonical Writings of the Old Testament Found in the Armenian Manuscripts of the Library of St. Lazarus* (Venice: Armenian Monastery of St. Lazarus, 1907), 140.

The latter sort of question might seem to better fit the context of the queen's visit; surely she did not travel all that distance for polite parlor games. But to understand what may really have happened here, one must return to the proverb (*mashal*), that one-line, two-clause saying in which ancient wisdom was carried:

———————————— I ———————————— II

The word for "riddle" in Hebrew, ḥidah, is the *mashal*'s closest cousin. Not only does the ḥidah apparently take the same form as the *mashal*, but the two words often appear together, as if synonyms or at least closely associated items (Ezek. 17:2; Hab. 2:6; Pss. 49:5, 78:2; Prov. 1:6). Thus, it seems altogether likely that what went on in this encounter was neither an exchange of riddles (in our sense) nor yet the asking of straightforward questions of the queen's own formulation, but something between the two, a request for clarification concerning a difficult *mashal* or two that the queen had heard but did not fully understand.

In order to see how this might be so, it is well to consider the only real "riddle" (ḥidah) exemplified in the Hebrew Bible, Samson's (Judg. 14:14). One day Samson went to inspect the carcass of a lion he had killed with his bare hands sometime earlier. When he arrived he found that in the meantime a swarm of bees had made their hive in the lion's body. He scooped some honey out with his hands and went on his way, but later, the incident inspired him to make up a riddle at a marriage feast:

Out of the eater came the eats, and out of the strong, the sweets.

JUDG. 14:14

At first glance, the utterance seems completely nonsensical. An eater does not *produce* food, "the eats," but consumes it; "strong" in Hebrew also means "bitter" and is thus the opposite of "sweet."

But that is just the point: the ḥidah, like the mashal, must be true if only you think about it long enough, ponder its words. The difference, of course, is that the mashal is a universal truth, whereas this ḥidah, at least, depends on guessing the precise situation (lion's corpse, beehive) in order to be true.* But from a literary standpoint the two forms are identical, and the operating instructions for both are also the same: just contemplate the words and you'll see how true they are.

Interestingly, when the marriage revelers manage to wheedle the details behind Samson's riddle out of his wife, they present their answer to Samson in the form of two questions:

> What is sweeter than honey? What is stronger than a lion?
>
> JUDG. 14:18

It was pointed out long ago that, while these words might be considered an adequate answer to Samson's riddle, they themselves could constitute another riddle, one answered with a single word: love. In any event, having thus been defeated by unfair means, Samson retorts with yet another mashal-like utterance (it even rhymes in Hebrew): "If you hadn't plowed with my heifer, you wouldn't have solved my riddle"(Judg. 14:18).

～

THE MASHAL, BASIC UNIT of all wisdom, is often a bit of a riddle, too. Consider, for example, the first of those proverbs listed earlier:

---

* This type of riddle (called a "Halslösungsrätsel" by literary scholars) is known in many different countries and settings. Its solution cannot be figured out by the ordinary listener or reader, since it depends on some private bit of information known only to the riddler.

A name is better than scented oil, and the day of death than the day of one's birth.

Eccles. 7:1

The first clause (we can call it Part A) seems quite indisputable: one's name, one's reputation, is better than any material possession, better even than precious oils, which, in biblical times, were scented with rare, imported spices to make perfume or lotion. Valuable as such scented oils might be, they could, in the world of biblical wisdom, scarcely match in value the worth of a person's own name.* But what about the second half of the proverb: how is the day of death better than the day of one's birth? Birth is almost always a happy occasion and death almost always a sad one. So in what sense can the day of one's death be "better"? Here, truly is the *mashal* as riddle. (But a biblical sage would say that every *mashal* is like a riddle in that it needs pondering in order to reveal its full sense.)

The precious oil mentioned in Part A is the clue to its true meaning. Such oil was valuable, so valuable that it was usually kept stoppered in little vials to protect it. In these vials it could survive for some time. Yet, even so, precious oils could— would—eventually go bad. As Ecclesiastes itself later mentions, one tiny, dying fruitfly can get into the oil and become the proverbial "fly in the ointment,"causing it suddenly to turn and putrefy (Eccles. 10:1). And if it was not such a fruitfly, then the mere passage of time would eventually do the same thing; no matter how valuable the oil, sooner or later it would turn, and what was worth hundreds of dollars one day would be quite worthless the next.

---

* Indeed, the truth of part A is only driven home by the near-perfect chiasmus of its sound, *tob shem mi-shemen tob.*

So too is it with the human being, or at least the human body. Sooner or later our physical existence gives out. This does not necessarily happen all at once, but eventually what had once been vigorous and full of strength begins to deteriorate, and the way of all flesh leads to the grave. Quite the opposite, says Ecclesiastes, is a person's name (by which he means not only a person's reputation—what other people know about him or her—but rather more abstractly the sum total of a person's accomplishments, the "what can be said afterward," a kind of condensation of everything that he or she has done). A name, in this sense, is not acquired at birth. The newborn baby quite literally has no name, and even after it has lived for a time, it has no name in the sage's sense. *That* kind of name only begins to be acquired as the person does things on earth, starts to determine through deeds what he or she really is. The more a person lives and does, the more that name grows and becomes more detailed and specific.

Now, quite unlike precious oil or the human body, a person's "name" in this sense is altogether immune to the inroads of time. A name—in this abstract sense of the sum total of all of a person's deeds—is immutable, so that eventually that name is all that remains of our earthly existence. Years, centuries after our death, the "name" (in this abstract sense of the sum-total significance of a person's doings) is what we are, what our life has amounted to.* For this reason, the proverb says, the day of a person's death may be a sad day, but it is indeed better in the sense that the process of building that name, which only began on the day of birth, is now at last complete. Thus, just as you concede, says Ecclesiastes, that a good name is better than precious oil (since precious oil is bound

---

*"Name" ought to be distinguished from "fame." In the proverbist's sense, one need not be famous to have a name, indeed, one need not even be remembered. The name is simply that abstract essence of one's being, one's significance, as it were, that continues even after death.

to go bad but the name is immune to decay) so you must also admit that the day of death, although the precious substance of the body has at last gone, is nonetheless better than the day of birth, for on this day the person's "name" is now complete and set for eternity.

~

TO PACK ALL THIS MEANING in a single line was the height of the biblical *mashal*, the fullest realization of the building-block line of biblical poetry. So such cleverly worded sayings really did amount to one-line poems. Pondered in the royal court, learned by heart and rattled off in series, they stumped, entertained, and enlightened successive generations. Their teachings were the very embodiment of divine wisdom, little spots on the highly detailed grid of God's set of plans for the world.

~

ANOTHER ONE-LINE POEM, this one from the Book of Proverbs, echoes Ecclesiastes' sentiments about the value of a person's "name":

> In the goodness of the righteous a city rejoices, and when the wicked disappear there is gladness.
>
> PROV. 11:10

At first one might think that this proverb simply presents a straightforward contrast: a city rejoices in the life of its righteous citizens and in the death of its wicked ones. But that is not quite the point. If such had been the proverbist's intentions, I think he would have written something more like:

> In the *lives* of the righteous [and not in their "goodness"] the city rejoices, and when the wicked *die* [and not "disappear," which is not precisely a synonym for death] there is gladness.

The fact that the proverbist avoided this obvious, and rather simple-minded, bit of parallelism, writing instead *goodness* and *disappear*, suggests a different interpretation. As a matter of fact, everyone in this proverb is already dead. The proverb's claim is that, even after their death, the righteous leave a legacy of goodness to the world, a goodness (in biblical Hebrew the word can, in fact, mean "abundance" or "wealth") from which people will continue to benefit long afterward, whereas the wicked, however harmful they may be during their lifetime, do not merely perish at the end but disappear without a trace: they leave no legacy.

In other words, this proverb's sentiment is quite the opposite of Marc Antony's in Shakespeare's *Julius Caesar*. The evil that men do, it says, can scarcely outlive them: as soon as they die they are powerless to harm us. The good that people do, by contrast, lives on after them, so that generations not yet born will reap the benefits of that good. The city that rejoices, in this proverb, thus stands for all of humanity: our true achievement is in what we are able to leave to them, whereas wickedness (which in Proverbs is often a synonym for self-indulgence or even foolishness) simply spends itself out and leaves nothing.

A person's name is the subject of another *mashal* in Proverbs:

> A good man's name [*zekher*] becomes a blessing, but the name [*shem*] of wicked men rots.

PROV. 10:7

This proverb uses (rather atypically) the fancier synonym first: *zekher* means "name," but is far less common than the word *shem*.

The proverbist prefers *zekher* here, however, because it comes from the same root as the word for "mention" or "remember." What Part A says, then, is that the mere mention of a person's name, if he was righteous, brings a blessing after his death. (It probably also means that, when a person has led an exemplary life, long after his death people will use his name as a blessing, that is, "I hope you grow up to be like so-and-so," or "May we all be granted to be like him.") This is not true, of course, with the wicked, but in saying so, Part B of this proverb carries an extra barb. For the whole distinction between "name" and "body" discussed earlier in connection with Ecclesiastes 7:1 was well known to everyone: the body decays and the name lives forever. But here, the proverbist pointedly contradicts this bit of received wisdom. Not only will the wicked man's name not be invoked as a blessing, but his name will rot along with his body; he will not be remembered, for there is nothing worth remembering, and so his name, despite its abstract quality, will "rot" as if it were flesh.

~

A GREAT MANY PROVERBS deal with "fools." A fool, in the world of wisdom, is not someone who is stupid any more than a "sage" or "wise man" is necessarily brilliant. But just as the wise man is someone who walks the path of wisdom—following the canons of restraint and patience that were the pillars of the wisdom outlook—so the fool is someone who does not follow the wisdom outlook, who does not live in accordance with wisdom's insights. Indeed, "foolish" and "wicked" are virtual synonyms in Proverbs, as are "wise" and "righteous." And just as humanity, according to the severe, abstract spirituality of this worldview, is uncompromisingly divided between the righteous and the wicked, so is it divided between the wise and the foolish, with no room in between for intermediates.

One thing fools do is scoff, but don't pay attention to their laughter, for:

> Like the sound of thorns under a pot, so is the laughter of fools.
>
> ECCLES. 7:4

Hebraists like to point out the play on words in this *mashal*: the word for "thorns" here, *sirim*, is very much like the word for "pot," *sir*. But beyond the pleasing sounds there is a point to this image. After all, the proverb could have simply been, "Like the sound of thorns in a roaring fire" or "Like the sound that thorns make when they burn." Why mention a pot? (For that matter, why not compare the fools' laughter to the braying of an ass or some other animal? That certainly would make for a closer comparison, and a more humiliating one.) But the thorns and the pot are there for a reason. One puts a pot on a fire in order to heat up its contents. For that, one needs good wood—solid tree limbs or even a nice, substantial log or two. If one puts the dried-out branches of a thornbush under the pot, they will crackle loudly and make a lot of noise, but they themselves will never suffice to warm up the food: they burn out too quickly and in any case supply little heat. So is it with the fools' laughter: it passes quickly and is utterly useless.

Here is a one-liner about the behavior of a fool:

> Lying lips cover over hatred, and a fool utters slander.
>
> PROV. 10:18

The "lying lips" in Part A are not lying about just anything—"The check is in the mail" and similar falsehoods are not the subject of this *mashal*. Instead, it is talking about hypocritical lies, specifically, those aimed at making oneself appear like a friend to someone who is in fact one's real enemy. Many proverbs condemn such behavior:

> He who hates dissembles with his lips, harboring treachery deep inside;
> though he makes nice sounds, don't trust him—seven abhorrences lurk in his heart.
>
> Prov. 26:24–25

"Hate" here, and in the previous example, means hidden, dissimulated hate. It is far better, in the biblical view, to confess one's hatred, indeed, to tell someone openly how he or she has caused offense, than to hate in secret:

> You shall not hate your brother in your heart [that is, in secret]; [instead,] openly reproach your fellow, and do not bear a sin because of him.
>
> Lev. 19:17

Thus, the "lying lips" of Proverbs 10:18 are covering over hidden hatred. But what about Part B of this proverb, "Lying lips cover over hatred, *and a fool utters slander.*" At first it might seem that the two parts are only vaguely related, each dealing with a different form of forbidden speech (since "uttering slander" is likewise disapproved in Proverbs). But the relationship is actually quite close, in fact, the lying lips of Part A belong to the fool of Part B. For the same person who covers over his hatred in front of his enemy, according to this *mashal*, will then go out and slander his enemy behind his back. Indeed, the point of this proverb is really to contrast the fool's reticence in the first case with his desire, his *need*, to talk and talk and talk in the second case. The contrast is a bit more explicit in Hebrew, since the expression "to utter slander" means more literally to "take out" or "send forth" slander, this verb thus being rather the opposite of "covering over."

The fool here, as usual, is not an idiot; he can be quite clever, in fact. But he does not live in accordance with the insights of wisdom. Nor, correspondingly, is there anything particularly profound about the behavior of a sage or wise man in the same circumstances: he simply does the opposite of the fool, neither covering over his hatred hypocritically nor broadcasting it to others behind his enemy's back. But if the "wisdom"of this proverb is simple, it was nonetheless phrased in such a way as to demand a bit of contemplation on the part of the listener before the relationship between A and B becomes clear.

A great many proverbs, like the previous one, focus on disputes that arise among people. Here is another:

> One who grabs a dog by the ears, a passerby who meddles in a dispute not his own.
>
> PROV. 26:17

Obviously, meddling in someone else's quarrel is not good, but what exactly is the point of this comparison? Someone who grabs a dog by the ears is, in the biblical world of unfailingly nasty dogs, in trouble. He won't himself get bitten so long as he holds on, but the minute he lets go, the dog, who had nothing against him before, is now likely to turn on him.* Indeed, if he lets go of just one ear, the dog will certainly bite the hand that still holds on to the other ear. So is it here with the third-party meddler. At first he was in no danger, but as soon as he grabbed on, he became a party to the dispute. Now he can't extricate himself, and he certainly cannot

---

*This same predicament was expressed quite independently in the Latin proverb *teneo auriculis* [or *auribus*] *lupum*, "I hold a wolf by the ears."

side with one party without expecting to have the other "bite" him. Beyond this obvious lesson, it seems that the proverbist takes delight in the fact that, while the passerby begins with the dog's ears—namely, speaking to the ears of the disputants—he is likely to end up getting it from their mouths.

Here is another one-line poem about disputes:

> The north wind gives birth to rain, and secret speech to an angry face.
>
> PROV. 25:23

It is clear enough that the north wind in the land of Israel is indeed usually a precursor to rain; you may not know it when it first starts to blow, but rain is on the way. And, of course, it is equally clear that whispering secrets (gossip, slander) usually leads to some kind of trouble, including someone's "angry face." But what possible connection is there between Part A and Part B? One might think that the proverbist could just as easily have said "April showers bring May flowers and secret speech an angry face." It so happens, however, that the word for "north" in Hebrew has a homonym that means "hidden" or "hiding." So a north wind is also a hidden, or hiding, wind, that is, a person's voice whispering secrets. And just as the meteorological "north wind" ultimately brings very unhidden results—the dousing rain—so "secret speech" will likewise end up producing very public consequences, "an angry face."

～

A GREAT MANY PROVERBS in the Bible have to do with wealth. Wealth is not a bad thing, it is not "filthy lucre," but it can lead astray. Specifically,

Who trusts in his wealth will fall, but the righteous like a leaf
will flourish.

PROV. 11:28

Trusting in one's wealth, or in any material thing, is a mistake;
however great its ramparts, the edifice of wealth can give way,
and he who stands on it will then plummet to the ground. By
contrast here, the righteous person is likened to the flimsiest
thing, a leaf, which in the Bible is utterly defenseless and gets
blown around by the wind (Lev. 26:36, Job 13:25). But the leaf
of the righteous is alive and will *flourish*. This word for "pros-
per," in Hebrew as in English, refers literally to the budding and
flowering of a plant. So although the righteous seem to be with-
out resources they will thrive.* As another proverb suggests:

The house of the wicked will be destroyed, but the tent of the
upright will flourish.

PROV. 14:11

Here too, the shelter of the "upright" (that is, the righteous) may
seem flimsier on the outside, but once planted it will flourish,**
whereas the apparently stronger dwelling of the wicked will
give way.

≈

A GREAT MANY PROVERBS function via the contrast between
inside and outside, what is in a person's heart (as the hatred seen
earlier) as opposed to what is on his or her lips.

---

*Indeed, the rich man's act of falling, *ypwl*, may be so worded as to suggest
ybwl, "withering," the opposite of "flourishing."

**Interestingly, tents, like trees, are "planted" in Hebrew.

Like thick glaze on a cheap pot, ardent lips and an evil heart.

Prov. 26:23

The thick glaze deceives the eyes: how the pot sparkles! But underneath is crumbling clay. So again, just as you know that A is true, recognize that B is true as well: however much the lips of a flatterer or hypocrite may say pleasing things, underneath them is an evil schemer. Pay no mind.

In the world of proverbs, the heart, the inside, is the domain of the wise, whereas the lips or the mouth belong to the fool:

The heart of the righteous meditates on its answer, and the mouth of fools babbles forth evil.

Prov. 15:28

Likewise:

The heart of the wise seeks out knowledge, the mouth of fools pursues foolishness.

Prov. 15:14

Nothing here is particularly difficult, but again, the real point lies in the contrast between "heart" and "mouth": the search for true knowledge is inside, internal, whereas foolishness is always on the surface, superficial.

In keeping with this, some proverbs present the inside and the outside as opposed to one another:

Better is affliction than laughter, for when the face is despondent the heart rejoices.

Eccles. 7:3

The idea here—quite the opposite of Proverbs 15:13 and 15:30—is that affliction is good for a person's insides, since it affords insight into the nature of our human existence, however much it may hurt on the outside and make for a despondent face.

Against this backdrop one can appreciate clever reversal achieved in a proverb cited earlier ("Where Wisdom Is Found"):

> To humans belong the plans of the mind, but from the LORD comes the spoken reply.
>
> PROV. 16:1

The phrase translated as "spoken reply" means, more literally, "the answer of the tongue." Thus here we have the usual opposition between inside ("mind"or "heart") and outside ("tongue"), but with a difference: here the outside is better! Human beings, this proverb says, can think or plan all they want in their minds or hearts, but God is the one who *speaks*, that is, He always has the last word.

~

TWO FINAL RIDDLES:

> *Just as a man does not control the wind, to stop the wind, so there is no control over the day of one's death. Moreover:*
>
> There is no delegation in [time of] war, and evil will not protect those who do it.
>
> ECCLES. 8:8

What is the relationship between A and B in the last sentence? And what is the relationship between both and the previous sentence? As any political scientist knows, delegations are there to *prevent* war: one side sends its diplomats to the other in a last-ditch effort to try to avoid hostilities. But once the armed conflict breaks out, diplomacy is done with, now it's war. The next exchange of delegations occurs (if at all) only after one side or the other is defeated and sues for peace. So is it with the evil man when the hour of his death has arrived. Before, he could indeed have done something. ("Control the wind" also means "control the breath," and that sort of control he certainly had, he could have spoken before. But now he no longer "controls the breath," that is, God has decided when he will draw his last.) So the time for talk—prayer, repentance, indeed, helping out the poor and otherwise demonstrating good faith—is now over; his evil* will help him no more.

> If the clouds fill up with rain, they will empty it on the earth,
>
> and if a tree falls to the south or to the north, wherever it falls,
>
> there it is.
>
> ECCLES. 11:3

This is in some sense a most befuddling pair of one-line poems, not because they are hard to understand, but because of the profound truth they embody. Both lines are about inevitability. The first is quite straightforwardly so: if the clouds fill up, inevitably they will empty (the two opposing verbs represent opposite, but complementary, actions). But as for the tree, there is nothing inevitable about *where* it will fall. Even as it sways in the wind on its very last day, a gust one way or another could decide its fate in quite opposite directions. But if there is no inevitability before its fall, once it has fallen, "there it is," inevitably, and there it will be forever.

---

*A shifting of the order of this word's consonants would yield "riches," and that might make better sense.

~

WE HAVE NO IDEA what the queen of Sheba really asked Solomon at their famous meeting. But it is a good bet that, in a conversation with anyone schooled in biblical wisdom, the subject of this or that *mashal* was bound to come up. True wisdom, that is, any true insight into the great divine plan underlying all of reality, could be, and was, packaged in this two-part sentence. These one-line poems were the basic building blocks of wisdom. No true sage existed who did not know hundreds of them by heart, and no worthy interlocutor existed who would not ask the sage for his *mashal*.

CHAPTER 10

ISAIAH 11:1−9

 HEN A SHOOT WILL SPRING UP FROM THE TREE
TRUNK OF JESSE, AND A SPROUT WILL RISE
FROM ITS ROOTS.

The spirit of the LORD will rest upon him, the spirit of wisdom and insight;

the spirit of counsel and courage, the spirit of knowledge and fear of the LORD.

Yes, he shall be guided by the fear of the LORD, not to judge by the way things appear, nor decide on hearsay or rumor.

He will judge the needy with righteousness, and bring fairness to the poor of the earth.

He will punish the arrogant at his word, put the guilty to death at his lips' decree.

Justice will be his regular clothing, and firmness his everyday dress.

Then the wolf will dwell with the lamb, and a leopard lie near a small goat;

the calf and the lion will pasture together, with a small boy to lead them.

The cow will feed with the bear, and their young will graze in one field;

the lion will eat hay like an ox.

A baby will play near the viper's hole, and a toddler will touch the snake's lair.

On My whole holy mountain, no evil will be done,

for the land will be brimming with devotion to the LORD, like the water that covers the seas.

AN IDEAL TIME

THE BIBLE RELATES THAT ISAIAH ṣon of Amoz became a prophet "in the year that king Uzziah died," that is, 742 B.C.E. In a visionary encounter, Isaiah was purified of his "unclean lips" and made a fit messenger of God (Isa. 6:1–8). At the time of this vision, things were still relatively calm in Judah, but all that was about to change. In far off Assyria, Tiglath Pileser III had ascended the throne. The man who later came to refer to himself as "king of the world" soon set about a program of military expansion and conquest that would ultimately spell the end of the Northern Kingdom of Israel and reduce Judah to quivering vassalage.

As so often in later history, the map of that part of the world was then a shifting checkerboard of alliances and enmities. When Tiglath Pileser* took on the lands to his west in 740–738 B.C.E., Israel and Damascus, off-and-on enemies, were both easily forced into the Assyrian fold and obliged to pay tribute. Now they were both in the same boat. Israel, the Bible reports, had to come up with a thousand talents of silver in payment to Assyria; "every man of means [that is, free landowner] had to pay fifty silver shekels for the Assyrian king" (2 Kings 15:20), a very hefty sum. As best anyone can tell, Israel's southern neighbor, Judah, was still untouched, but its citizens must have cast a worried glance at these events, all the more so after 734 B.C.E., when Assyrian troops circled around and down the Mediterranean coast, spreading their conquest as far as the Egyptian border at what is now Wadi el-Arish.

---

*Sometimes he is also referred to in the Bible as "Pul, king of Assyria": 2 Kings 15:19, 1 Chr. 5:26.

Damascus and Israel did not willingly suffer the Assyrian yoke. In 733 B.C.E. the king of Damascus, Rezin, tried to organize an alliance of vassal states to oppose Tiglath Pileser. He soon enlisted the help of Pekah, king of Israel, and the two of them together then naturally turned to Israel's former other half, Judah, to join in. Ahaz, the young and inexperienced king of Judah, hesitated. It was one of those decisions that, at a distance of nearly three millennia, is difficult to second-guess. Was there some sort of unreported agreement between Assyria and Judah that kept Ahaz from going in with his northern neighbors? Or was Ahaz worried about the ultimate intentions of Damascus's Rezin? Or perhaps those of Pekah, an upstart king who had ascended the throne of Israel by assassinating his predecessor (2 Kings 15:25)? We will probably never know. What we do know is that the prophet Isaiah approached the vacillating Ahaz with some unsolicited advice: Stay out of it. Don't ally yourself with either side, not with Assyria and not with Pekah and Rezin—even though the latter pair were apparently threatening (or had already undertaken) an invasion of Judah to "persuade" that country to go in with them:

> And the LORD said to Isaiah, "Go and meet Ahaz, you and your son Shear-Yashub, at the edge of the upper pool's ditch, by the road of the fuller's field, and say to him: Be careful, take it easy! Don't lose your nerve and don't be afraid of those two smoldering half-burned sticks, [I mean of] the wrath of Rezin and Aram,* and the son of Remaliah [that is, Pekah].** Insofar as Aram has plotted evil against you,

---

*A general name for Damascus and environs.

** To call someone by his last name, that is "son of X," rather than by his first name was usually a form of disparagement in ancient Israel.

along with Ephraim* and the son of Remaliah, saying: "Let us go up to Judah and breach it[s walls] and conquer it for ourselves; then we can set up the son of Tabeel as king there," thus says the Lord GOD: It will never happen, it will never come to pass. For at the head of Aram is Damascus, and at the head of Damascus is [only] Rezin. . . . And the head of Ephraim is Samaria [the capital], and at the head of Samaria is [only] the son of Remaliah. If you don't believe, then you won't be left."

ISA. 7:3–9

With this last, striking mashal (in Hebrew the words corresponding to "believe," ta'aminu, and "be left" [more literally, "made firm"], te'amenu, sound very similar) the prophet presumably turned on his heel and went. But Ahaz did not believe. When Pekah and Rezin marched their armies into Judah and set up a siege around Jerusalem (2 Kings 16:5), Ahaz appealed to Assyria and Tiglath Pileser for help, contravening the strict neutrality enjoined in Isaiah's message. Predictably, Assyria did march in to help Ahaz, but in the process Judah, too, became an Assyrian vassal, forced to pay tribute (2 Kings 16:7–9). Fleeing one enemy, it had fallen into the hands of another.

Tiglath Pileser III died in 727, but not before conquering Damascus and laying it to waste, as well as taking away a good chunk of the territory of Northern Kingdom, Israel, and annexing it to his empire. He did leave Samaria, Israel's capital city, and its immediate environs independent. However, even this last vestige of Israel did not have long to live; it fell to Tiglath Pileser's successor, Shalmaneser V, in 722 B.C.E. In keeping with imperial policy, many of the inhabitants of the conquered nation—partic-

---

*Another name for Israel.

ularly the upper classes—were deported and resettled elsewhere in the Assyrian empire. At the same time, other peoples (including conquered populations from the east and north) were moved into Israel's territory by the Assyrians. All that truly remained of the once mighty United Monarchy of David and Solomon was its southern component, the Kingdom of Judah. The northern part was now a colonial hodge-podge of different populations and nationalities; even centuries later it was to be decried as a "non-people" (Sir. 50:26).

IN THE MIDST OF ALL THIS political turmoil, perhaps contemplating the very collapse of the Northern Kingdom of Israel, Isaiah of Jerusalem uttered the well-known words that open the eleventh chapter of his book. What he meant by "a shoot will spring up from the tree trunk of Jesse" seems clear enough. Jesse was, after all, the father of David, founder of the Davidic dynasty that still ruled Judah in Isaiah's time. The immediate sense of this reference is thus that the royal dynasty is to undergo some dramatic renewal: a great new king will spring from the royal stock. This was certainly good news, though it is hard to imagine that the description that follows could not have been taken as reflecting badly on the present or immediately past rulers. For if the new king was going to "judge the needy with righteousness" and not decide things on appearances or hearsay, did not this imply that such was precisely the way Judah's kings *had* been deciding cases until now? But if that was the implication, well, prophets were not in the business of flattering anyone, even (indeed, especially) kings. In any event, many scholars have seen in this description of a future ideal leader the announcement of the impending ascension of the heir to the throne, presumably

Ahaz's own son, the great Hezekiah. He would be the king to inaugurate, in the midst of all Judah's troubles, a golden age. Indeed, scholars have connected this offspring of "the tree trunk of Jesse" with another passage that appears slightly earlier in the book of Isaiah:

> A boy has been born to us! We have been given a son, and majesty is set on his shoulders.
>
> He has been given the name "Mighty-God-counsels-wondrous-things," "Eternal-father-is-a-peaceful-ruler."
>
> There will be no end to the greatness of majesty nor to peace, on David's throne and over his kingdom,
>
> setting it firm and sustaining it, in justice and righteousness from now henceforward; the LORD of Hosts will zealously see to it!
>
> ISA. 9:5-6

Perhaps the most striking thing nowadays about these two passages would not even have been worthy of comment in ancient times, so obvious did it seem: a new golden age could only be inaugurated by a new golden ruler. That is to say, it was not that *conditions* would somehow change, the economy pick up, or the international situation suddenly fall into a peaceful lull. Life worked from the top down. Only a great new ruler could change things, but such a ruler could indeed do that, righteousness and justice and peace *could* quite conceivably be forced into being by his advent.

~

THOUGH MOST MODERN SCHOLARS connect these passages to Isaiah's own time, a different purpose appeared in them to early Christians (and many contemporary ones): they seemed to refer to the events recounted in the Gospels, the birth of a promised Savior. Indeed, numerous passages in the book of Isaiah were, and are, read in the same light. When, for example, the prophet wished to press home the point that Ahaz had nothing to fear from Pekah and Rezin's threatened invasion, he did so via a striking illustration:

> Therefore, let my Lord give you a sign: Suppose a young woman is [now] pregnant and gives birth to a son. She should call his name "God-is-amidst-us." He will be eating butter and honey by the time he knows how to reject what's bad and take what's good, for even before the child knows how to reject the bad and take the good, the land whose two kings you fear will be a wasteland.
>
> ISA. 7:14–16

A divine "sign" was sometimes a miraculous event, but sometimes, as with Cain's "sign"* (Gen. 4:15) or that of Moses on Mount Horeb (Exod. 3:12), merely a divine pledge of some kind. If that is the case here, then the pledge is simple: a child who has already been conceived and is soon to be born will, in its early development, mark off the time required for safety to return to Judah. Once little babies start to crawl, they put whatever they find into their mouths; it takes a few years before they know "how to reject what's bad and take what's good." But before this baby even reaches that point, Isaiah says, Damascus and its ally, Israel, will have been laid waste, while things in Judah will be

---

*That is to say, the famous sign or "brand" of Cain was not, as later interpreters liked to imagine, a mark set on his forehead, or a set of horns, or any other physical sign; it was the divine pledge made in the previous sentence, "Anyone who kills Cain [or "a Kenite," a member of Cain's tribe] will suffer vengeance sevenfold."

fine, people will be eating "butter and honey." In other words, don't worry, Ahaz; peace and prosperity are only a few years down the road, so don't get involved on either side. Although the above translation, "Suppose a young woman is [now] pregnant," accords with the Hebrew text, some scholars suggest an equally plausible reading, "Behold!" in the sense of "Look! The young woman whom we all know is pregnant," in which case the child to be born might indeed be the same royal heir whose existence is mentioned in Isaiah 9:5–6 and 11:1–5, and the "young woman" Ahaz's own bride.

In the Christian interpretation mentioned, however, this birth announcement is understood as intended for the far distant future. In this reading, the word translated as "young woman" was itself turned into a source of controversy. The Hebrew 'almah does indeed designate a girl or young woman in the Bible. As such, the term apparently says nothing specific about the woman's virginity. Solomon's harem, according to the Song of Songs 6:8, boasts "sixty queens, eighty concubines, and innumerable 'alamot." However, when the verse from Isaiah was first translated into Greek by Jews (long before the rise of Christianity), for some reason they rendered this Hebrew term by the Greek parthenos, a word that usually meant specifically a virgin. Perhaps they did so because the biblical word for "sign" was now understood to mean, unequivocally, "miracle"; surely a virgin who gives birth would be a miraculous sign. In any event, the virgin birth soon became a Christian teaching (Matt. 2:20–23). One early Christian treatise, Justin's Dialogue with Trypho, records a booklength debate between a Christian and a Jew concerning various passages and ideas in the Hebrew Bible. It is not long before they get to discussing this famous verse in Isaiah. To the Jew's interpretation of "young woman" Justin objects:

Also the words, "Behold, the virgin shall conceive and bear a son" were spoken in advance of Him . . . . But you [Trypho] dare to pervert the translations which your own elders made at the court of King Ptolemy in Egypt [that is, the old Greek translation of the Bible, which reads "virgin" here] and say that the text does not have the meaning as they translated it but "Behold the young woman will conceive"—as if something of importance were being signified by a young woman bearing after human intercourse, which all young women do, save for the infertile, and even these God can, if He will, cause to bear.

DIALOGUE WITH TRYPHO, 84

IF ONE READS ISAIAH 11:1-9 in the context of Isaiah's own times—and keeping in mind, of course, that change moves from the top down—its message of hope would certainly have been an understandable one. To have a great new king might indeed change everything, not only obvious injustice and oppression, but the grinding corruption and stagnation that can eat away at everyday life from the inside. One who had the gifts of wisdom and insight, and the strength of character of a born leader, could indeed inaugurate a brand new day.

But what could be the significance of those suddenly peaceful predators in the second half of this prophecy, carnivores that now eat only grass and hay? Many have seen in these words a political message. If so, there is no doubt who, from Judah's standpoint, the "lamb," the "small goat," and the "baby" really were. For, from the beginning, the people scattered in the rugged Judean hills or on the adjacent fertile plains had never been free of the threat of foreign domination. Dependent on unpredictable rainfall for their survival, their numbers were always relatively small. Egypt, by contrast, with its great river's annual overflow, had always been able to support a huge population and could thus always march out a powerful army against the dirt farmers to its northeast. On the other side of Judah/Israel, the land between the two great rivers, the Tigris and the Euphrates, had also always hosted a large population, supported by a sophisticated system of canals and waterways; these peoples too had often been tempted by the little strip of territory on the seacoast and nearby hills. And to the north of that strip, the city-states along the Mediterranean, as well as the vast territories of what is now Syria and Turkey, were no less menacing. Was it not obvious, under the circumstances, that Judah's safety would only be realized when its normally fearsome neighbors were turned into vegetarian lions and defanged asps?

Yet if such was the immediate resonance of these words, they have always had another one as well. The road ahead is infinitely long. Will not the day sometime come, even if it is not yet visible, when things will at last be set aright and a new and perfect order will reign among the nations of the earth? This was the full promise that Isaiah's words would carry long after his own time, and the whole history of messianism (Jewish and Christian, socialist and Aquarian) emanates in large measure, though of course not exclusively, from these peaceful animals in Isaiah's vision. Surely the lamb *will* lie down in safety with the wolf someday, and in the age of brain implants and the genetically engineered barnyard, that day may not seem far off. Can the same be said of the (usually neglected) closing words of Isaiah's prophecy?

CHAPTER 11

PSALM 23

HE LORD IS MY SHEPHERD; I SHALL NOT WANT.

He maketh me to lie down in green pastures; He leadeth me beside the still waters.

He restoreth my soul; He leadeth me in the paths of righteousness for His name's sake.

Yea, though I walk through the valley of the shadow of death, I will fear no evil,

for Thou art with me; Thy rod and Thy staff they comfort me.

Thou preparest a table before me in the presence of mine enemies; Thou anointest my head with oil; my cup runneth over.

Surely goodness and mercy shall follow me all the days of my life; and I will dwell in the house of the LORD forever.

"And Obscure as that Heaven of the Jews"

THE OTHER TRANSLATIONS IN THIS BOOK are my own, but I did not wish to forgo here the well-known, and altogether stunning, translation of Psalm 23 that appears in the King James (or "Authorized") Version of the Bible. First published in 1611, this translation perfectly captures the serene, measured tone of confidence of the original Hebrew and has justly won the hearts of generations of Bible readers. It would be difficult to communicate better this psalm's directness and simplicity.

Of course, scholars know more now than they did in the seventeenth century about the subtleties of Hebrew syntax or the meaning of particular words and expressions, so it might be worthwhile to explain a few points in connection with this famous translation. Thus, "the LORD is my shepherd, I shall not want," compressed as it is in English, does not yet capture the telegraphic style of the Hebrew. These nine English words are only four in Hebrew: "LORD my-shepherd; not I-lack." Nor does the English quite cover all the ambiguities of this assertion in the original. The reason is that, apart from the absence of tenses (in our sense) in Hebrew verbs, poetic style in the Bible often works by omitting those little words and particles that otherwise would make explicit the relationship between adjacent clauses. Their omission invites the reader in Hebrew to fill in the blanks, at least mentally. Consequently, "LORD my-shepherd; not I-lack" could be understood as "Since the LORD is my shepherd, I do not lack anything," "With the LORD as my shepherd, I will never be in need,"

"The LORD shepherds me so that my needs are met," and conceivably quite a few other things as well.*

In the next verse, "maketh me to lie down" is literally correct, but the expression was used particularly of shepherds grazing their sheep (Jer. 33:12, Ezek. 34:14, Song of Songs, 1:7), so something like "graze" or "pasture" might better capture the feel of this verb in the original. Likewise, "in the paths of righteousness for his name's sake" well translates the metaphorical intentions of this expression, but not quite the basic meaning appropriate to the human-as-sheep speaker. That basic meaning would be more like "He"—the divine shepherd—"guides me on the right path in keeping with his name." That is, like any shepherd, God is concerned that not a single one of his flock go astray, so He keeps me going on the straight path. As for the "valley of the shadow of death," scholars have long been aware that this phrase literally refers only to a valley of "darkness" or "blackness"; death certainly lurks in the background but its presence here should perhaps not be overstated. Finally, there is just the touch of irony lost in the King James version of the last line. Literally, it means something more like "Goodness and kindness alone will *pursue* me," or, more pointedly, "My only pursuers will be goodness and kindness." That is, with God as the speaker's shepherd, there will be

---

*On this point of Hebrew grammar sixteenth- and seventeenth-century scholars were actually quite well informed, and it is thus interesting to observe some of the variety in English translations of this verse in the years that preceded the King James version: "The LORD is my shepherd, therefore can I lack nothing" (The *Great Bible*, 1540); "The LORD governeth me, and I shall lack nothing" (A *Latin-English Psalter*, 1540); "My shepherd is the living LORD; nothing, therefore, I need" (from the metrical—"fourteeners"—psalter of Thomas Sternhold and John Hopkins, 1567); "God is my shepherd, therefore I can lack nothing" (*The Bishops' Bible*, 1568); "Our LORD ruleth me, and nothing shall be wanting to me" (*Douai Bible*, 1609). All these *ands* and *therefores* are attempts to make more explicit the unstated relationship of Parts A and B in this Hebrew line.

no natural predators to fear: divine beneficence alone will be at his heels.

Putting all of this together, and with all deference to the classic King James text, I might offer the following, less as a substitute translation than an explicative restatement:

> Since the LORD is my shepherd, there is nothing I lack.
>
> He takes me to graze in grassy fields, He leads me along peaceful streams;
>
> He restores me, guiding me on the right path in keeping with His name.
>
> Even when I go through the darkest valley, I am not afraid.
>
> For You are with me: Your rod and staff give me comfort.
>
> You set a table for me, right in the face of my enemies;
>
> You anoint my head with oil; my cup overflows.
>
> Goodness and kindness alone will pursue me, all throughout my life,
>
> and I will dwell for a length of time in the house of the LORD.

A BOOK OF BIBLICAL POETRY can scarcely fail to point out some of the fundamental differences between the way poems work in other literary traditions and in the Bible. One thing that is often crucial in the psalms is the moment when the speaker turns from the somewhat more distant, and formal, third-person way of speaking *about* God to the direct, second-person "You" (or, sometimes, the reverse). This moment of transition, if noticed at all, must strike an American or European reader as odd: why isn't the psalmist more consistent, making everything "He" or everything "You"? But the switch in persons is quite conscious (it happens as well when underlings address a king, for example) and, as in this psalm, can be quite dramatic.* "For You are with me: Your rod and staff give me comfort" is the moment at which the speaker at last lifts his eyes to confront God face-to-face. As for the "rod" and "staff" mentioned, either word might reasonably do for a shepherd's crook; if both are mentioned it is because of their contrasting associations in Hebrew. A "rod" is at least sometimes an instrument of chastisement, as in "the rod of His wrath" (Isa. 10:5, Prov. 22:8; cf. Job 21:9, Prov. 22:15). The word used for "staff," by contrast, means, literally, a "leaning stick" or "support." In mentioning both, the psalmist does not mean to imply that the divine shepherd actually sets out with two different wooden sticks; he means instead to say that whether it chastises or supports him, God's guidance gives him comfort.

This moment of transition sets up a second one. Without preamble, the shepherd-sheep metaphor that has been the whole substance of the psalm until now is dropped: "You set a table for me, right in the face of my enemies; You anoint my head with oil; my cup overflows." Again, by the standards of our own poetry, such a switch is disturbing: why not carry the sheep metaphor through to the end? But clearly that does not bother the psalmist. In general, since almost every line of biblical poetry is end-stopped and quite independent, each is felt to stand on its own in a way not common in other literatures (though it might be helpful to think of the rhyming couplets of Dryden or Pope as an equivalent in English). Consistency or even continuity from line to line is not crucial. And so, now addressing God directly, the psalmist simply speaks as a human being of human things. You provide, he says, not only what I need to survive—food—but "set a table for me," feed me lavishly, even in the menacing pres-

*See, for example, Pss. 19, 22, 27, 32, 33, 35, and so forth.

ence of my enemies. (In biblical society, everyone who was any-one had enemies.) Indeed, you "anoint my head with oil," an act that sounds rather messy nowadays but one that, in the ancient world, was very much prized because of the exquisite, and pow-erful, fragrance carried by the oil. (People who could afford it reg-ularly used anointing oils.) To the words "my cup overflows" there was no need to add *with wine*, for everyone knew that that was *the* drink of ancient Israel—and wine proverbially "glad-dens the heart" (Judg. 9:13). Thus, the psalmist says, I am not just taken care of, as a sheep is cared for by its shepherd; I am given every comfort. Indeed, my only "pursuers" are goodness and kindness.

~

WHAT IS IT about the picture presented by this psalm that so speaks to readers' hearts? Certainly the meaning of this psalm has changed over the centuries, so much so that even some of its images now need to be explained. No doubt even saying "the LORD is my shepherd" meant something rather different in a world in which "the LORD" was not recognized by everyone as God. Moreover, the whole reality of shepherds and their flocks is nowadays remote from the experience of most readers; in this respect the psalm cannot speak to our own lives as it did to those of past readers. But there is one aspect of this psalm that has always remained and has always made it almost unique. Here the psalmist does not, as so often elsewhere, approach God with a request: Help me, forgive my sin, crush my enemies, do not let me die. Nor, as also frequently, does he offer God thanksgiving after the fact: You did help me, and I am grateful. Nor is it a psalm that celebrates God's grandeur and mighty deeds. It is just about ordinary daily life, a psalm about You and me: You are my shepherd. In biblical times, no less than nowadays, this assertion might appear altogether foolish. What biblical speaker, living in a world in which the dangers of famine and disease, military invasion, economic collapse, or sudden death, were certainly no less threatening than in our own day, could contemplate his existence and see only grassy fields and peaceful waters? But that is what he does see, and say. In so saying, he is asking for nothing, he does not even offer thanks as such. Indeed, that might be the particular nuance of the first line: Since You are my shepherd, I will never have anything to ask for; and having no occasion for special requests, I will likewise have no reason for giving extra-ordinary thanks, I am thankful for whatever happens.

BUT THEN THERE ARE the very last words of the psalm and the whole new problem that they introduce. It is far from clear what "I will dwell for a length of time in the house of the LORD" really means. The word translated "dwell" appears to be derived from the common verb that means both "sit" and "settle" (hence "stay" or "dwell"), but if so, it is an unusual form of the verb.* Alternatively, it might be parsed as an entirely different verb, one that means "return." (The trouble with that proposal is the preposition "in the house of the Lord." One does not return in someplace but to someplace.) As for where this dwelling or returning is to take place, the "house of the LORD" is the usual way of referring to God's earthly abode, His Temple. But this is problematic as well. No one, properly speaking, dwells in the "house

---

*That is, it has apparently been shortened, wšbty in place of wyšbty. Some have therefore suggested that the verb be understood as a gerund, that is, "and my staying [will be] in the house of the LORD," which would better suit the letters wšbty. See also Ps. 27:4 and next note.

of the LORD" except for God Himself, though priests of course served there and ordinary Israelites visited from time to time. Yet the psalm specifically says that the speaker will be there for a "length of time" (literally, "length of days").* Now, in Hebrew a "length of time" is always a *long* time. In fact, this phrase is sometimes used to mean "a long life," both in the Bible (Deut. 30:20; Ps. 21:5, 91:16; Prov. 3:2) and in Phoenician inscriptions; otherwise it can mean simply a long period of unspecified duration. So who is this human being who will be dwelling in the "house of the LORD" for a long period of time? Indeed, is the act of dwelling there part of—an example of—the goodness and kindness that will pursue him; that is, is the form

_____ I _____ II

to be understood here in the sense of "A, as a matter of fact, B," or is it rather a case of "A, and in addition to that, B"; that is, will the psalmist dwell in the house of the LORD *after* having been dogged by goodness and kindness "my whole life long"?

If it is the latter, then this line must be understood as referring to the afterlife. The psalmist asserts that God's fostering protection will last not only throughout this life, but that after death he will dwell in the house of the LORD—not literally an earthly temple, but metaphorically "with God," indeed, perhaps in that other place of God's dwelling, heaven—for a "length of time,"

---

*Psalm 27 contains a curiously analogous phrase. It says: "One thing I ask of the LORD, and request it earnestly: to dwell in the house of the LORD all the days of my life, to behold the LORD'S glory and to frequent his temple." It would seem on the basis of this text that "dwelling" in the temple did not mean actually living there but going there often, being a devotee of God. (Though even this is far from clear: the verb translated as "frequent" meant more normally to "inquire of," "contemplate," or "distinguish.")

which could mean eternally. This may indeed be the sense of the psalm; it is certainly how many readers of the psalm understand it today. Truthfully, though, the matter does not depend on this verse alone, but on what the Hebrew Bible elsewhere says about life after death. Do people, according to the Hebrew Bible, indeed "go to heaven" after death? And does everyone go there, or only the righteous? If the latter, then what is the fate of everyone else?

~

THESE QUESTIONS ARE PARTICULARLY DIFFICULT because the biblical evidence is sparse and not all of one piece. Toward the end of the biblical period, clear references to the afterlife begin to appear, but before that the picture is somewhat cloudier. A number of biblical texts do speak of the dead residing in a place called "Sheol." It is hard to gauge the extent to which these texts intend Sheol as a reality, a definite place, and to what extent they are simply referring figuratively to the "realm of the dead," as a modern-day person might speak of the Underworld or Hades without intending all the ancient mythological baggage associated with these names. In any case, Sheol was somewhere *underneath*. People "went down" to Sheol, perhaps because bodies were sometimes (though not always) buried beneath the surface of the earth. Apart from residing there, the dead did not appear to do much in Sheol. "The dead do not praise the LORD, nor do any who go down to 'Silence' [another name for Sheol]" (Ps. 115:17). But the truth is that, apart from such passing references as this one, the Hebrew Bible does not appear to have an articulated teaching about Sheol. Israel's ancient Near Eastern neighbors, in Egypt and in Mesopotamia, preserved detailed theories about the abode of the dead and the fate of those who go there, but what happened in Sheol is largely a blank. Indeed, some of the other names by which this abode of the dead is known—"the pit," "Abbadon [destruction]," or "the dust"—suggest that it was not a place of continued existence at all, but simply the locale of nonexistence that follows death, the grave.

However, a number of biblical texts suggests that those who are in Sheol can return to the world of the living. Hannah, in her famous song of praise, describes God's ability to reverse reality at will:

> A barren woman [now] gives birth to seven, while the mother who had many children is bereft.
>
> The LORD kills and brings back to life, sends down to Sheol and raises up again.
>
> The LORD makes poor and makes rich, both humbles and exalts.
>
> 1 SAM. 2:5–7

The verb to "bring back to life" in Hebrew is ambiguous; it can also mean to "make alive" or merely "keep alive." But there is not much ambiguity about "sends down to Sheol and raises up"; this verse certainly is talking about bringing back to life one who was dead. So, another description of God's powers ought to be read in the same light:

> Behold now that I, I Myself, am, and there are no gods alongside Me.
>
> I put to death and bring back to life; those I crush I can heal, but no one escapes my power.
>
> DEUT. 32:39

Many modern commentators shy away from the idea of God bringing the dead back to life and argue that such passages are not to be taken literally. But certainly the idea of resurrection from

Sheol is there, however it was intended to be understood. A whole chapter of the Bible, 1 Samuel 28, recounts how King Saul in desperation goes to a medium in order to have the prophet Samuel raised from the dead so that he can consult him. According to the narrative, Samuel does indeed emerge from the dead; his first words to Saul are, "Why did you disturb and raise me up?" (1 Sam. 28:15)

In the ancient world, people's thinking about the resurrection of the dead was influenced by another factor: bones. When a person dies, his or her flesh soon rots, but the bones stay on undisturbed. Centuries later, there they still are. In the great divine economy—"For dust you are, and to dust you shall return" (Gen. 3:19)—the survival of people's bones was a puzzle. Why did they not disintegrate along with the rest of the dead person? It certainly seemed that their survival must be intended, part of the way in which the world has been arranged. And so, from ancient times, many different peoples had cared for the bones of their ancestors. Sometimes they collected the bones together after the flesh had disappeared and then buried (or reburied) them, sometimes they even gathered them together in special boxes (ossuaries) to preserve them intact for eternity, carefully labeling the sides or tops with the name of the deceased and stern warnings or curses for whoever opened them. Why this effort? It had not required a great mental leap for people to conclude that if God had arranged for these bones to survive, the purpose might be to reassemble them later on, turning them back into the full person to whom they once belonged. After all, even with living people, flesh comes and goes; we are sometimes fatter and sometimes thinner. So there did not seem to be anything *essential* about flesh. Only the bones counted.

When the prophet Ezekiel, rocked by the events of his own time, doubted about the future of his people,

The hand of the LORD came upon me and took me out by the spirit of the LORD and set me down in the midst of a valley that was full of bones. And He made me pass over them, around and around, and I saw there were very many of them, scattered all over the valley, and that they were very dry. And He said to me, "Son of man!* Do you think these bones can come back to life?" And I said, "My Lord, GOD, You are the one who knows." And He said to me, "Prophesy over these bones and say to them, 'O dried up bones! Hear the word of the LORD. Thus says the Lord GOD to these bones: I am causing [My] spirit to enter into you so that you may live again. I will put sinews on you and set flesh over you and cover you over with skin and put breath into you so that you come back to life; then you will know that I am the LORD.'" . . . And I prophesied as I had been told, and as I was prophecying there was a sound, a rattling, and the bones began moving closer together, one bone to another, and I saw sinews on them and flesh over them and skin covering them over on top. . . . And He said to me, "Son of man, these are the bones of the whole house of Israel."

EZEK. 37:1–11

What Ezekiel saw was a vision of the resurrection of the people of Israel, but the vision no doubt resonated with what many people had in any case supposed for centuries: that death is not necessarily final, indeed, that the very fact of our bones' survival indicates that we may someday be reassembled and resurrected physically. So the Book of Isaiah could proclaim:

Let your dead come back to life! Let their corpses rise up again!

ISA. 26:19

---

* God's usual way of addressing Ezekiel. The Hebrew expression means simply "human being," with perhaps the nuance of "mere mortal."

Sometime later, the Book of Daniel gave the Hebrew Bible's most explicit statement concerning resurrection of the dead:

> Many of those that sleep in the dust of the earth will awaken, some to eternal life, others to condemnation and everlasting horror.
>
> DAN. 12:2

Clearly, then, the Bible did here and there countenance the resurrection of the dead in some form. But how did it work exactly?

Many peoples have identified the "breath" or "wind" in our lungs not only as that which animates us and makes living persons out of what would otherwise be dead flesh and bones, but also as our very innermost self, the fleeting, immaterial essence of every human being. But when that essence is breathed out and departs forever, does it just disappear? Again, from ancient times and in different corners of the globe, people have maintained that this human *spirit* (from the Latin term for "breath" or "breeze") continues to exist outside of the body it once inhabited. In the Bible, as we have seen, this breath of life is said to come from God. He literally breathes it into Adam's nostrils (Gen. 2:7) and so makes him alive. Likewise, at the end of life, "the dust [that is, the human body] returns to the ground as it was, while the spirit returns to God, who gave it" (Eccles. 12:7; see also Isa. 42:5, Job 34:14, Jonah 4:3). As an old conceit would have it, people's souls are gathered back to God as the last rays of sunlight are gathered back into the sun as it sets.

This divine breath, coming from God, might naturally be expected in every case to return to Him after death and, in this sense, live forever. But if such is the nature of the afterlife, a number of biblical texts suggest that only those who have led a righteous existence will so benefit:

The wise man's is the road of life upward, that he may turn from Sheol underneath.

PROV. 15:24

One who heeds instruction is [on] the road to life, but he who neglects reproof leads astray.

PROV. 10:17

The Book of Proverbs, like all wisdom writings, is concerned with death, with what will happen to people after their brief sojourn among the living. But however much the worldview of Proverbs may be one of abstract essences and altogether schematic, it is nonetheless an earthly one. Perhaps in keeping with this, Proverbs does not openly speak of life after death or a last judgment. One might thus understand the references to the "road of [or "to"] life" in the verses cited above (and elsewhere) to refer simply to the path of the righteous in this world. But "the road of life *upward*," as opposed to "Sheol underneath"? And the "road *to* life"? Perhaps here are the slightest hints that the life being referred to is not merely terrestrial existence but the *destination* of the road in question, that is, life after death. If so, then there is the further implication that that road is not open to all, but only to the "wise," the one who "heeds instruction." In the same vein, the last verse of Ecclesiastes asserts that God "will bring every one to judgment concerning all his conduct, whether it be for good or ill" (Eccles. 12:14). The sense seems to be that God will determine the nature of everyone's deeds (even those apparently hidden) to decide for the good or the evil. This does indeed sound like a kind of last judgment; those who receive the "good" judgment will presumably be rewarded after death. The same is true of the verse cited earlier from Daniel, "And many of those that sleep in the dust of the earth will awaken, some to eternal life, others to condemnation and everlasting aversion" (Dan. 12:2). If such a distinction is made among the dead, is not the implication that God will *judge* people sometime in the future and assign them to their eternal fate on the basis of their past deeds?

~

THE IDEA THAT THE SOULS of the righteous will go to a place called Paradise is not found as such in the Hebrew Bible. This idea is actually a development of an early interpretive tradition surrounding the story of the Garden of Eden in Genesis 2 and 3. In that story, God puts Adam and Eve in a special garden with fruit-bearing trees. From the biblical text itself, the garden appears to be an altogether physical, earthly place located somewhere in the ancient Near East. Four rivers are said to issue from it, of which two, at any rate, are identified as the Tigris and the Euphrates (Gen. 2:14), located today in Iraq. Certainly the presence of these rivers, as well as that of fruit-bearing trees, would seem to indicate that Eden was a magnificent garden somewhere on earth; how can a river flow, or a tree grow, in the sky? When the Hebrew Bible was first translated into Greek toward the end of the biblical period, the Greek translators referred to the Garden as a "paradise" because that was the common Greek word for a luxurious enclosed orchard, the sort that nobles in those days planted on their vast estates. Thus, neither the Hebrew Bible nor its ancient Greek translation contained any indication that the Garden/Paradise was anything other than an earthly orchard.

But certain elements of the story made ancient biblical interpreters wonder. After Adam and Eve were expelled from the Garden, God did not destroy it. Instead, He placed cherubim and a flaming sword at its entrance "to guard the way to the tree of life" (Gen. 3:24). If the Garden was being guarded and preserved, presumably God intended to keep it for some future use; and what was the "tree of life" in its midst meant for if not to feed (and perhaps thus keep alive) those righteous souls who had been granted life after death? So it was that the age-old teachings about the soul's return to God after death and the reward of the righteous came now to focus on this Garden. "Paradise" became the place where the blessed would go after their earthly passing.

Even as the place of repose of righteous souls after their death, Paradise certainly could be located on earth, and many ancient writers from the early postbiblical period maintained that it was.

> And both [Adam and Eve] were buried according to the commandment of God in the regions of Paradise, in the place from which God had found the dust [from which Adam was formed, Gen. 2:7].
>
> APOCALYPSE OF MOSES, 40:6

> [An angel tells Baruch:] "When God caused the flood over the earth . . . and the water rose over the heights of fifteen cubits, the water entered Paradise and killed every flower.
>
> 3 BARUCH, 4:10

But there were some indications in the Bible itself that this final resting place was not on earth but in heaven. After all, heaven— though in Hebrew there is no separate term for "heaven," texts simply use the common word for "sky"—has always had a special significance in human thought. It is higher than earth, "up there," hence a superior, presumably dominant station vis-à-vis earth. From heaven one can look down on all that happens on earth (and, so it was supposed, also hear everything that is said down there). Its great, open expanse has always suggested that which is beyond, free of, the bonds of earthly existence and the laws that govern ordinary life. So it was that the righteous Enoch and Elijah were understood to have ascended into heaven and to live there still (Gen. 5:24, 2 Kings 2:11); presumably, the proper place for immortality was far above the changeable things of this world. Similarly, the Book of Isaiah refers to the reward of the righteous in these terms:

> He who walks righteously and speaks uprightly, who despises the gain of oppressions, who shakes his hands lest they hold a bribe, who stops his ears from hearing of bloodshed and shuts his eyes from looking upon evil—he will *dwell on high*, his refuge will be craggy fortresses; his food will be given him, his water will be sure. Your eyes will behold the King in his splendor, they will *see the earth from afar.*
>
> ISA. 34:15–17

The highlighted words suggested that the reward of the righteous was not to be found on earth but in heaven. In this passage, and in others, only the very literal-minded will confuse the metaphysical heaven with the actual stratosphere. But this metaphysical sense was nonetheless tied to the physical "sky," and Paradise *was* spoken of in the Bible as if an actual garden. So it was that the reward of the righteous came to be thought of, especially by the literalist, as an orchard above the clouds.

> And those men took me from there, and they brought me up to the third heaven. And they placed me in the midst of Paradise. . . . And I said, "How pleasant is this place!" The men answered me, "This place has been prepared for the righteous."
>
> 2 ENOCH, 8:1, 9:1

≈

As with the reward of the righteous, so with the punishment of the wicked. In one passage, the Book of Isaiah asserts that

> a burning place [Tophet] had long been prepared. . . . Its pyre made deep and wide, with fire and wood in abundance; the breath of the LORD, like a stream of brimstone, burns within it.
>
> Isa. 30:33

Elsewhere in the same book:

> For as the new heaven and the new earth that I will create will endure before Me, says the LORD, so will your descendents and your name endure. And at each new moon and each sabbath in its time, everyone will come to bow down before Me, says the LORD. And when they go out they will see the dead bodies of the men who have sinned against Me, how their worms will not die and their fire will not go out, and they will be a source of horror to all.
>
> Isa. 66:24

Passages such as these suggested to many that those found unworthy of paradise would not simply *not* go there, but would suffer in its opposite, a place of eternal torment and burning. This, like "Paradise" itself, was not an idea found in and of itself in the Hebrew Bible, though biblical support for it (as the above) was found in later times.

≈

Some decades ago, the cliché about the Hebrew Bible was

that it really has no notion of an afterlife or the return of the soul to God or a last judgment or a world to come. But such a claim will not withstand careful scrutiny. The truth evidenced above is that each of these rather distinct ideas can be located in the Hebrew Bible; one difficulty, however, is that there is little indication of how (if at all) they were conceived to overlap or work together. This much is clear: both later Judaism and Christianity, heir to these teachings, passed them on within the framework of their own faiths. While many know this about Christianity, a surprising number of people erroneously believe that Judaism has no doctrine of resurrection or the world to come; indeed, they sometimes suppose that the absence of such teachings in Judaism is a faithful reflection of the Bible's own teaching. They are wrong on both counts.

If the last words of Psalm 23, "I will dwell for a length of time in the house of the LORD," refer to the soul's rejoining God after death, the form of reference is certainly strange: as was seen, the words for "dwell," "house of the LORD," and "length of time" all pose a problem. It is more reasonable to suppose that they express the psalmist's confidence that he will, during his lifetime, often "dwell" in God's temple, or, perhaps, "return" there again and again. But the idea of an afterlife, if it is not stated in Psalm 23, is certainly to be found elsewhere in the Hebrew Bible. In many of the passages cited it is as plain as day.

CHAPTER 12

JEREMIAH 12:1–6

OU WILL ALWAYS WIN, O LORD, WHENEVER
I LODGE A COMPLAINT AGAINST YOU;
STILL, I WOULD ADDRESS YOU ON A
MATTER OF LAW.

Why is it that wicked men prosper, why do liars and back-
stabbers thrive?
You must plant them if they take root; if they flourish and then
bear fruit,
You must be listening to their words—but not, somehow, to their
thoughts.
Yet You, LORD, know me thoroughly; when You look You see
my heart.

Drag them off to slaughter like sheep, set them aside to be killed!
How long will the land be parched, every green blade of grass
turn dry?
Because of the people's corruption the birds and beasts have all
died,
yet they—the wicked—keep saying: "No one will call us to
account."

[God's answer:]

If you race on foot and they beat you, how can you win against horsemen?

If you topple over when things are fine, what will you do when the Jordan floods its banks?

Your brothers and your family, even they can turn against you, even they can denounce you.

So don't believe them now, no matter how nice they might sound.

WHY DO THE WICKED PROSPER?

I WOULD HAVE LIKED TO PRESERVE at least a faint echo of the usual translation of this passage's famous first line, "Thou art just, O LORD, when I complain against Thee," but in truth, Jeremiah's words have an entirely different ring in biblical Hebrew. The Hebrew ṣaddiq can indeed mean "just" or "righteous," but this term has another, technical sense that is being invoked here: it refers to the winning side in a legal case, the person in whose favor the judges decide. So in biblical times Jeremiah's opening sentence sounded more like: "You always win, O LORD, whenever I take You to court; still, I must institute proceedings against You one more time." Of course, this legal metaphor is just that, a metaphor. There is no court of justice to which God may be summoned. But it was a striking way for Jeremiah to begin his indictment of divine justice: Why indeed, if You are in charge of the world, does the way of the wicked *ever* prosper?

The question of life's injustice was hardly a new one in Jeremiah's day. It had been around for centuries and centuries, in fact, long before monotheism. But in a polytheistic world, controlled by competing divine forces—whether simply the "gods," or, as in old Iranian and certain other systems of thought, paired deities of good and evil, or even a more-or-less equally matched God and Satan—the problem had an answer of sorts: the bad power won out in this or that case. For true monotheists, alas, the same question has no obvious answer. "I am the LORD, and there are no gods beside Me," God says (Isa. 45:5); in keeping with this, I am

> The shaper of light and creator of darkness, the One who makes
> well-being and creates evil—
>
> I, the LORD, make all these things.
>
> ISA. 45:7

These lines (and many others in the Bible) clearly impute to God responsibility for all that happens on earth, including all evil. Indeed, a student of biblical parallelism might well bring out the sharpness of this verse with a slightly freer, but in another way more accurate, translation: "*Just as you will concede that I am the shaper of light and creator of darkness—since both things do exist in the world that I created, indeed, My creation of both light and darkness "in the beginning" is well known—so you must also concede that I am the one who creates the moral equivalents of both light and dark, namely, I am the One who makes well-being and creates evil.*" The maker of all things must thus be responsible for evil and injustice too.

But if so, why? Why, the biblical monotheist asked, do the wicked prosper. And certainly equally troubling, why do the righteous suffer? One answer frequently given in Israel was that the workings of divine justice may not always be apparent to human eyes. After all, humans live only a certain number of years, while God was deemed eternal. In keeping with this, God is sometimes said in the Bible to "visit the sins of the fathers on the children, to the third and fourth generation" (Exod. 20:5, 34:7), that is, to punish vicariously, hence, nonobviously. Was it not therefore the case that the ultimate setting aright of injustice—and perhaps also the ultimate goodness of apparently needless suffering—was sometimes unperceived by human eyes?

Such an answer was in particular championed by the sages of ancient Israel. If the wicked seemed to go unpunished, ancient wisdom explained that the divine plan had not yet worked itself out—but ultimately, justice would triumph. In the meantime, a sage ought to wait patiently. Similarly, human suffering also called for patience. Suffering that appeared to be undeserved might indeed be just a matter of appearances, for who really knew the inner life of a person? Perhaps not even the person himself. Moreover, precisely because divine justice may not be carried out at once or obviously, people sometimes erroneously conclude that there is no reward or punishment:

> Since the verdict for an evil deed is not swiftly rendered,
> men therefore resolve to do evil.
>
> ECCLES. 8:11

Human beings, in this same view, may also fail to understand the relationship between sin and punishment because sin has a cumulative effect: God finally brings about a person's death, some biblical texts suggest, not in response to the last misdeed, but because of the accumulation of many sins:

> For we perish because of Your wrath, and by Your anger we are whisked away,
>
> [after] You have set out our sins in front of You, and our hidden things by the light of Your face [that is, examined by divine wisdom].
>
> PS. 90:7–8

An extension of this answer (but no real change in direction) involved the idea of an afterlife or the resurrection of the dead. Both beliefs are certainly old, and neither is altogether foreign to the Hebrew Bible, though they are hardly prominent there. If, after their lives are over, human beings are still to be judged,

For God will bring every creature into judgment on every hidden
thing, whether good or evil.

ECCLES. 1 2 : 1 4

then it is certainly not within man's grasp to assess divine justice.
Perhaps (as Jews and Christians both held) a righteous person's
sufferings in this world are a down payment on his or her imme-
diate reward in the next, while a flagrant sinner's prosperity dur-
ing his lifetime might be nothing but a prelude to an eternity
of punishment. Finally, there was simply the enormous gap
between man and God undergirding all such answers. What
God tells Job in response to his book-long protest of apparently
undeserved punishment is not that all will eventually be set
aright (though that is how things do turn out in Job's case).
Instead, God's answer focuses on Job's, and all human beings',
ignorance: since we know so little about God's ways, our con-
clusions are all basically hot air.

~

SOME MODERN THEOLOGIANS, moved to despair, have suggested
that God does indeed love humanity and wants only good for it,
but that even He is powerless to prevent evil from afflicting good
people. But this is essentially a return to the old, polytheistic
view. Such a God may be altogether loveable, but He is not really
God. And so one is left with inscrutable injustice. What is partic-
ularly striking in the Bible is that injustice is not swept under the
rug. It is unfair, Israel's prophets and sages say. There is always
something heroic, thrilling, even, in their speaking the truth.

Why do the wicked live on? Growing older, they only get richer.

They reproduce, smile on descendants,

while they themselves live securely—no rod of God's ever strikes them.

The bulls in their fields rut on demand, and their cows give birth without fail.

Their own infants gambol like sheep, their children dance in a round,

playing on harp and timbrel, singing to the sound of the pipe.

They spend out their days in comfort, then peacefully go down to Sheol.

To God they say, "Leave me alone. I don't need Your religion.

What is the Almighty, that we should serve Him? What good does it do to pray?"

Yet all that they have didn't come from themselves—the fate of the wicked is too much for me.

How often is their light snuffed out, as their downfall at last overtakes them?

Let God, in His anger, make them hurt! Let them be like straw in the wind, like chaff that the storm carries off.

"God saves punishment for their children"? Let Him punish the guilty one, so *he*'ll know!

Let his own eyes behold his downfall, let him taste the Almighty's displeasure.

What does he care, anyway, if those who come after live less?

Meanwhile, should he outsmart God or act like some heavenly judge?

Oh, one man dies in perfect condition; how tranquil he was, at his ease.

His haunches were full and plump, his bone marrow rich and moist.

Another man dies with gullet unfilled—he never had enough food to eat.

Now the two together lie in the dirt, as the worms in the grave devour them.

JOB 21:7–26

❧

JEREMIAH'S BRIEF EXCHANGE with God is thrilling in another way, not so much for what the prophet says, but for the answer he receives. Lurking in the background is that other meaning of Jeremiah's opening words, "You are *just*, after all"—forget about who wins in court, why would You *want* to be on the side of injustice? Perhaps indeed, the only thing that one can do is simply accept what God gives. Job did not need to wait for God's answer to understand this truth. His opening insight on his own catastrophic fall is basically what anyone would have been taught in the great eastern academies of wisdom: "The LORD gave and the LORD has taken away, blessed be the name of the LORD" (Job 1:21).* But if that is how a human being is to respond to suffering, it still leaves unanswered the question of divine injustice. Whatever they might teach in Mesopotamia, neither Job (that pseudo-Edomite crypto-Israelite) nor Jeremiah can quite make their peace with such an approach.

The answer Jeremiah gets is hardly the magnificent response delivered to Job from the whirlwind, nor even some shorthand

---

*A more explicative translation of this bit of biblical parallelism might read: "Whether the LORD gives or the LORD takes, blessed be the name of the LORD."

version thereof. Surely this is significant. After all, Jeremiah is an educated man, indeed, a temple priest. He may not be a professional sage, but certainly he, like any other adult of his time and station, had heard the things that ancient sages say about humanity's short lifespan or its inability to see the big picture. In such circumstances, God might well have answered Jeremiah with a brief allusion to these themes. How remarkable, then, that what Jeremiah hears is rooted not in wisdom's metaphysics but in the here-and-now: "Things are going to get a lot worse, and you had better realize it." Here is no dry discourse on the meaning of suffering, but a snatch of an actual conversation: first Jeremiah said this, then God answered in a way that must have caught the prophet completely off-guard. "If you topple over when things are fine, what will you do when the Jordan floods its banks?" This hardly contributes to the debate on unjustified suffering or the apparent prosperity of the wicked, but it provides something else, actual footage of the real prophet and how God answered his question one day.

CHAPTER 13

PSALM 137

Y THE RIVERS OF BABYLON WHERE WE SETTLED,
WE WEPT WHEN WE THOUGHT OF ZION.

On poplar trees there, we hung up our harps,

since there our captors asked us to sing, and our masters
demanded entertainment —

"Sing us one of those Zion songs."

How can we sing a song of the LORD in a foreign land?

If I forget you, Jerusalem, let my right hand wither;

let my tongue go dry in my mouth if I stop speaking of you,
if I don't think of Jerusalem even at my greatest joy.

Please, O LORD, pay back the Edomites for the day of Jerusalem's
fall,

the ones who said, "Tear it down! Tear it down to its
foundations!"

O Babylon, you destroyer! Lucky the one who does back to you
what you did to us!

Lucky the one who takes your little babies and smashes them on
the rocks!

The Fall of Jerusalem

LOVED FOR ITS PICTURE of steadfast devotion in the midst of suffering, though sometimes also questioned for its closing fury, Psalm 137 has always occupied a central place in the book of Psalms. The facts that stand behind it are well known. In the seventh regnal year of the neo-Babylonian king Nebuchadnezzar II (that is, 597 B.C.E.), in the month of Kisilimu, Babylonian troops mustered and began their march toward the territory of the Jews. According to a contemporaneous Babylonian chronicler,* they "encamped against the city of Judah [Jerusalem] and seized the city on the second day of the month of Adar. He [Nebuchadnezzar] took the king [Jehoiachin] prisoner. Then he appointed another king of his choosing [Zedekiah] and received much booty from there, which he sent back to Babylon." Included in this first shipment of spoils were, according to the biblical account, all the funds accumulated in the king's treasury as well as the monies of the Temple and its golden ornaments and other valuables, plus "all the noble men, seven thousand of them, and a thousand craftsmen and smiths—all of them warriors and fighters" (2 Kings 24:16).

Thus weakened, the puppet government of Zedekiah seemed to have little choice but to do Babylon's bidding. And so it did, for a time. But then, heartened by troubles elsewhere in the Babylonian empire (and, probably, egged on by Babylon's rival, Egypt), Zedekiah revolted, apparently believing that Nebuchadnezzar's army would never be able to intervene with full force

---

*Translated in D. J. Wiseman, *Chronicles of Chaldean Kings* [626–556 B.C.E.] in the British Museum (London, 1956), tablet B.M. 21946.

against him. He was wrong. In 588 Babylonian troops marched back into Judah and prepared to take Jerusalem. The procedure in such circumstances was brutally simple. The attackers would surround the (usually heavily fortified) city while its citizens huddled inside. The attacking army would then try to smash through the city walls or gates with heavy battering rams, or sometimes scale the walls with ladders, or else try to dig their way through underneath. At the same time they would also institute a siege, building high siege towers all around the city and preventing anyone from entering or exiting.* Those behind the city walls would try to ward off the enemy soldiers and survive as best they could, consuming the grain and other edibles that had been stored away beforehand and hoping that the enemy's patience, or lines of supply, would give out before they themselves did. Sometimes it went one way, sometimes the other.

The siege of Jerusalem was particularly cruel; the people, knowing the bitter fate that awaited them, held out in the face of horrendous suffering. The biblical book of Lamentations records what it was like.

> My eyes have no more tears and my insides are like clay.
>
> My feelings are numb at my people's catastrophe,
>
> as little babies, infants, lie helpless in the streets.
>
> They whine to their mothers, "I'm hungry!" "Something to drink!"

---

*Ezekiel mentions some of these tactics in his depiction of Nebuchadnezzar in the process of deciding who first to attack among his western neighbors: "For the king of Babylon paused at a fork in the road, where two roads diverge, to decide by lot. He shook arrows, read teraphim, and inspected the liver [all forms of divination]. The omen against Jerusalem came up in his right hand: to set up the battering rams, to cry 'Havoc!' and let loose the trumpets of war, move the battering rams to the gates, to cast up mounds, to build siege-towers" (Ezek. 21:26–27; some Bibles, 21:21–22).

but they're left like the helpless corpses in the city streets,

as they languish in their mothers' arms.

·

Even jackals offer the breast to suckle their young,

but not my people; they have turned crueler than an ostrich in
the desert.

A baby's tongue is stuck to the roof of its mouth from thirst

and little children beg for bread, but no one gives them a crumb.

People who once fed on dainties are wasting in the streets,

and those who went about in purple now sift garbage.

This nation's sin must be greater than Sodom's,

which was crushed in a flash, untouched by human hands.

Her [Jerusalem's] rulers were purer than snow and whiter than
milk,

with limbs that were ruddy as coral, frames of sapphire.

Now they are blacker than soot, unrecognized in the streets;

their skin lies shriveled on their bones, dried up like wood.

The ones killed in battle fared better than those killed by hunger:

at least they oozed [blood] from wounds and [not from lack of]
grain.

Tenderhearted women boiled their children with their own
hands.

Then they ate them as food. [This] is my people's catastrophe.

LAM. 2:11–12, 4:2–10

The siege went into its second year and still the Jews held out.
But finally hunger, thirst, and the crushing summer heat over-
came them. Jerusalem's walls were at last breached; the end was

now in sight. King Zedekiah and his troops took flight by night through the broken walls, hoping to find safety in the desert or, perhaps, on the far side of the Jordan.

> But the Babylonian army went after the king in pursuit and caught up with him at the plains of Jericho; all his troops scattered and left him. They seized the king and brought him to the king of Babylon at Ribla; there they put him on trial. Then they slaughtered Zedekiah's children in front of him, and they put out Zedekiah's eyes and bound him in bronze chains and took him to Babylon.
>
> 2 KINGS 25: 5–7

Back in Jerusalem, the Babylonians inflicted similar revenge on the city itself, burning down the great Temple as well as the private houses in the city, then tearing apart sections of the city walls stone by stone so that no one could dwell there in safety again. Those inhabitants who had not been killed were dragged off as prisoners and marched across the desert to Babylon. A dark new chapter was opening in the history of the people, one that seemed quite possibly its last.

❧

IT MIGHT SEEM STRANGE to say that the catastrophe was as devastating theologically as politically, but this was true. For four centuries Jerusalem had stood unvanquished. Often threatened, sometimes reduced to political vassalage, it had nonetheless always survived, while elsewhere whole empires rose and fell. Even the apparently invincible Assyrian army that had swept over Israel's Northern Kingdom and brought it to an end did not manage to conquer Jerusalem, though it apparently came close.

What is more, during the same four centuries a descendant of King David had always sat on the throne in Jerusalem—four hundred years.* Few monarchies elsewhere in the ancient world, or, for that matter, in Europe in later times, could match this record of continuity and stability.

For both these unusual circumstances a ready explanation was at hand. Jerusalem would never fall, and the house of David would never be replaced, because both of them had been chosen by God. God's own house was the Temple in Jerusalem; surely he would not allow an army of aliens to enter it or even to conquer the city in which it was located. As for the royal house of David, it was God who had originally placed David on his throne and had guaranteed the survival of his dynasty forever (2 Sam. 7:11–16). How then could the Davidic king be toppled?

True, there were people in Jerusalem who questioned these divine guarantees. Some of them, no doubt, were gnarled political realists. Whatever the "men of God" might wish, they said, facts are facts. The Babylonian army is a formidable force, and it will get its way no matter what we do. Interestingly, though, one of the principal naysayers was a man of God himself, the prophet Jeremiah: "Don't put your trust in the lies that say 'the Temple of the LORD, the Temple of the LORD, the Temple of the LORD [is here]'" (Jer. 7:4). Having God's Temple in your midst is no guarantee. After all, wasn't there a temple of God in Shiloh before it was overrun?

> "Just go to my holy place in Shiloh, the place where I established My name at first, and see what I did to it because of the

---

*By comparison it is worth pointing out that the American republic has, as of this writing, been in existence only a little more than two centuries. Four hundred years of a single regime may not look like much as a number in a history book, but in the minds of the people living under it, it seems like an eternity.

wickedness of My people Israel. And now, since you have done all these [sinful] things, says the LORD—though I warned you day after day, yet you did not listen, and though I called out to you, you did not answer—therefore I will do to the Temple which is called by My name and in which you trust, I will do to this holy place which I gave for you and for your fathers, just as I did to Shilo. And I will cast you off just as I cast off your brothers, the whole family of Ephraim [that is, the Northern Kingdom]."

JER. 7:12–15

One need not speculate about how these words sounded to the professional optimists and their followers in Jerusalem. The Bible itself recounts what happened to Jeremiah after he delivered this message:

The priests and prophets and the people all heard Jeremiah say these things in the house of the LORD. When Jeremiah had finished saying everything that the LORD had told him to say to all the people, the priests and the prophets and all the people seized him and said, "Now you shall be put to death! How can you prophesy in the name of the LORD and say that this house will be like Shilo, or that this city will be destroyed and without inhabitants?" And all the people bitterly accused Jeremiah in the house of the LORD. . . . And the priests and prophets said to the officials and the whole people, "This man is to face the death penalty. He prophesied against this city, as you yourselves have heard with your own ears."

Then Jeremiah said to all the officials and to the whole people: "It is the LORD who sent me to prophesy against this house and against this city and to say everything that you heard. Now, if you change your evil ways and obey the LORD your God, then

the LORD will rescind the evil sentence which He has pro-
nounced against you. As for me, look, I am in your hands. You
can do with me whatever you want. But understand that if you
put me to death, you will be shedding innocent blood [and it
will be] on yourselves and on this city and its inhabitants. For
the LORD did truly send me to you to say these things directly
to you."

JER. 26:7–15

Jeremiah was not, in the end, put to death. His courage and his
calm as attested above are probably all that saved his life. Still,
the message that he brought was no less acceptable to his coun-
trymen: God is not necessarily on our side. Our sins will be pun-
ished at great cost; God will not abide with us under any
conditions. Someone who, like Jeremiah, believed in the exis-
tence of one God alone could not attribute the vicissitudes of this
world to some grand theomachy (battle of the gods). If there is a
single divine will, then it alone is responsible for everything that
happens, even the cruelest evil.

～

ONE OF THE STRIKING TRAITS of the book of Lamentations—
ascribed by tradition, incidentally, to Jeremiah's own author-
ship—is its unflinching portrait of God as the enemy. The title of
the book is in that way misleading. It is not just a book of laments
over the fall of Jerusalem, but an assignment of blame. It stares
into the horror and says, again and again: You did this to me. The
Babylonian army was simply a shill, a decoy in the shadowy
game of divine punishment:

[*Jerusalem speaks*:]

O you who pass by, stop and look awhile:

Is there any pain like this pain of mine,

which the LORD made me suffer on the day of His wrath?

From on high He let loose the fire, and sent it into my bones.

He set a trap for my feet and down I fell.

Now He has left me desolate, infirm the whole day long.

His hand has yoked me to my sins,

and the yoke sits on my neck and saps my strength;

my Lord has given me over to undefeatable enemies.

•

He drew His bow like an enemy, held firm His bow-hand like a foe;

then He killed all the lovely ones;

in the tents of Zion, He spewed out His anger like fire.

My Lord has become like an enemy, destroying Israel,

destroying all her citadels and laying waste her fortresses,

making great the mourning and grieving in Judah.

He has stripped down His little hut and stopped the festival,

the LORD has put an end in Zion to festivals and sabbaths,

and in His wrath has set aside both king and priest.

My Lord has abandoned His own altar, rejected His sanctuary;

He has handed over to the enemy the walls of its citadels;

yes, voices were heard in the LORD's house as loud as on a festival.

The LORD hatched a plan to destroy Zion's wall, then He
measured it;

His hand did not flinch at its destruction . . .

·

Look O LORD, look well—who is it You have treated this way?

Are not women eating their own children, their babies?

Are not priest and prophet slain inside my Lord's own Temple?

Young boy and old man lie sprawling in the streets together,

girls and boys are cut down by the sword.

You killed them on the day of Your wrath. You slaughtered.
You had no mercy.

LAM. 1:12–14; 2:4–8, 20–21

Many people miss the point of Lamentations. If they read it at
all, they tend to recoil from passages like the above. Who would
delight to hear that "My LORD has become like an enemy"? But
one should consider what this assertion and the others like it real-
ly meant in ancient Israel. The speaker of these words saw the
greatest of horrors, the very worst things that can happen in this
world, people slowly starving to death in the streets—his own
family starving to death. Seeing this, he said "God." He did not
say this out of virtue or even out of what is today called "faith."

He simply looked and said what he saw: My intimate, there You are, now my enemy. In this he was a bit like the psalmist cited elsewhere herein,

> Where can I go from Your spirit, or how can I get away from You?
>
> If I could go up to the sky, there You would be, or down to Sheol, there You are too.
>
> Ps. 139:7–8

Sheol, the realm of the dead, was not far from where the speaker of Lamentations actually stood, and there, presiding over these dead bodies rotting in the street, was not the Babylonian army or any of the other grim shapers of politics and human affairs, but You. This was the dilemma, and sometimes the horror, of living in God's world. But he had no choice.

It is certainly no accident that the book of Lamentations is written in the most self-consciously literary style there can be in the Bible. That is to say, in common with a few psalms (25, 34, 37, 111, 112, 119, 145)* and one section of Proverbs (Prov. 31:10–31), Lamentations is an acrostic poem, or, rather, a series of them, in which each line of the poem begins with a successive letter of the alphabet.** Indeed, the third chapter is a triple acrostic: the first three verses begin with "A," the next three with "B," and so forth. Now, acrostics were a highly ornamental form of composition, and in that sense also the most obviously plotted out, *arranged* form of poetry in Hebrew. Acrostics had a further

---

* Pss. 9–10 also seem to bear the mark of an original alphabetical construction.

**The only exception is the last of its five chapters, about which more presently.

.nuance as well. The alphabet, much more in biblical times than now, bespoke the world of education and wise scribes. (Though the evidence on this is necessarily sparse, literacy does not appear to have been very widespread at the time of the Babylonian exile; even the names of the letters could not be presumed to have been known widely.) Alphabetical acrostics said "wisdom."

There may seem to be something grotesque in shaping verses about rape and cannibalism to match an alphabetical grid. But it is also an act of control, a way of saying: "I will fit everything that happened into this orderly framework." Making this catalogue of horrors alphabetical may have also served to make it scribal, wise. Of course, the tone of Lamentations is very far from the gnomic detachment of Proverbs. But it shares with it the profound conviction that life must always make sense, and then follows that conviction down into life's darkest corridor. In this sense, the form of the book is perfectly consonant with its sustained, unflinching apprehension of God.

～

WHAT HAPPENED TO THE JEWS after the fall of Jerusalem is also described in Lamentations, in its last chapter, which focuses not on the fate of those Jews who were led into exile in Babylon, but on those (apparently few) who were allowed to remain behind:

> Remark, O LORD, what has become of us, stop and consider our downfall.
>
> Our lands have been given to strangers, foreigners live in our houses.
>
> We have become like fatherless orphans, and our mothers are like widows.

We pay money for our water, our firewood comes at a price.

We are shoved around by the neck; tired out, we are given no rest.

Even the Egyptians gave help [to our ancestors], the Assyrians supplied enough food.

Our ancestors sinned and passed on; now we are paying for their deeds.

Slaves rule over us, with no one to save us from their hands.

We earn our bread at our peril in the parching desert heat.

Our skin glows like an oven from the ravages of hunger.

Women are raped in Zion itself, girls in the towns of Judah.

Our leaders are hanged by their hands, our elders put to shame.

Boys are put to work grinding, or stagger under loads of wood.

The elders have left off their meetings, and young people their songs.

Joy is gone from our hearts, our dancing is turned to mourning.

The crown has fallen from our head. Alas, alas that we sinned.

LAM. 5:1–16

At the height of their sufferings, many wondered if indeed they had not reached the end of the road:

You, O LORD, will rule forever; Your throne exists in every age.

But do not, then, forget us entirely! Do not forsake us for a long, long time.

Let us return and go back to You, LORD. Restore us as we were before—

unless You have completely rejected us, having grown exceedingly angry.

LAM. 5:19–22

~

THE AUTHORSHIP AND HISTORICAL SETTING of Psalm 137
have, since ancient times, been the subject of some speculation.
One old tradition, well known, attributes the authorship of the
whole book of Psalms to King David. But if David did write
Psalm 137, his description of the Babylonian exile was certainly
prophetic, since the events themselves were still far in the future
during his lifetime. Perhaps for that reason a second tradition
existed, one that ascribed the authorship of this psalm not to
David but to another, later figure—once again, the prophet
Jeremiah. This tradition is reflected in some ancient manuscripts
of the old Greek translation of the Bible, which actually print the
heading "to [or "of"] Jeremiah" at the beginning of the psalm.
Other ancient Greek manuscripts read "To David, through
Jeremiah," apparently seeking to harmonize both traditions by
implying that, while the original author of all the psalms may
indeed have been David, it was Jeremiah who actually spoke the
words of this psalm on the occasion of the exiles' departure to, or
entrance into, Babylon. (The same tradition is found in later, rab-
binic sources.)

However, a close reading of the words may indicate that even
this later historical setting is a bit too early. The sufferings of
exile described in this psalm seem to have already passed.
Babylon is "there" and "then," not here and now:

> By the rivers of Babylon where we settled, we wept when we
> thought of Zion.
>
> On poplar trees there, we hung up our harps,
>
> since there our captors asked us to sing, and our masters demanded
> entertainment—"Sing us one of those Zion songs."

Even the lines that immediately follow these,

> How can we sing a song of the LORD in a foreign land?
>
> If I forget you, Jerusalem, let my right hand wither;
>
> let my tongue go dry in my mouth if I stop speaking of you,
>
> if I don't think of Jerusalem even at my greatest joy.

while at first they sound like an oath spoken in the present tense, seem on reflection to be, in the context of the psalm, a later report of what had been said in Babylon in answer to the preceding command, "Sing us one of those Zion songs." In other words, this psalm as a whole situates itself in the period just after the Babylonian exile has come to an end.

If so, then it is striking to consider the difference between this psalm and the spiritual world of the book of Lamentations, which may precede it by, at most, a few decades. But what a difference! Here, God is no longer the enemy; the Babylonians themselves are the authors of our suffering. Even what preceded the exile—the destruction of Jerusalem "to its very foundations"—is not a divine act but an altogether human one, and its perpetrators, Edomite and Babylonian, will, the psalmist hopes, one day pay dearly for their crimes. It is only in the context of this hoped-for revenge that God's name is invoked. Nor is it difficult to understand why such a difference should exist. The exile has come to an end; we are back in Jerusalem now. The imponderable, the inscrutable, which is God's, has turned into a merely human, understandable evil. After years of being too big, it can now be grasped for what it was. All that is still just beyond the psalmist's reach is revenge, for which he earnestly prays.

Is not this difference reflected as well in poetic form? I have already described the tight acrostics of the first four chapters of

Lamentations. The fifth chapter, set in the period just after the destruction, says nothing of God-the-enemy. God is mentioned only in the closing lines (5:19–22, cited above), in words that ask Him not to forget His people forever. Perhaps it is only a co-incidence, but this is also the only chapter of Lamentations that is not an alphabetical acrostic. The acrostic form is evoked, so to speak, by the fact that the number of verses in it is the same as that of an alphabetical acrostic (twenty-two); it *could* have been an acrostic, the author seems to say, but it is not quite.

If the last chapter of Lamentations thus represents a certain loosening of the controlling poetic hand, that hand is almost absent from Psalm 137, one of the "prosiest" psalms in the Bible. Here, even the rough equivalences of the standard form

—————————————— I —————————————— II

have been all but dispensed with. A line like

> By the rivers of Babylon where we settled, we wept when we
> thought of Zion

is longer in Hebrew than the great majority of lines of biblical poetry, as is the three-part line that follows a little later,

> since there our captors asked us to sing, and our masters demanded
> entertainment—"Sing us one of those Zion songs."

On the other hand, even the relatively short or normal-sized lines like

> On poplar trees there, we hung up our harps,

or

How can we sing a song of the LORD in a foreign land?

lack the niceties of Part A and Part B, the connectedness amid disjunction, that is the heart of biblical prosody. We *can* pause in the middle, so we do, but the spring, the fulcrum, of the poetic line is not there. Perhaps the reason is that there is no need here for the tight logic of Part A, Part B. By the rivers of Babylon we suffered but held firm; we said we would not forget Jerusalem, and we didn't.

~

INTERPRETERS, ANCIENT AND MODERN, have frequently been troubled by the central gesture of Psalm 137:

> On poplar trees there, we hung up our harps,
>
> since there our captors asked us to sing, and our masters demanded entertainment—"Sing us one of those Zion songs."
>
> How can we sing a song of the LORD in a foreign land?

Is it reasonable to suppose that these captive singers, having been told to perform a song of Zion, could simply refuse to comply? Surely the Babylonians had the means to make them sing if they wanted. But even if they were somehow allowed to refuse, what was the significance of their hanging their harps (lyres, more accurately) in trees? This was a decidedly strange thing to do under the circumstances! If truly they were refusing to sing, they should have simply left their harps wherever they were. And even if one supposes that they had been holding their harps all along (or had taken them up now at the Babylonians' insistence), they could certainly have better symbolized their refusal to sing a song of Zion by putting their harps back down or even smashing them to bits in their fury. Why (and how) hang them in trees?

Wrestling with these questions, one medieval commentator, Menahem ben Solomon Meiri of Provence, suggested a surprising interpretation: the singers did not refuse at all. The phrase "on poplar trees there" could also be understood as "by poplar trees there" or "next to poplar trees." (The Hebrew word 'al is ambiguous, and it is the same word that, all agree, means "By the rivers of Babylon" in the first line.) As for "hang," this word can, Meiri argued, sometimes also mean "stretch" or "extend" in Hebrew. Thus what the text is really saying is that there, in Babylon, next to some poplar trees, the Jewish singers stretched the strings of their harps as they tuned them. They had no choice, since the Babylonian soldiers escorting them,

> once they were in their own territory, had begun to rejoice and make merry. And they had in their possession all the instruments of the Temple, so they ordered that they [the Jews] sing from the songs of Zion. And they were forced to do so. They took out their harps and put them in their hands to tune their strings and pegs and pull them. . . . [Thus] they forced them to sing a song of Zion.

Meiri's interpretation is hardly the only one put forward, however. Other interpreters saw the gesture of hanging the harps as symbolic. Prophecy, which was sometimes induced by strumming the lyre, was held by some to have been impossible on Babylonian soil. Hanging the lyres in the trees was, in a sense, turning them into Aeolian harps, to be played on directly by earthly breezes rather than through the divine inspiration that had previously animated their strings. Early Christians saw the reference to the trees here as a symbol of the crucifixion and the harps as the harp of David. But the real intentions of the text will probably always be in dispute.

~

ONCE THE EXILE WAS OVER, the move from Babylon back to Jerusalem might seem like an easy step. With the way open for the exiled Jews to return home, would they not now jump at the chance? But it was not so (see "The Match"); the move from despair to hope is rarely easy. How can someone, having seen the Jews suffer the very worst at God's hand, go back to where he was before—not physically, but in his heart? For some the answer was certainly to remain in Babylon, and to remain in despair; indeed, they had no choice. Perhaps, then, it is wise to see in Psalm 137 something of a spiritual step as well (though this is rarely said about that psalm), a step in what is always a very long journey. Lucky the one, a biblical sage might have said, who can walk the whole way from "My LORD has become like an enemy" to "Lucky the one."

CHAPTER 14

PSALM 119

APPY ARE THOSE WHOSE PATH IS PURE, WHO WALK IN ACCORD WITH THE LORD'S TEACHING.

Happy are those who keep His statutes and appeal to Him with their whole heart —

those who have not acted wrongly, but follow His paths.

You have admonished us about Your precepts, to keep them carefully.

Oh, if only my ways were straight, to adhere to Your laws!

Then I would never be ashamed, when I consider all Your commandments.

I approach You with an upright heart as I learn Your just rules.

Let me keep Your laws. Do not abandon me completely.

But how can a fellow straighten his way and follow Your words?

I have begged You with my whole heart, do not let me stray from Your commandments.

Deep in my heart I have buried what You said, so that I not sin against You.

Blessed are you, O LORD; teach me Your laws.

By myself I have recited all of Your rules.

I like better the path of Your statutes than any riches.

Let me speak some of Your precepts and behold Your paths.

I take pleasure in Your laws. Let me bear Your words in mind.

Be compassionate with Your servant so that I may live and keep Your words.

Open my eyes to contemplate mysteries from Your teachings.

I am a wayfarer in the land. Do not conceal Your commandments from me.

Constantly my soul is overcome with longing for Your rules.

You have confounded the accursed ones who stray from Your commandments.

Keep me from calumny and dishonor, for I have kept Your statutes.

Though princes may condemn me, Your servant only speaks of Your laws.

Yes, Your statutes are my delight, my closest friends.

My soul is down in the mud—bring me back to life in accord with Your words.

I have told of my ways so that You might help me; direct me with Your laws.

Let me discern the path of Your precepts and speak of Your mysteries.

My soul is dragged down with sadness; uphold me in accord with Your words.

Draw me away from the path of falsehood and grace me with Your teaching.

I delight in the path of faithfulness, I am mindful of Your rules.

I have been drawn to Your statutes, LORD, do not let me be shamed.

I hasten down the path of Your commandments since it gives my mind discernment.

Show me, LORD, the path of Your laws so that I may execute them accordingly.

Educate me to keep Your teaching so that I may observe it with my whole heart.

Lead me on the road of Your commandments, for it is my enjoyment.

Make me earnest for Your statutes and not for worldly gain.

Turn my eyes from illusion; may Your ways keep me alive.

Make what You said come true for Your servant, since it enforces Your worship.

Let me not be put to shame, as I fear, for Your rules excel all.

I am so eager for Your precepts; keep me alive by Your righteousness.

LORD, let Your graciousness find its way to me; let Your salvation be as You said.

Then I will have a reply for those who shame me, since I will have had faith in Your words.

Do not withhold a word of truth from my mouth, since I follow Your rules.

And let me keep Your teaching steadily, forever and ever.

So I will walk about freely, since I have inquired into Your statutes.

If I talk about Your precepts, even around kings I will not be forsaken.

I am fulfilled in Your commandments; I love them.

I worship Your commandments out of love; let me fathom
Your laws.

Grant Your servant a word, for You have offered hope to me.

Your word gives me new life, and this consoles me in my affliction.

Though the wicked gloat over me, I have not strayed from Your
teaching.

I have always thought of Your rules, LORD, and have gained
comfort from them.

Outrage seizes me at the wicked ones who give up Your teaching.

Your laws became the songs I sing as I go about my house.

At night I make mention of Your name, LORD, so that I may
guard Your teaching.

All this has been given to me, since I keep Your statutes.

Since the LORD is my portion, I promise to hold fast to Your
words.

I have hoped for You with my whole heart; be gracious as You
have promised.

I have looked hard at my ways and returned to Your statutes.

I have hurried and not dawdled to keep Your commandments.

Though the wicked hold me back with chains, I have not neglected
Your teaching.

At midnight I get up to honor You for Your just rules.

I am a friend to all who fear You, holding to Your precepts.

Your kindness, LORD, fills the horizon; teach me Your laws.

You have been well inclined toward Your servant, in accordance with Your word.

Inform me of what is right to do, since I have trusted in Your commandments.

Before I was punished I was ignorant, but now I am keeping Your word.

You are good and do good; instruct me in Your laws.

The wicked invent falsehoods about me, but I will keep Your precepts with my whole heart.

Their minds are ignorant and gross, but for me, Your teaching is a pleasure.

It is well with me when I am humbled, so that I may be informed of Your laws.

Your instruction is better for me than thousands of gold pieces or silver.

Your hands made me and joined me together; instruct me so that I may learn Your commandments.

Those who fear you will be joyful when they see me, since I have faith in Your word.

I know, LORD, that Your rules are just, and that you have punished me properly.

Now may Your kindness bring me joy, in keeping with Your promise to Your servant.

Let Your mercy overtake me so that I may live, for Your teaching is my joy.

Let the wicked be put to shame, since without justification have they wronged me; as for me, I will speak of Your precepts.

May those who fear you return to me, those who know Your judgments.

Just let my heart be pure in Your laws, so that I not be put to shame.

My soul is keen for Your salvation; I have faith in Your word.

My eyes keep longing for what You speak, as if to say "When will You comfort me?"

Though I am dried out like a wineskin in smoke, I still know Your laws.

How long will Your servant keep living? When will You give my enemies what they deserve?

The wicked have set a trap for me, which is not in keeping with Your teaching.

All Your commandments keep steady; help me since I am falsely pursued.

They [my pursuers] have all but killed me, but I still have not abandoned Your precepts.

Bring me back to life, as suits Your kindness, so that I may observe the statutes You have decreed.

Your word, O Lord, is forever, located in heaven.

Your faithfulness lasts from age to age; You established earth so that it endures.

All the living are Your servants; they stand ready at Your orders today.

Were not Your teaching my delight, I would not last in my affliction.

Never will I leave off Your precepts, since through them You keep me alive.

Save me, for I am yours; I have looked deeply into Your precepts.

The wicked hoped to do away with me; I linger over Your statutes.

I see a limit to everything made, but what You command is large beyond measure.

How much do I love Your teaching! I mull over it all day long.

Your commandments make me discerning—more than my enemies—for they are always with me.

I have passed all my masters in learning, since Your statutes are what I study.

I have become wiser than my elders, for I have maintained Your precepts.

I have made my way from any evil path so that I might keep Your word.

From Your rules I have not moved, for You are my teacher.

How soothing are Your words to me, sweeter than honey to my mouth.

My mind grows sharper from Your precepts; that is why I hate any path of falsehood.

Your word lights my steps, and illuminates my nighttime path.

I have sworn to keep Your righteous norms, and I will keep my word.

I am near the bottom, LORD; keep me alive as You have promised.

Accept with favor, LORD, the offerings of my mouth, and notify me of Your rules.

I lift up my soul to You, and Your teaching I have not neglected.

The wicked set a trap for me, but from Your precepts I have never strayed.

Your statutes are my possession forever, for they are next to my heart.

In my heart I have undertaken to observe Your laws, now and forever.

I hate divisive offshoots, because I love Your teaching.

You observe and watch over me; I have faith in Your word.

Out with you, wicked ones, and let me keep my God's commandments.

Support me as You promised so that I may survive, otherwise my hope will disappear.

Open Your hand to me and save me, so that I may always think about Your laws.

You reject all who do not obey Your laws, for their falsehood and their lies.

You cast off the obdurate like dross; rightly do I love Your precepts.

My skin bristles from fear of You, I am overawed at Your rules.

I practice justice and right, do not leave me to those who would persecute me.

Pledge that Your servant will be well—do not let the wicked oppress me.

I pine away for Your salvation, and for the promise of Your victory.

Treat Your servant in accordance with Your kindness and let me pore over Your laws.

I am Your servant; make me perceptive so that I may keep Your statutes.

When it was time to take the LORD's part, they violated Your teaching.

I do indeed love Your commandments, more than precious gold.

All Your precepts—all of them—I hold to be right, and I hate any false path.

Your statutes are quite wondrous; for that reason my soul carefully guards them.

To quote Your words is enlightening, and even the foolish are brought to understand.

Winded and out of breath, I am still in quest of Your commandments.

Attend to me and be kind to me, quite as You do with those who love Your word.

Quicken my steps as You promised, and do not let evil rule over me.

Quell the oppression against me, so that I may keep Your precepts.

Quench Your servant's thirst for knowledge: teach me Your laws.

My eyes have wept quantities of tears for those who do not keep Your teaching.

You are righteous, LORD, and Your rules are just.

You have made Your statutes righteous too, steady and unbending.

Rage overcomes me when my enemies treat Your words with neglect.

Your word refines and purifies, and Your servant loves it well.

Though I am belittled and rejected, I do not neglect Your precepts.

Your righteousness is forever, and Your teaching is faithful.

Though pain and distress ravage me, Your commandments are my delight.

Your statutes are righteous forever—let me understand them so that I may live.

I have called out with all my heart. Answer me, so that I stay faithful to Your laws.

I call out to You to save me, so that I may keep Your statutes.

At first light I get up in supplication to You, for I have faith in Your word.

My eyes greet the night watches to study Your words.

Take heed of my voice in keeping with Your love; O LORD, make me survive by Your rules.

Those who pursue sinfulness may draw close, but how far they are from Your teaching!

You stand nearby, O LORD, and all Your commandments are faithful..

Of Your statutes I long ago learned that You had established them forever.

See how low I have been brought and set me free, for I have not neglected Your teaching.

Take up my cause and redeem me, keep me alive as You promised.

Salvation is far from the wicked, for they have not thought through Your laws.

Lord, Your mercy is truly great; keep me alive by Your rules.

My pursuers and enemies are many, but I have not turned from Your statutes.

When I see traitors I end up fighting, because they do not keep Your word.

See how I trust in Your precepts; Lord, preserve me in keeping with Your love.

Truth is what Your word stands for, and all Your just laws are forever.

Those with power pursue me undeservedly, but my heart fears only Your words.

I am uplifted by Your word like someone who just found a great fortune.

I hate, I despise untruth; it is Your teaching that I love.

Seven times a day I utter Your praises, because of Your righteous rules.

Well-being belongs to those who uphold Your teaching; they do not falter or fail.

I set my sights on Your help, Lord, and I have undertaken what You command.

My soul is used to keeping Your statutes, and loves them very much.

I have kept Your precepts and statutes, for none of my ways is unknown to You.

May You value this prayer of mine, Lord; make me know Your word.

Let my request come before You: save me by virtue of what You have said.

My voice speaks Your praises, for You teach me Your laws.

My tongue utters Your very words; all Your commandments are just.

May Your hand be there to help me, for I have been vigilant about Your precepts.

I have been very eager for Your salvation, LORD, and Your teaching is my delight.

I have veered off like a lost sheep—but come after Your servant, for I have not violated Your commandments.

TO KNOW GOD

HOW CAN ONE COME TO KNOW GOD? To this question many answers have been given over the ages. It is scarcely my intention here to add a new one to those already proposed, but rather to approach this old question from a slightly different angle. What would the idea of coming to know God have meant to someone in biblical times, and how would a biblical Israelite have reacted to such an idea?

Of course, "biblical times" extended for more than a thousand years, and a great many things changed over that period. But one might start by noticing that, in general, people in the Bible do not seem to "come to know" God at all. Certainly all sorts of things were done in later ages (vigils and contemplative exercises, prayers for enlightenment, self-mortification), initiatives undertaken by the worshiper to help bring him or her into direct contact with the Deity, but none of these is present as such in the Hebrew Bible. On the contrary, what emerges from an examination of biblical texts is that it is almost always God, and not human beings, who initiates contact.

"Depart from your homeland" are God's first words to Abraham (Gen. 12:1–3). Before this was said, no contact whatsoever between God and Abraham had been mentioned; certainly Abraham did nothing, according to the Book of Genesis, to encourage God's speaking to him. The same is true of Jacob, Moses, and other ancient figures; God simply addresses them, in person or in a dream. Many prophets relate how it was that they came to hear, or see, God for the first time, and it is always God who approaches them; there is no hint of the prophet having done anything beforehand in order to, as it were, allow him to come to know God or be known to Him. On the contrary, these prophetic call narratives seem inevitably to stress just how unprepared, and unwilling, the prophet was. Thus Isaiah was mortified when he suddenly found himself in God's presence (Isa. 6:1–4); he believed himself not only unworthy but liable to be killed, and he would certainly have preferred to be elsewhere. The prophet Samuel was so unprepared to be addressed by God that He had to call him no fewer than four times before he realized that it was God who was speaking to him; since he had no idea what God's voice sounded like, he thought his human superior, the priest Eli, was the one summoning him (1 Sam. 3:1–10). In these and many other cases, there is not the slightest hint that the person involved did anything (or had done anything previously) to come to know God, to initiate this divine-human encounter.

NOW ONE MIGHT ASK WHY this is so. Were not Abraham and the other patriarchs (and matriarchs), Isaiah and the other prophets, eager to know God on their own before He addressed them? Why should they have been so passive? And ought not the Bible somewhere to have presented readers with a model for their own piety, some instruction about how they might actively set out to know God?

Part of the answer, I think, is connected with the great reserve any biblical Israelite would have had with regard to God. Any contact with God was a potentially frightening thing. (In a way, the ongoing divine-human contact in the lives of prophets and patriarchs may be somewhat misleading, since, by definition, these are extraordinary individuals.) Of course, ordinary Israelites might have been curious about what God was going to do; perhaps a few individuals also might want to know God's secrets, how He governed the world; many doubtless wanted to know what God desired of them. But to know God in the sense that, I think, most contemporary people understand this phrase—to enter personally into God's living presence, to speak and be spoken to—was a thought that would have been profoundly frightening.

In fact, fear is the first reaction of many of the individuals mentioned above when God does address them. At the time when God first identifies Himself to Moses at the burning bush, "Moses hid his face, because he was afraid to look at God" (Exod. 3:6). At Bethel, after his vision of God,

> Jacob woke up from his sleep and he said, "The LORD must indeed be in this place, though I did not know of it." And he took fright and said, "How fearsome is this place! This is the very house of God and the gateway to heaven."
>
> GEN. 28: 16–17

The Israelites similarly quake when they encounter God at Mt. Sinai. Though Moses tries to reassure them and get them to approach the mountain, "they trembled and stayed back" (Exod. 20:18–21). All of these biblical figures (and dozens of others) might have agreed with the sentiments found in the prophecies of Habakkuk, "O LORD, as soon as I hear of You [coming] I take fright" (Hab. 3:2), or those of Psalm 119 above, "My skin bristles from the fear of You." One can well imagine why ordinary Israelites would not seek, at least in the modern sense, to come to know God.

Besides, to know God presumably meant to go where He was, to the temple in which He was deemed to reside. From the beginning the very notion of a divine residence on earth—a temple, the "house of the LORD"—was not understood to limit God physically, to mean that if He was "there" He could not therefore be elsewhere. God certainly manifested Himself outside of the temple and heard the prayers of people far removed from His dwelling place. But the temple was nonetheless His place, and it was where one would normally go in order to, as it were, encounter God. Precisely because contact with God was so potentially dangerous, the temple was a highly controlled environment. Priests officiated there; they exercised the only important functions in the temple, offering sacrifices and coming close to the holiest area. Since their high calling was decreed hereditary, acquired by birth, an ordinary Israelite could only aspire to watch at a distance. Moreover, the strict laws of purity, and the simple fact of the temple's being a *place*, somewhere other than one's normal sphere of activity, made it necessarily remote from most people's daily life.

Of course ordinary Israelites did go there. As we know from biblical and postbiblical sources, they streamed into Jerusalem for the festivals, and some of them delighted to go there at other times as well to offer sacrifices of their own free will. When they were in need of help, people would often make a vow to God—"If only You give me such and such, then I will make such and such an offering"—and then they would go to the temple to fulfill what they had pledged. Sometimes, too, people simply went to the temple in desperation, in order to, as it were, come to God's attention so that He might intervene directly in their lives. But even under such circumstances they probably behaved the way a person would before a king of flesh and blood under similar circumstances. That is, one might seek to emerge from the sea of faces for a time to press one's request, but one certainly did not expect, or desire, to become God's intimate thereafter as a result. So Hannah, desperate to have a child, goes to the temple at Shiloh and prays to God (1 Sam. 1:11). Her wish granted, she returns to the temple, offers her thanksgiving, and then disappears; we never hear of her interacting with God again. The fact that God had intervened personally into her life and granted her request hardly made her an intimate of God henceforth. Once satisfied (or not), a suppliant would naturally disappear back into the crowd. Precisely because of the setting, and the fearful nature of the divine-human encounter, this was probably the only way most people could conceive of it being in any case.

From all this it might seem that most Israelites did not "come to know" God at all, that the relative remoteness, and fearfulness, of God kept them from leading a God-centered life. But this is to misunderstand totally the essence of Israel's religion, in fact, to misunderstand what was meant by the "fear of the LORD." Far from being an impediment on the way to coming to know God, the fear of the LORD was understood in the biblical world as the sine qua non of any true approach to Him. God was apprehended in the biblical world first and foremost by being "feared."

IT IS IMPORTANT TO DISTINGUISH—because the Bible does—two concepts that might at first seem identical: the "fear of God" and the "fear of the LORD." The "fear of God" actually has nothing to do specifically with the religion of Israel. Indeed, in the face of a certain ambiguity in Hebrew, it probably would not be wrong to translate it as "fear of God/the gods." That is to say, worshipers of other deities are also presumed to have the "fear of God," since what this term fundamentally means is "common decency," the sort of minimally ethical behavior that can be expected from anyone on the globe who believes that human whims are not supreme. Thus, Joseph, pretending to be an Egyptian official, reassures his brothers with the words "I fear God" as he releases them and sends them back to their father, Jacob (Gen. 42:18). By this he does not mean to imply that he is really one of their coreligionists (nor do the brothers understand his assertion as such). Rather, what he says is what any Egyptian might say under the circumstances: "I too have common decency; I too fear God/the gods." Similarly, Abraham explains to the non-Israelite Abimelech that he had to engage in deceit with regard to Sarah because "I said to myself, 'There is no fear of God in this place'" (Gen. 20:11). Abraham certainly does not expect Abimelech's subjects to be worshipers of the God of Israel. What he means is that, whoever they worship, people ought to have at least the "fear of God/the gods," but he was afraid that even this minimum decency could not be assumed in Abimelech's kingdom. The Egyptian midwives refuse to carry out Pharaoh's order to kill the Israelite male babies because, we are told, they at least had such minimal morality, "they feared God" (Exod. 1:17). Similarly, common decency alone ought to prevent someone from putting a stumbling block before the blind (Lev. 19:14), or ill-treating the aged (Lev. 19:32), or taking unfair advantage of people (Lev. 25:17, 35–36), or attacking the defenseless (Deut 25:18). Observing such basic norms is consistently described as "fearing God."

It should be obvious that "fear" here (as so often with biblical emotions) really stands for the external expression—that is, "acting fearful"—of an internal state. The "fear of God" is fundamentally the awareness of God's existence and power, the awareness that, ultimately, the human is not supreme. With that awareness goes the realization that one's own self-interest cannot therefore reign unchecked, that a certain basic decency is required of every human being...or else. There is indeed real fear in the "fear of God," but the phrase fundamentally refers to an awareness and the attitude that results from it.

The "fear of the LORD" has a somewhat different meaning. The LORD, of course, is specifically the God of Israel, and so the "fear of the LORD" is practiced within the context of the religion of the people of Israel. But it is not, therefore, simply the Israelite equivalent of the more generalized "fear of God." Rather, the particular nuance of the "fear of the LORD" is that it constitutes the basics, the entry-level awareness, of biblical religion. "Fear of the LORD" is what an ancient Israelite saw as the first step in coming to know God.

One would not normally think that something like "fear" can be taught. Yet the Bible says again and again that the "fear of the LORD" is precisely the thing that one does teach:

> "Come, children, and listen to me, let me teach you the fear of the LORD."
>
> Ps. 34:12

In the study of wisdom, the first lesson to be learned was . . . the fear of the LORD:

> The beginning of wisdom is the fear of the LORD.
>
> Ps. 111:10

> The fear of the LORD is the beginning of knowledge.
>
> PROV. 1:7

> The fear of the LORD is the beginning of wisdom.
>
> PROV. 9:10

The book of Deuteronomy, in particular, stresses that the fear of the LORD is something that one learns:

> And I [God] caused them [the Israelites] to hear my words, so that they might learn to fear Me the whole time that they should be alive upon the earth, and so that they might teach their children.
>
> DEUT. 4:10

> so that you may learn to fear the LORD your God forever.
>
> DEUT. 14:23

> And [this Torah] shall be close to him [the king] and he shall read from it his whole life long, so that he may learn to fear the LORD his God, to keep all the words of this Torah and these laws, to follow them.
>
> DEUT. 17:19

> Assemble the people, the men and the women and the children, and the sojourner within your midst, so that they might hear and learn and fear the LORD their God, and be careful to do all the provisions of this law. And let their children, who do not know, hear and learn to fear the LORD their God all the days that they shall live on the land.
>
> DEUT. 31:12–13

Note also:

The king of Assyria brought in people from Babylon and

Cuthah . . . and he settled them in the towns of Samaria in place of the Israelites. . . . And when they first settled down they did not fear the LORD, and the LORD dispatched lions against them which killed them. . . . Then the king of Assyria gave an order: "Send there one of the priests whom you have exiled and let him teach them the law of the god[s] of the land." So one of the priests came . . . and settled in Bethel, and he taught them how to fear the LORD.

2 KINGS 17:24–28

What did one learn by learning the "fear of the LORD"? Presumably, the fear of the LORD was similar to the fear of God/the gods in that it started with a recognition that God is indeed the powerful king. Both kinds of "fear," in other words, represented a kind of minimum, Step One, the basics. But the fear of the LORD could not end with an awareness, or even refraining from certain actions; one could not simply stand at a distance. The God of Israel demanded things of human beings. He told Abraham and others what to do; to prophets He confided a message; and of ordinary human beings He demanded that certain basic norms be respected and certain actions be performed. So one had to learn the rules, the sacrifices to be offered, the behavior that was prescribed, and the behavior that was proscribed. If the "fear of God" was something like a universal (and minimal) morality, the "fear of the LORD" consisted, in biblical Israel, of those fundamental steps to be followed collectively as well as individually by those who are in the LORD's fealty.

The way one approached God, as the last passage cited above makes explicit, was by coming to serve Him. The "fear of the LORD" thus designated both a state of mind and what that state of mind leads to, the practice of the service of God. It is certainly no accident that, in many of the other passages cited, the fear of the

LORD is directly connected—as if virtually synonymous—with keeping divine laws and statutes. So also:

> And this is the commandment—the laws and the rules—which the LORD your God commanded to teach you to do in the land to which you are crossing over to possess, so that you fear the LORD your God, keeping all his laws and commandments which I am commanding you.
>
> DEUT. 6:1–2

> The LORD commanded us to do all these laws in order to fear the LORD our God.
>
> DEUT. 6:24

> Fear the LORD your God and serve Him and cling to Him and swear by his name.
>
> DEUT. 10:20 (SEE ALSO: 6:13)

~

THE TORAH, OR PENTATEUCH—the first five books of the Bible—is full of divine laws, things that God commanded the Israelites to do in their daily lives. Many people tend to misunderstand the very nature of these laws; especially nowadays, the idea of being commanded to do this and not do that seems to people an imposition, and a formalistic one at that, in what ought otherwise to be a natural and unimpeded relationship between God and the human being. But for biblical man, it *was* the relationship. Only in carrying out the Divine King's orders could his servants aspire to grow close to Him, grow to know Him. Of course, biblical religion was not a static thing; no generalization will hold equally true for all centuries. But certainly the passages cited from Deuteronomy and other texts above make it clear that to keep all the laws and statutes and ordinances of the Torah was, from ancient times, Israel's highest calling. Indeed, God is said to have initiated His formal connection with Israel by presenting them with a group of *laws*: the Ten Commandments (Exod. 19–20). This list of dos and don'ts, the text makes clear, was the starting point of God's closeness to His people, the filaments that would bind these human beings to God. Thus, if the temple was the domain of the priest and hence only visited now and again by ordinary Israelites, the daily round of keeping God's laws is presented in the Torah as the domain of every person. It was the way in which one concretized and put into practice the "fear of the LORD," that fundamental awareness that was the beginning of wisdom.

It is certainly significant that this "fear of the LORD" found expression not just in things having to do directly with God, but in the realm of the ordinary and commonplace, in everyday life. That is to say, the "fear of the LORD" might conceivably have consisted only of regulations about temple worship and sacrifices, or about remaining strictly and exclusively devoted to God. But, from the beginning, that is not all that God demanded. It is true that the Ten Commandments start with God's requirement that He be recognized and held in exclusive reverence— "You shall have no other gods beside Me"—and the prohibition of image making that follows is presumably likewise connected to this concern. But soon enough the focus turns to relations among human beings: the honoring of one's parents, the prohibitions of murder and adultery and theft. Why should God even care about such things? But this was also part of what the "fear of the LORD" entailed. It was a way of acting not just in the sanctuary but at home or in the marketplace, a way of going about daily life.

It is noteworthy that fear was not the only emotion involved. In many biblical passages, Israel's requirement to fear God is conjoined with that of loving God:

> But now, Israel, what does the LORD your God demand of you, save that you fear the LORD your God, follow all His ways and love Him; that you serve the LORD your God with your whole heart and soul, keeping the commandments of the LORD your God and His laws which I am commanding you today, for your benefit.
>
> DEUT. 10:12

In our own notion of things, fear and love are almost opposite emotions, but according to such texts as the above, they are closely related. And just as with fear, so love, too, sometimes means something other than what it might seem at first.

It was pointed out some years ago,* that the word "love" is sometimes used in the Bible in the sense of "be loyal to," "be exclusively devoted to." This biblical usage parallels the use of the same verb in certain ancient Near Eastern treaties. "You will love Assurbanipal as yourselves," stipulates an Assyrian treaty between King Esarhaddon (seventh century B.C.E.) and his vassals, demanding their unswerving loyalty to his son Assurbanipal. Clearly, the vassals were not supposed to be enamored of Assurbanipal's personality: the sole intention is that they not deviate in their loyalty, and especially that they not be tempted into making any alliance with a rival empire or power. So similarly, when God commanded the Israelites to love Him "with all your heart and all your soul and all your might" (Deut. 6:5), these words must have resonated with the language of international diplo-

---

*W. L. Moran, "The Ancient Near Eastern Background of the Love of God in Deuteronomy," *Catholic Bible Quarterly*, 25 (1963), 80.

macy. God was, after all, the Great King of whom one stood in awe and to whom one owed absolute and undeviating loyalty: in other words, fear and love are hardly opposites here, but close relatives.

But that is hardly all there was to the love of God. If the "fear of the Lord" (and never, incidentally, the "love of the Lord," a noun phrase that does not exist in the Hebrew Bible) was the entry-level awareness and the putting of that awareness into practice, there was obviously more than this, more even than "love" in the sense just seen. In other verses the relationship between man and God is presented in the intimate terms of the family. In the same book of Deuteronomy, God is a "father" to Israel (Deut. 8:5), and they are his "children" (Deut. 14:1); God carries them like an eagle carrying his young on his wings as they learn to fly, and they are dearer to Him than the pupil of His eye (Deut. 32:10–11). It is the book of Psalms, as we have repeatedly glimpsed, that most openly speaks of God as an intimate, the One who is closest to the psalmist and always will be. "Even if my mother and father should abandon me," he says, "the Lord will take me up" (Ps. 27:10). He is the One who knows the psalmist inside out, and always has:

> For You have been my benefactor since the womb, my support even at my mother's breast.
> I have been cast upon You since birth, and since my mother's womb You have been my God.
>
> Ps. 22:10–11

> For You are my benefactor, my Lord, the One I have trusted in, O Lord, since I was young.
> From birth You have sustained me, from my mother's womb

You have been my hope; You are the One I praise continuously.

Ps. 71 : 5–6

Such verses must appear striking. What need was there to claim—and what plausibility was there in such a claim—that God had always been the psalmist's support, even from the time before his birth? But behind such words lies an apprehension of God that is far, far away from what is conventionally thought about biblical religion: God is so close to me, so close to my soul. So God is likewise the One whom the soul yearns for, longs for, like a deer for water; He is the shepherd who attends to all needs.

> God, You are my God. I am so eager for You.
>
> My soul thirsts for You; I yearn for You with all my being in a dry and parched land without water.
>
> If only I were seeing You in the sanctuary, beholding Your glorious might!
>
> Your good favor is better than life itself; let my lips praise You.
>
> Let me bless You while I am yet alive and pray to Your name.
>
> Though my soul is filled up as with a feast, my lips and mouth keep praising.
>
> I even mention You on my bed, in the middle of the night I mumble about You.
>
> Since You are my help, I rejoice in Your protection.
>
> My soul clings to You. Your hand holds me up.

Ps. 63 : 2–9

The fear of the LORD, it is tempting to say, apprehended God on the outside. He was *there*, the Great King, and He is to be worshiped and served. But in the world of the soul, the great Outside and inside meet. God was no longer remote; He was the "living God," right here. And so, the God of the "fear of the LORD" was no longer only outside and no longer only fearsome. It is in the psalms that one finds the fullest expression of this spiritual truth.

~

THIS BRINGS US TO PSALM 119.

The psalms, once composed, apparently had an ongoing role in the life of ancient Israel. Indeed, many modern scholars have sought to discover in the words of this or that psalm clues as to how, and under what circumstances, it might have been used and reused over the life of biblical Israel. Many psalms, for example, seem appropriate for festivals, and it is not hard to imagine that back then, as in later times, these celebrations of God's interventions in history, or hymns to His greatness, would have been performed at the time of Israel's great pilgrimage festivals, presumably at a temple. A great many other psalms consist principally of requests, those made on behalf of either a single individual or of the whole nation: "Save me from my enemies," they say, or "Cleanse me of my sin," or "Do not let me die." It is not always clear whether such requests ought to have been uttered only in a temple or whether some other setting was implied, or no special setting at all. Their purpose, in any case, is clear: they ask for help (although these requests also often contain praise of God and expressions of closeness to Him). Other psalms give thanks for help already given. For such psalms the temple setting may have been expected; now at his leisure, the worshiper could make his way to God's house to offer thanks; perhaps in connection with the payment of a vow. But then there are other psalms that have no clear purpose or occasion: they ask for nothing, and they give thanks for nothing in particular. They simply offer praise and appreciation—to God the shepherd who guides my steps. They are altogether general and occasionless. In fact, a number of them begin by suggesting that they are what elsewhere was called *laus perpetua*, the regular, ongoing praise of God at all times, without any particular reason:

> Let me bless the LORD at all times, may His praise be in my mouth continuously.
>
> Ps. 34:2

> I will exalt You, O king, my God, and I will bless Your name forever and ever.
>
> Let me bless You every day and praise Your name forever and ever.
>
> Ps. 145:1–2

It is interesting that the two psalms from which these opening lines are taken are both (like Lamentations 1–4 seen earlier) alphabetical, that is, each line begins with a successive letter of the Hebrew alphabet. Here, as elsewhere, this alphabetical arrangement gives the psalms a certain ornate quality and, perhaps, a "scholarly" flavor as well. But in connection with the theme of eternal praise with which they both begin, the very alphabetical organization may also suggest something like "the praises of God, A to Z." In other words, the very fact that the psalmist has no specific reason for starting out works well with the alphabetical structure. I will praise You by the letters of the alphabet, and having gone through the whole thing, what can I do but turn around and start all over again?

The most ambitious alphabetical psalm of this sort is Psalm 119. It is written in stanzas of eight verses, that is, each of its first eight lines starts with the Hebrew letter corresponding to A, each of the next eight lines with the Hebrew letter corresponding to B, and so forth. The result is a mammoth psalm of 176 lines, far and away the longest psalm in the whole Bible. It is surprising—precisely because of its length—that this psalm has been as popular as it has over the years. Who could find time to recite it, and even if so, why it and not eight or ten other, shorter psalms? Yet people have always found time to recite it, and among Jews and Christians its recitation has enjoyed a favored place in various liturgies, for reasons that are not difficult to discern.

A psalmist undertaking to praise God at such length might have resolved to treat different subjects, indeed, to turn to the great themes that are elsewhere central in the Book of Psalms: the creation of the world, God's interventions in the history of Israel, divine mercy and forgiveness, punishment of Israel's enemies, and so forth. There is scarcely a hint of any of these themes in this psalm. Instead, it seems to say only one thing again and again: Let me understand and keep Your laws faithfully. Indeed, along with "laws" appears a host of synonyms (statutes, precepts, rules, words, teachings, ways, and commandments), just as, along with "understand" and "keep" are other, similar verbs (see, behold, observe, uphold, delight in, be faithful to, and so forth). And there are other terms that recur frequently: the laws (and this word's variations) are in the psalmist's "heart," though they also constitute the "path" or "road" on which he goes. These ideas, too, are stated repeatedly.

The result is a psalm that is somewhat reminiscent of a type of poem that flourished in medieval Provence, the *sestina*, so called because each line of its six-line stanzas would end with one of the same six words that end each line of the other stanzas. Sestinas produced their dizzying effect via recombination, in which the same words keep being rearranged to create new, or

not-so-new, formulations. The dual constraints of Psalm 119—
its alphabetical acrostic structure, and its continuous restatement
of a single theme in slightly differing combinations of words—
give it a similarly dizzying quality. The recombinations are not
artful or deft exactly, nor, for that matter, is the way in which the
alphabetical acrostic is carried out; but that is not the point. The
psalm is an act of devotion, and in reciting it the worshiper is
brought to duplicate the self-dedication to God that stands
behind the act of composing this psalm in the first place.

What the psalm says is: *I want to serve You, I want to do every-
thing that Your laws say to do. Make me understand, let me go along the
path.* But to do that is no easy task; indeed, here it is all-consum-
ing. For the spiritual world to which this psalm belongs might be
expressed visually by the painting style of German expressionism
from the beginning of the twentieth century (or, in another way,
Russian or Polish graphic art from a slightly later period). Here,
too, everything is stripped down to essentials; everything is spir-
itual. The surrounding world is dark and menacing, but through
it all shines a brilliant, highly textured beam of yellow-white
light. There is nothing simple about following God's ways, since
dark reality threatens to engulf and overcome at every turn;
God's teachings must be wrested out of the blackness. It is the
same world as that evoked in Daniel's words of praise after God
has revealed to him the sense of a certain dream:

> May the name of God be blessed from eternity to eternity, for
> wisdom and might belong to Him.
>
> He changes the times and seasons; He deposes kings and
> establishes kings.
>
> He gives wisdom to the wise, and knowledge to those who have
> understanding.

He reveals the deep and hidden things; He knows what is in the darkness, and the light remains with Him.

Dan. 2:20–22

The one who speaks Psalm 119 aims only to do God's bidding, but to do so, the psalm maintains, is an unceasing act of struggle and rededication. The speaker stands utterly alone. Around him are only the "wicked," with whom, of course, he has no commerce. Are they nonetheless the source of the threat looming against him? He asks God endlessly not for this or that thing, but only to be "saved" or "kept alive"—as if he were at death's door—and, along with that, to be brought to understand God's laws. Like the thought of God Himself, the commandments fill the psalmist with fear (v. 120).

Indeed, one of the more surprising features of this psalm is that it often speaks of God's teaching (laws, statutes, and so forth) in the same terms that other psalms reserve for God Himself. Verse 48 says literally "I lift up my hands to Your commandments." In biblical times, lifting up one's hands (toward heaven) was an attitude of prayer (Exod. 9:29, Ezra 9:5, Ps. 63:5), just as clasping one's hands together was in slightly later times. But here, the gesture is directed not to God but to His commandments. (That is why I translated this phrase "I worship Your commandments.") "Do not conceal Your commandments from me," another verse says (v. 19); but the usual request elsewhere is that God not conceal His own *face* (Pss. 13:2, 27:9, 44:25, 69:18, 102:3, 143:7), that is, that He be merciful. Similarly, the speaker of Psalm 119 is said to "love," "cling to," "trust in," "hope in" God's laws, which, he also asserts, "keep me alive," are "eternal, established in heaven," and so on—all things that are said elsewhere in the Book of Psalms about God.

This observation would seem to be most important when

considered in the light of the foregoing discussion. For if, else-
where, the "fear of the LORD" is inevitably expressed in the
keeping of divine law, Psalm 119 tightens this connection to the
point of identification. What God has said for humans to *do* is, in
this psalm, itself Godlike; the divine commandments become an
embodiment, a hypostasis, of God's presence on earth. Thus the
way to apprehend, to "come to know," God is not simply *through*
keeping His commandments, as if these were only a means to an
end, but *in* them. God is, as it were, manifest in divine law.
Indeed, to apprehend the commandments themselves is, in this
psalm, scarcely less daunting than to apprehend God elsewhere,
since their true meaning is hidden and must be wrested from
them through great effort, perhaps even through divine revela-
tion.

If this idea is not explicit in other psalms, it rests on one that is.
The constantly reiterated request—"Teach me Your laws," "Let
me not forget Your teachings"—might have been the motto of
almost any ancient Israelite who wished to draw close to God.
And having undertaken this Step One, such an Israelite would
surely have endorsed the other, oft-restated sentiment of this
psalm: "How I love Your teaching [Torah], I speak of it the whole
day long." God is present, connected to a person's daily exis-
tence, through the filaments of His laws. As Moses says to the Is-
raelites toward the end of his final address to them, "Certainly the
commandent [to keep these laws] that I am giving you today is
not something that is beyond you, nor is it out of your reach. . . .
No, this thing is very close to you indeed; it is in your mouth and
in your heart to do it" (Deut. 30:11–14).

CHAPTER 15

THE SONG OF SONGS

(SELECTIONS)

'M THE DAFFODIL FROM SHARON, THE LILY OF
THE VALLEY.

"Like a lily in the thistles, so are you compared to other girls."
Like an apple tree in the pines, so is my love compared to other
boys:
I can lounge in his shade, and the fruit is good to taste.

His left hand under my head and his other hand around me—
I swear to you Jerusalem girls, by the deer and mountain stags,
don't start up, don't get started with love until it's time.

•

Here he comes, he's on his way—
running down the mountains, jumping over streams—
my love is like a deer or mountain stag,
standing now, waiting at our wall,
looking in through the windows, peering through the lattice.
My love called out and said to me,
"Time to go, my darling, time for us to go.
The winter's over now, the rain has come and gone.
Buds have started sprouting and the time to prune is near;
you can hear turtledoves in these mountains.

Fig trees are blossoming, and the vines are ripe with fruit—
Come, my darling, my beauty, it's time to go.
My dove, nestled in the rocks, hidden among the stones,
let me see what you look like, let me hear your voice,
because I know your voice is sweet, and I know how nice you
look."

.

My love is mine and I am his. He grazes in the lilies.
Before the day drifts in and the shadows flee,
go, run like a deer or mountain stag on the cleft hills.

One night, in my bed, I looked for my true love—
looked for him but could not find him.
So I'll search the town, the streets and squares, looking for my
love—
I looked for him but could not find him.

The town watchmen saw me on their rounds—
Have you seen my own true love?
No sooner did I leave them than I found my love;
I've got him now and will not let him go,
not until I've brought him home, brought him to my room.
I swear to you Jerusalem girls, by the deer and forest stags,
don't start up, don't get started with love until it's time.

Who's this up from the desert? Like clouds of dust,
a wave of perfume and spices, all the merchant's powders.

It's Solomon's royal train, sixty bodyguards around it, Israel's best;
every one of them is armed and skilled at war,
each with sword on hip (for protection late at night).
Solomon got himself a carriage, made of wood from Lebanon.
The posts are set in silver and the spreads are made of gold,
with purple seats and insides covered over with leather from
Jerusalem.
Come out, you girls of Zion and see King Solomon,
see the crown his mother gave him on his wedding day, the day of
his delight.

"You are so beautiful, my love, your eyes like doves behind a veil.
Your hair is like a herd of goats, streaming down Mount Gilead.
Your teeth are like a flock of ewes freshly washed in the brook,
every one perfectly paired, none bereft.
Your lips are like a crimson thread, and your mouth is so sweet,
your forehead like pink pomegranate behind your veil,
your neck like David's tower, fashioned to perfection,
with a thousand shields hung around it, all the soldiers' bucklers.
Your two breasts are like two fawns, twins grazing in the lilies.
Before the day drifts off and the shadows flee,
I'll go off to Spice Mountain, to the fragrant hill.
Everything about you is beautiful, there's not one thing that's
not."

•

Come my love, let's go out to the fields and spend the night in the
grass,

then wake up to the vineyards, and see if the vine has sprouted,
or if the blossoms have budded and the pomegranates bloomed.
That is where I will give you my love.
The mandrakes are full of scent, and at our doorway, every delight,
both old and new, my love, I've put aside for you.

If only you were my brother, a child of my own mother,
then I could throw my arms around you in the street and kiss you,
and no one would say a thing.
I'd take you and lead the way to my mother's house,
I'd give you mulled wine to drink or pomegranate juice.

His left hand under my head and his other hand around me—
I swear to you Jerusalem girls, don't start up, don't get started
with love until it's time.

·

Make me a locket on your heart, a signet on your arm.
For love is as strong as death, and as harsh as Sheol.
Its flames burn like fire, a holy burning.
Deep waters can't put love out, and rivers will not drown it.
If a man gave all his family's wealth for love, would anybody
blame him?

·

Solomon had a vineyard in Ba'al Hamon which he farmed out to
the watchmen;
each would pay a thousand silver pieces for its fruit.

"I have my own vineyard right here,
so keep the thousand, Solomon, and here's two hundred for the
watchmen.
As for you, my darling, down in the gardens,
people are listening, let them hear your voice."
Run, my love, run like a deer,
or like a mountain stag on the sweet-smelling hills.

SEA OF LOVE

[*On its canonization:*]

SHE WAS SO BEAUTIFUL. Seeing her for the first time, he would remember long afterward, had an eerie feeling of recognition to it, as if she had always been in his mind, *so* beautiful . . . But then afterward, by himself again, he began to doubt what had happened. It seemed as if the whole thing had been some sort of a dream or, perhaps, a misunderstanding.

He would never forget that feeling of rushing through streets or shaded alleyways, down corridors—desperate, laughing at his own seriousness, his pettiness—he kept going over things again and again in his mind, as if he had only one purpose in life, the next meeting, the next time with her; always on his way, impelled like some unusual species of animal from the far side of the forest, ordered now by the seasons or the movement of the stars to think about no one but her.

Years passed, decades. So much had changed. Now he was old, surrounded by achievements and big children. But the more he thought back, the more it seemed obvious that everything had begun in, or had been a kind of playing-out of some complicated analogy to, that desperate rush. Could it be that love really was so important? How strange for *him* to be thinking this, and thinking of it now, as he combed gray hair. But wasn't "I love you," in the end, the oddest of assertions and also the most human, the one that spoke the most for our having been here at all?

Even in considering what now seemed to him most real, didn't he sometimes catch himself as once again the breathless, hurrying animal? It was strange to think of oneself like that, in fact, like *her* sometimes, waiting to be found or gotten to. "I called out but he did not answer me." Love was always risky, but there was never any choice, no real choice. It must be that what happens deep in the heart always leaves one stunned, defenseless, so that one is suddenly merely there, existing for that moment in the bewildered simplicity of oneself.

If this is true, the canonizer thought, who or when isn't it true of? Aren't we all, in the end, citizens of the same republic, fish in one great sea? Indeed, if the camera could pull back far enough, was it not that way on a still larger scale? "All those who yearn for the LORD" were sometimes happy—unmatchably happy—but sometimes left wondering, left wandering dreamily about the city, free to go anywhere but chained to one purpose with absolutely no alternative, "I sought the one whom my soul loves, I sought him but I could not find him." He liked to think of himself sometimes as a fingernail, an eyelash, of that beautiful woman who drifts about remembering, "Set me as a locket on your heart."

That was why the Song now seemed to him so right. Other people might see it differently, but for him the Song would always be the essence of—that is, the sadness, but also the warm and steady drive of, most of all the discreteness, the smallness of—being nothing but a human being. It was a most generous unfolding, the blessed little details of the way it happens again and again. Indeed, the more he listened to it, the more it seemed just perfect, as if everything there were meant to teach about what just now he had come to know fully: love is so, so strong, though sometimes also so bitter; you always have to take a chance; the opposite of death is not life, but birth. So what else is worth it? "You can keep the thousand, Solomon, and take another two hundred for the watchmen," because if someone gives the wealth of his whole house for love, could anyone blame him? Of course, other people might punctuate it differently.

> All the sacred writings are canonical. [Reporting another tradition on this topic,] Rabbi Yehudah said: The Song of Songs is canonical, but the status of Ecclesiastes is contested. Rabbi Yose said: Ecclesiastes is not canonical and the status of the Song is contested. . . . Rabbi Akiba said: Heaven forbid! No one ever contested that the Song is canonical. For the whole world altogether is not as worthy as the day on which the Song of Songs was given to Israel. If all the sacred writings are holy, then the Song of Songs is the holy of holies.
>
> MISHNAH, YADAYIM 3:5

CHAPTER 16

MICAH 7 : 8–20

O NOT REJOICE OVER ME, MY ENEMY!

Though I am fallen, I will yet rise; though I sit in darkness, the
LORD *is my light.*

Just now I bear the Lord's anger, for I have indeed sinned against
Him;

but He will take my side again and set my case aright.

He will take me out to the light; I shall witness His vindication.

•

Who is a God like You, forgiving sin and passing over
transgression on behalf of the remnant of His people?

He will not maintain His anger forever, for He delights in
kindness.

So He will once again have mercy on us and destroy our sins—

may You cast all their misdeeds into the depths of the sea,

and remain true to Jacob, steadfast to Abraham, as You swore
to our ancestors in days of old.

GOD'S CHARACTER

IT WAS OBSERVED EARLIER that nothing in the Bible ever really sets out to say in systematic fashion who God is, or even to demonstrate that He is. For the most part, biblical texts concern themselves only with what God did or what He said. Yet, for all that, God could hardly be said to be faceless or inscrutable in the Bible. Again and again Scripture relates that God intervenes on the side of right and justice, that He is thus fair and compassionate, powerful and great, punishes the guilty, defends "the stranger, the widow, and the orphan"—all of these seem to tell something about God's very essence, His traits of character, as it were. Indeed, though different parts of the Bible were written down in different periods and social settings and political circumstances, the idea that God is fundamentally good, that He cares for humanity and upholds what is right, seems everywhere to be maintained.

But doesn't that go without saying? Perhaps not. After all, the world must have always struck human beings as a place in which justice and injustice seem to coexist; the cruelty of life persists despite divine compassion, and the poor and the helpless remain poor and helpless, no matter what the Bible says about God's allegiances. Would it not have been more reasonable for Israel's prophets and sages to conclude that God is quite inscrutable? Sometimes He makes things turn out right, but sometimes He doesn't. Surely such an assertion would not have diminished His greatness or His dominion over all that happens, and it scarcely would have made His worship, or obedience to His words, any less crucial in biblical times, since His disfavor would be no less fearsome in this view. Yet this is not what they said. Time and again they came back with the same message: despite what might sometimes appear, the divine will is not neutral or capricious.

In the book of Exodus, after Israel commits the sin of worshiping the statue of a golden calf, Moses pleads for forgiveness on behalf of the people. But having been assured of God's forgiveness, he persists with a further request: "Show me, I beg, Your glory [physical being]." God offers to comply, in a fashion (on the whole passage, see "The Death of Baal"), though we are never told directly that Moses did actually catch sight of God in the manner described. Instead, the text goes on to say that Moses climbed up Mt. Sinai to encounter God again.

> The LORD came down in a cloud and stood with him there, and he [Moses] called upon the name of the LORD [that is, worshiped Him]. Then the LORD passed in front of him and proclaimed: "The LORD, the LORD! a God merciful and gracious, slow to anger and of great kindness and faithfulness, keeping kindness for thousands, forgiving sin and transgression and misdeed. Yet He does not [always] utterly acquit, but may visit the sin of parents on their children and children's children, on the third and even fourth generations."
>
> EXOD. 34:5–7

What can the placement of this passage mean? Apparently, it was important for Moses to catch this glimpse of God's inner nature, just as it was important for him to see God from the outside, if only from behind as He passed by. Indeed, more than one commentator has suggested that this revelation of God's inner traits is really the response to Moses' earlier request to see God's outer "glory." In any case, the apparent shifts and turns in this description—God forgives, but not everyone and not always; God is faithful and kind, but punishes even to the fourth generation—might indeed seem to suit well the inconsistent reality seen by most human beings. Yet from earliest times, people could not help noticing that here, as elsewhere, mercy and strict justice are not evenly matched; there is no balanced neutrality with regard to God. Even from these quick pencil strokes a face emerges: here, too, God is overwhelmingly good, His mercy, in an old phrase, precedes (and overwhelms) His anger.

This piece of news might hardly seem stunning, but in biblical times it apparently was. At the heart of everything, it seemed to say, Israel's great God was neither indifferent nor above the fray. What could be said about God's very nature was thus not nothing, but something after all. Numerous other passages in the Bible echo the description of God found in Exodus 34, as if cherishing its very existence. (Not surprisingly, many of these passages evoke specifically the "good" traits revealed to Moses):

[Moses said:] "And now, I pray you, let the power of the LORD be great, as You promised, saying, 'The LORD is slow to anger and of great kindness, forgiving sin and transgression. Yet He does not [always] utterly acquit, but may visit the sin of parents on their children, on the third and even fourth generations."

NUM. 14:17–19

Return to God, for He is merciful and gracious, slow to anger and of great kindness, and relenting from [inflicting] evil.

JOEL 2:13

I know that You are merciful and gracious, slow to anger and of great kindness, and relenting from [inflicting] evil.

JON. 4:2

And You, O LORD, merciful and gracious God, slow to anger and of great kindness and faithfulness . . .

PS. 86:15

He made known His ways to Moses, His acts to the people of Israel: Merciful and gracious is the LORD, slow to anger and of great kindness. He will not chide forever, nor keep His anger for all times. He does not deal with us as befits our sins, and has not requited us in keeping with our transgressions.

PS. 103:7–10

He has left a remembrance of His miracles, gracious and merciful is the LORD.

PS. 111:4

Light shines for the righteous amidst darkness, [God is] gracious and merciful and good.

PS. 112:4

Gracious and righteous is the LORD, and our God is merciful.

PS. 116:5

Gracious and merciful is the LORD, slow to anger and abounding in steadfast love.

> Ps. 145:8

But You are a God ready to forgive, gracious and merciful, slow to anger and of great kindness, and You did not forsake them.

> NEH. 9:17 (ALSO: 9:31)

For gracious and merciful is the LORD your God; He will not turn His face from you if you return to Him.

> 2 CHRON. 30:9

~

ANOTHER PASSAGE ALLUDING to God's well-known "traits" is the one from Micah cited above. Micah was a prophet of the eighth century B.C.E., but little is known of his personal life or circumstances. He apparently lived through the tumultuous events associated with the rise of Assyrian power and its conquest of the Northern Kingdom (Israel) as well as its later assault on the Southern Kingdom (Judah), his homeland. Like the Book of Isaiah, Micah's collection of prophecies seems addressed to the events of different periods and settings. The excerpted passage might be understood as a personal statement, but most scholars take it to refer to the whole nation; indeed, some have suggested that it is really a liturgy intended to be recited in public, perhaps with contrasting choirs or voices. All this is highly speculative, however, and little can be said for certain about the circumstances underlying its composition or, for that matter, its relationship to the previous sections of the Book of Micah. What is clear is the strength of belief that stands behind the words translated above—as well as their rather interesting connection to the list of divine "traits" found in Exodus 34:5–7 and the other passages previously cited.

One thing that is remarkable about the part of this Micah passage that alludes to God's mercy (for here, as elsewhere, God's punishing "to the third and fourth generation" has been passed over in silence; it is only divine mercy that counts) is the subtle way that it moves in and out of direct address to God. The passage in Exodus 34 was all in the third person: *He* is "a God merciful and gracious, slow to anger," and so forth, yet "*He* does not utterly acquit." Here, by contrast, the speaker turns directly, intimately, to God in the second person: "Who is like You?" he asks. Then, as if in answer, he alludes back to all that had been said of old, and God subtly slides into the third person. While the gerunds "forgiving" and "passing over" could refer to either a second- or third-person subject, "His people" is unequivocal: God has become the "He" of that famous passage in Exodus 34. It is to be noted that the prophet up to this point has also referred to himself and his countrymen in the third person—not "us" but "them." This changes, however, in the ensuing lines: this God about whom I am speaking will "again have mercy on *us* and destroy *our* sins." Now Israel and its sins are the focus, the foreground. But then comes a further change: God is again "You" and Israel is again "they." The whole passage, in other words, weaves in and out, until everything comes together at the end: Only in the last words is God "You" and Israel simultaneously "we."

> Who is a God like *You*, forgiving sin and passing over transgression on behalf of the remnant of *His people* [not "us"]?

He will not maintain *His* anger forever, for *He* delights in kindness.

So *He* will once again have mercy on *us* and destroy *our* sins—

may *You* cast all *their** misdeeds into the depths of the sea,

and remain true to Jacob, steadfast to Abraham, as *You* swore to *our* ancestors in days of old.

This shifting focus of the passage serves the overall question it addresses: Who is God in relation to us, and what are we to expect from Him? Clearly, the opening lines acknowledge that the speaker is in distress, fallen and sitting in darkness. This is indeed God's punishment, the text says, and not mere happenstance: "Just now I bear the LORD's anger, for I have indeed sinned against Him." But this state of affairs does not lead to despair; punishment does not spell an eternal sentence of rejection:

With your staff [*that is, your anger*], be a shepherd to your people, the sheep of your own land.

Let those who dwell alone in the forest, next to the farmlands,

graze in the Bashan and Gilead, as in days gone by.

MIC. 7:14

The author of these lines maintains what Exodus 34:5–7 maintains: that divine punishment and divine reward are not evenly balanced, that God's mercy will be extended even to those who suffer His punishment. "He will take my side again and set my case aright. He will take me out to the light; I shall witness His vindication."

In line with this, the question that opens this extended allusion to God's famous traits is also worthy of comment: "Who is a

*Some texts read "our" here.

God like You?" Now, questions in biblical Hebrew often really have the force of negative assertions. This is true of all manner of questions and not just those evoking God; time and again, especially in psalms and other highly rhetorical compositions, "Who?" really means "No one," "What?" means "Nothing," and so forth. So Micah's query, "Who is a God like You?" is really an assertion that no other deity is comparable to Israel's God. Yet it is striking to think of this question in its overall context. Somewhat earlier, nearly the same words had been uttered in connection with God's miraculous deeds at the crossing of the Red Sea, when the Israelites were saved and the pursuing Egyptians drowned. There, "Who is like You among the gods?" (Exod. 15:11) was a natural expression of awe at God's power to work external, visible miracles, saving a fearful cohort of refugees from bloodthirsty pursuit. In the sweet, simple spirituality of the Micah passage, by contrast, God's incomparability has to do with all that is inside and unseen. No other deity, the text says, has ever been so forgiving or so willing to wipe the slate clean—as if this, as much as the more obvious manipulation of reality, were altogether miraculous in the prophet's eyes.

ISAIAH 60

 [*Spoken to Jerusalem:*]

RISE, SHINE! FOR YOUR LIGHT HAS COME,
THE LORD'S GLORY IS DAWNING UPON YOU.

For though darkness may cover the earth, and shadows envelop
the nations,

over you the LORD shines like the sun, and His glory is breaking
upon you.

Then nations will troop to your light, and kings to the gleam of
your sunrise.

Lift up your gaze and look! Together, they all hasten toward you,

your sons coming back from afar, and your daughters held tight to
the side.

When you see it, your face will glow—though inside, your heart
may be fearful

that a mass from the seas will engulf you; for a great throng of
nations is coming.

The dust raised by camels will swirl—camels from Midian and
Ephah, even from Sheba they'll come—

with incense and gold on their backs, announcing the glories of
God.

Flocks will arrive from Kedar, and Nebayot's rams for your
service;

they will rise to My altar in favor, as I care for My glorious house.

Who are these flying in like a cloud, like doves that return to their
dovecote?
To Me the outposts are gathered, with ships from Tarshish at their
head,
bringing your sons from afar, their silver and gold alongside,
for the sake of the LORD your God, the Holy One who adorns
you.

Foreigners rebuild your walls, and even their kings come to
serve you:
for if in My anger I struck you, then with love I am taking
you back.
Your gates will always be open, night and day they will never
be shut,
as the wealth of nations streams in, with their monarchs leading
the way.

Any nation or any kingdom that fails to serve you will perish;
yes, those nations will be destroyed.
So Lebanon's glory will enter—all its evergreen, cypress, and
pine—
to adorn the place of My Temple, and make My foothold revered.

Then the sons of those who oppressed you will come bowing and scraping before you;
your former tormentors will fall at your feet.
"City of the LORD" they will call you, Zion the Holy of Israel.

Instead of your being abandoned, with no traveler coming to stay,
I will make you a source of unending pride, a joy for all generations.
Suckled with milk from the nations, you will drink at royalty's breast.
Then you will know I have saved you; the LORD, Jacob's Power, redeemed you.

[In the Temple:]
In place of copper I will put gold, and in place of iron will be silver;
copper will come in place of the wood, and iron in place of the stone,
And I will make Peace your blueprint, with Righteousness as your foreman.
No one will cry out "Thieves!" in your land, no crime will be done in your borders,
but Salvation will stand at your walls, and Praise will protect as your gates.

[The new light:]
No more will sunshine brighten your days, nor the moonlight glimmer at night,

but the LORD will be your unending light, and your God will be your glory.

So your Sun will never go down, and your Moon will not wax or wane,

But the LORD will be your unending light, and the days of your mourning will end.

And your people—all of them righteous—will inherit the land forever,

the little shoot that I planted. I created them for My glory.

The smallest of them will turn to a tribe, and the least to a mighty nation.

I am the LORD. . . . I will hasten it when it is time.

THE MATCH

BABYLON, THE SPLENDID CITY. The Ishtar Gate, fashioned for the queen of Heaven, is decorated with gazelles, dragons, wild bulls, and oddly delicate lions, all on a glimmering background of lapis lazuli bricks. Inside the walled capital, huge statues of Bel-Marduk and Nabu hunch menacingly over the tiny visitor. O Nabu, guard my progeny! Bel's temple, ascending skyward on its seven-storey base, overshadows even the royal palace; beyond it, terraced gardens and the brilliantly colored colonnades. King Nebuchadnezar in his mercy has decreed. The King has, for the *akitu* festival, granted. But off in the hot, dusty slums, along the outskirts and next to canals and rutted roadways, a hopeless colony sinks in its exile. Babel, Chebar, Tel Abib. There is no point in going on, they say. Why should we talk about our children?

Chapter 60 of the Book of Isaiah is a single unit. Its theme, the new light, is announced in its opening words and then returned to again at its end. But it is also part of a larger group of chapters, 40–66. Those to whom these chapters were addressed must have scarcely been in a mood to listen. Their spirits, dragged down by decades of exile, had grown accustomed to disappointment and despair. And so, the first task had also been the hardest: to wake them up, to make them begin to hope again. Tell them about the ransom.

A voice was saying, "Speak up!" so I said, "What should I say?"

[*Say:*] "Humanity is only grass, and all its glories are like a little wildflower.

Grass dries up and the flower withers, for the breath of the LORD blows over them."

So yes, the people are grass, and the grass will dry and the flower will wither.

But the word of our God will prevail forever.

Climb up on the highest hill, you sentinel of Jerusalem, and shout it, don't be afraid!

Tell the townships of Judah, "Look, look there! Your God is coming!"

Look, the LORD your God is coming in strength, with His powerful arm triumphant!

Look! He is bringing His bounty with Him, the reward even goes before Him.

And oh, He will guard His flock like a shepherd, in His own arms He will pick up the lambs,

and carry them next to His breast, as He leads their mothers alongside.

•

So now, thus says the LORD—your creator, Jacob, and your maker, Israel—

do not be afraid. I am paying your ransom. I have pointed you out by name, you're Mine.

When you go over the water, I will be with you; over rivers— they will not sweep you away.

Even if you walk in the midst of fire, you won't be burned, conflagrations will not even singe you.

I am the LORD your God, the Holy One of Israel, your savior.

I would have given Egypt as your ransom, Ethiopia and Saba in exchange for you.

Since you are very precious in My sight, honored even, and I love you,

I am willing to give people in exchange for you, whole nations for
your life.

So do not be afraid, I am with you.

Now I will bring your children from the east, and from the west I
will gather you up.

I will say to the north wind, "Come on!" and to the south wind,
"Don't hold back!

Give Me My sons from afar, and My daughters from the ends of the
earth!"

~

So get out of Babylon, leave Chaldea!

Say it, shout it out with joy and broadcast it to the ends of the
earth!

Say: "The LORD has ransomed his servant Jacob!"

ISA. 40:6–11; 43:1–6; 48:20–21

BUT HOW, THEY ASKED, could God have let us be taken
prisoner in the first place? Why did He allow His Temple—*His
Temple*—to be reduced to smoldering ruins, then abandon those
inside to be dragged off to cruel exile?

For this the dreamer gave no answer, except that God is very
big. What difference could human might make to God?

Who has measured the oceans in the palm of his hand, or checked
the heavens with his yardstick?

Who has put all the earth's soil in his bushel basket, or weighed
the mountains on his scale and the hills in his market balance?

Who can gauge the LORD's own spirit? And who is His adviser
that can tell of it?

To whom does He go for consultations? Who directs Him or
teaches proper procedure?

Let such a person tell Him what to do and inform Him of all He needs to know.

Look, the nations are a drop from the bucket, they weigh as much as the dust on a scale.*

The islands He can flick off like a mote; all the Lebanon will not supply Him kindling, its animals do not equal one lone offering.

The nations all together are nothing for Him, insignificance itself and less than zero.

So to whom will you compare God?

ISA. 40:12–18

~

WHEN THEY BEGAN to take heart and understand that Babylon would be behind them, he turned to their destination, the Jerusalem they had left half a century earlier. It too needed to be roused from its sleep:

Wake up, wake up, Jerusalem, get up!

You have indeed swallowed a dose from the LORD, drunk from the cup of His wrath. You drank the flagon's drug to its dregs.

(Yet of all the sons she gave birth to, not one is there to lead her,

not even one to hold her hand, from all those whom she brought up.)

Two there are who call to you—but not one to mourn:

---

*Our expression, "drop in the bucket," is based on a misunderstanding of this verse. The biblical image is of someone bringing up water in a bucket from the riverbank. Inevitably, a little will spill on the way up, but it is a negligible amount not worth going back for, a "drop from the bucket." Similarly, when one goes to the market to buy vegetables or grain, no one insists on wiping the scales of the bits of dust fallen there from a previous customer's purchase—the "dust on a scale" is also an insignificantly small amount.

Crime and outrage call, oh yes, and hunger and war—but there
is no one to comfort you.

Your sons have fallen senseless to the ground, felled at the
crossroads like a deer in a snare.

They are full of the wrath of the LORD, your God's rebuke.

But hear now this, my poor one, you who have drunk, but not
of wine:

Thus says your Lord GOD, your God who takes the side of His
people:

I hereby take the potion from your hand, the flagon of My wrath;
you shall drink no more.

Instead I give it to your persecutors, the ones who said to you,
"Down on the ground, so we can walk on top,"

and you did make your back like the ground, like a roadway for
whoever passes by.

Get up from the dust, get up and leave your prison, Jerusalem,

undo the chains from your neck, poor prisoner, Zion.

For thus says the LORD:

You were sold for nothing at all, so your redemption will cost
nothing either.

ISA. 51:17–52:2

Without much effort he could imagine, from where he stood, a
distant messenger running along the hilltops to announce the
exiles' return:

How beautiful on the mountains are the feet of one who brings the
news,

a message of well-being and announcement of good fortune,

bringing news of triumph, saying to Zion, "Your God is king indeed!"

Isa. 52:7

~

WHAT HE SAID AT LAST TO BOTH—to Jerusalem and to the exiles—was that a new light was dawning. An old metaphor. Still, the way he said it made it sound as if he actually saw *something*, no metaphor at all but a great glow somewhere, up a little funnel in time through which he had somehow slipped for a moment and come back with a message about the light.

> Lift up your gaze and look! Together, they all hasten toward you,
>
> your sons coming back from afar, and your daughters held tight to the side.

The mass movement of exiles on their way home. This thought never failed to move him. Cheap cases hasped with a rope, cloth pack slung over the back, and the red-faced, screeching children who ride on their stringy-haired mothers' sides; exhausted travelers not happy, but happy to be going back. She bends down, straightens up, wipes her face. A timeless gesture, so that for an instant the background shimmered and blurred, and Babylon seemed to give way to something strange... Where *does* the uplifted gaze lead to? But then he saw them again massed together and leaving, heading out in great caravans across the desert. They didn't leave, it seems, because of what he said, but what he said had made them think they had a chance, though some of it sounded positively goofy:

> The dust raised by camels will swirl—camels from Midian and Ephah, even from Sheba they'll come—

with incense and gold on their backs, announcing the glories
of God.

Jerusalem turned to Dromedary Central. Forget the dust, think of
the manure! But here was the point: dumb animals themselves an-
nounce the praises. They don't say a thing, but somehow, in a
way he couldn't quite recall or figure out just now,* all those
riches and spices were being carried in on the glories—or was
that "lorries"?—of the LORD, streaming there from some distant
point. History itself has a way, or ought to have a way, of praising
God by its outcome, though the difficulty was that history always
keeps on going; every victory song, as an old rabbinic commen-
tary observes, is termed a *shirah*, the feminine form of the word for
song, because it always gives birth to something else after itself.
Still, if all these camels and conveyances were not history's out-
come, they were at least good news, an end to Jerusalem's aban-
donment, the beginning of something altogether new.

> Who are these flying in like a cloud, like doves that return to their
> dovecote?
> To Me the outposts are gathered, with ships from Tarshish at their
> head.

---

* "A prophet utters nothing on his own, but all that he says comes from else-
where, the echo of Another's voice.... For when the light of God shines, the hu-
man light sets; when the divine light sets, the human dawns and rises. This is
what regularly happens among prophets. The mind is evicted at the arrival of
the divine spirit, and [only] when that departs does the mind return to its ten-
ancy... For indeed, the prophet, even when he seems to be speaking, is really
silent, for his organs of speech, mouth and tongue, are wholly in the employ of
Another, to show forth what He wishes." (Philo of Alexandria, *Who Is Heir*,
259–266). Similarly, Maimonides: "Among the parables of the prophets there
are many whose meaning is not interpreted in the vision of prophecy itself, but
whose purpose is [only] known by the prophet after he awakens." *Guide of the
Perplexed*, 2:43.

Standing on land that, by coincidence, would one day be an inter-
national airport, he watched a convoy of ships gliding in on great
outriggers, reminiscent in a way of large silver clouds, ferrying
voyagers from afar, though it was not clear why they circled about
and did not dock directly, since even doves returning to their dove-
cote will, exhausted after the long voyage, slip perfectly and with
nary a pause into their assigned stations. In any case, these had
come from Tarshish—the name probably means "foundry," and
there may have been half a dozen sites so named by Phoenician and
other mariners up and down the whole Mediterranean and even
beyond. Jonah hopped a boat for Tarshish, but no one today
knows where he was heading. The search for tin, in particular,
sent ancient traders to the remotest destinations, since none was to
be found in the immediate environs of ancient Israel. In context,
the mention of Tarshish here and elsewhere suggests a distant sea-
port; Tartessus in Spain has been proposed.

> Then the sons of those who oppressed you will come bowing and
> scraping before you; your former tormentors will fall at your feet.
> "City of the LORD" they will call you, Zion the Holy of Israel.

The theme of reparations, *Wiedergutmachungsgelt*.
The foreign minister laid a wreath. "I am honored and moved
more than words can express," he wrote in the guest book, " . . .
and to the memory of all those who." The flowers, held in place
underneath by a hidden metal frame, sparkle in the sun. Is any-
thing worth it? A room full of shoes. A room full of human hair.
Later, at a press conference, in neutral English, he expressed par-
ticular satisfaction at being in Jerusalem on this occasion. "This
holy city," he said, smiling. "Zion, Israel's holy place," wrote
the dreamer. Al-Quds, y'al Quds-u. (Cut to: My friend Zhorzh
"translating" from a record the best-known political song of

Feiruz, the Arab torch singer: "Oh now she is angry . . . Wait a minute! Now she is not so angry . . . Oh, now she is angry again.")

"At your feet" they ought to have fallen, Edom and Moab and Babylon, and if they didn't, perhaps the time was not yet right. But justice demanded something, *something* should have happened right then, sixth century B.C.E., as the straggling returners set themselves up again, met not by a penitent Edom but one that had come to encroach in their absence, farm their lands and drink from their cisterns, and now comported itself as a proprietor. This was not right, but the scene kept seeming to shift just as justice started to be done, leaving him befuddled and quite disoriented. Sometimes, he felt as if he were looking south when he was actually looking north.

~

> Instead of your being abandoned, with no traveler coming to stay,
>
> I will make you a source of unending pride, a joy for all generations.

The poor city was no longer poor. But where had its wealth come from? He went back over his notes:

> Your gates will always be open, night and day they will never be shut,
>
> as the wealth of nations streams in, with their monarchs leading the way.

This, of course, made sense; all those who trooped through the darkness to see Jerusalem would bring with them what they could, and if it was not quite the "wealth of nations," perhaps room should be left in that phrase for sacrificial offerings of the sort that visiting dignitaries present to the local shrine. Certainly that was what ought to happen in Jerusalem too, for "My house will be called a house of prayer by all peoples" (Isa. 56:7). Still, this wealth also suggested what he had said a few verses earlier about her sons' silver and gold; it was obviously connected:

> bringing your sons from afar, their silver and gold alongside,
> for the sake of the LORD your God, the Holy One who adorns you.
> Foreigners rebuild your walls, and even their kings come to serve you

He recalled having watched (another dream?) a family from the distant islands disembark, later unpack the crate of garish furniture, Brazilian leather sofa and matching chairs, glass-and-chrome coffee-table, glass-doored bookshelves, gold-plated service for twelve, computers, hockey game, acres of clothes. Was there any end to this abundance? The next morning, before dawn, he watched the buses of construction workers streaming in from Hebron, and the cleaning ladies walking the back way around the Bethlehem checkpoint, through Tantur, to Gilo. Astonished, he had written those three lines.

> Instead of your being abandoned, with no traveler coming to stay,
> I will make you a source of unending pride, a joy for all generations.

True enough, though this bit of good news was also worrisome, since an eternal source of pride for the one is inevitably an eternal irritation for the other, and so the proprietors tend to see-saw. Where would it all finally end and pride give way to joy?

> Suckled with milk from the nations, you will drink at royalty's breast.

(No withered British monarch, but real French *Mirages*, Deutschmarks, pesetas, and Swiss francs, the State Department and the steel worker in Ohio. They all paid tribute; still he felt it important to add):

> Then you will know that I have saved you; the LORD, Jacob's Power redeemed you.

~

BUT WHAT "NEW LIGHT" could be better than the old one? That delicious Jerusalem sunlight smeared on the swabbing tops of pine trees or on stately palm fronds swaying in the breeze; sunlight that is baked into dusty roads and stone walls and the sides of yellow buildings, or reflected off the half-raised windows of the little toy train chug-chugging its way around the side of a mountain, then the sharp report of sun off the railroad ties as it rides by. No new light could top the old light, so bright at noon that people there squint out of habit, indoors and out, only to relax into the exquisite glow of mid- and late afternoon. Unless what was meant was indeed the old light, but touched now with, not a new intensity, but a timbre or tone simply not perceived before, so subtle that it came over one unawares until, just now, one was struck, one was dumbstruck, as the new light came rising up around one to the ears and left a tingling there, left one warm and involved in the new glow and in everything it touched.

"Sweet is the light, and it is [also] a pleasure for the eyes to see the sun" (Eccles. 11:7). But the light was too strong now for mere contemplation. He stared resolutely forward for a time, dazed but full of energy.

No more will sunshine brighten your days, nor the moonlight
glimmer at night,

but the LORD will be your unending light, and your God will be
your glory.

So your Sun will never go down, and your Moon will not wax or
wane,

but the LORD will be your unending light, and the days of your
mourning will end.

Then on the foothills visible, far in the distance, the legs of
someone running, running—how beautiful! How lovely, Neve
Ilan. And Telstone, Abu Ghosh, how beautiful! He thought: I
will never, never forget this, never again feel faint, feel doubt.
Thus the feet on pavement beat with a logic of their own. The
light so bright now that one dare not look ahead but only side-
long as the miles whiz by, Nabi Samu'il, Giv'at Ze'ev, Ramot!
Warm air flows unimpeded to the lungs, to the pumping legs.
Nothing you see was unimagined. Arriving suddenly at the cen-
tral bus station and Binyanei ha-Umah, he continued at an easy
gallop:

And your people—all of them righteous—will inherit the land
forever,

the little shoot that I planted. I created them for My glory.

The smallest of them will turn to a tribe, and the least to a mighty
nation.

I am the LORD. . . . I will hasten it when it is time.

All of them righteous? That can't be right. Perhaps the judicial
sense is meant, then, winners in a lawsuit get to hold the proper-
ty forever. Or perhaps—how vague poetic syntax is!—an
implied condition: when your people are all of them righteous,

then will the land be theirs forever; in the meantime . . . Here he paused, convinced that the words contained legitimate grounds for query, a request for further clarification, since so much hung on the answer, as he rounded the big curve behind Jaffa Gate, glanced quizically at the tourist stands, and headed on toward the Armenian Quarter. . . .

Too late. Caught up in the rhythm he was. No, there would be no turning back now, even though he knew that the little shoot was *very* little, that the righteous were not the only righteous; still, the light was overwhelming, blinding really, suns could rise and suns could set, the light would never go away and he would never sleep until "inherit the land forever," yes, that was one true thing he said, sleep in my little garden patch, tree of my planting, forever. Be comforted, my people. When its time comes, he said, it will not happen slowly.

∽

HOW BOOKS WILL LAST! Dog-eared, shedding, they pad through generations reproducing, never lost for good. . . . It was a scene of pastures without caption, a sylvan world entered and recollected, then set down; misinterpreted, it kept on edging up to itself—as had the dreamer, when one day it was there, a little in front and above him, and his mind reached up and got it. So natural and uninterrupted, that gesture, that what could make him follow through and finish the getting? Not an appreciation of its worth, its strangeness, because that could not be noticed; but he brought it back again, a match; through the densest ambience, souvenir.

CHAPTER 18

ECCLESIASTES 12

EMEMBER YOUR CREATOR IN THE DAYS OF YOUR
YOUTH, BEFORE THE TIME OF AFFLICTION
COMES, AND THE YEARS APPROACH ABOUT
WHICH YOU WILL SAY, "I TAKE NO PLEASURE
IN THEM."

Before the light of the sun goes dark, and the moon and the stars;
and the clouds return [empty] after the rain;

in the days when the guards of the house start to tremble, and the
strong men are crooked,

and the grinding women give out, because they are few, and the
women watching at the window grow dark;

the double doors are closed in the marketplace, since the sound of
the grinding mill has gone low;

and a bird's chirping is heard, for all the daughters of song have
been brought down.

Any height inspires fear, and a journey seems fraught with danger.

Then will the almond tree blossom, and the grasshopper drag
along, and the caperbush bud—

for a man has gone off to his eternal home and the mourners have
made their turns in the square—

until the silver cord is snapped and the golden bowl is crushed,

and the pitcher is broken at the spring, and the jug is shattered at
the well,

and the dust rejoins the earth as it had been before, and the spirit returns to God who gave it.

"So fleeting," said Koheleth, "everything is so fleeting!"

Not only was Koheleth a sage, but he also taught the people wisdom;

he studied and investigated, and prepared many proverbs.

Koheleth sought to find out pleasing sayings, and to write straightforward words of truth.

The words of sages are like prods, and like nails well planted are those of teachers; they were given by one Shepherd.

But beware, my son, of more than these things:

for there is no end to acquiring books, and much studying tires a person out.

The end of the matter, when all has been heard: Fear God and keep his commandments, for this is all of being human.

For God will bring everyone to judgment concerning all his conduct, whether it be for good or ill.

FOR EVERYONE, A SEASON

THE LAST ENEMY, OLD AGE. "I have seen everything in my fleeting days" (Eccles. 7:15), one says. But having gone so far and seen so much, what does one have left now but to look the short distance ahead?

When we are very young and we first understand about death, the idea seems horrible, monstrous. *Me not be?* But being is what I am just brimming with! To think of a tombstone some-where with my name on it, grass, and just nothingness . . . But then we forget about death, at least for a while. It is bad, but it is also far away. When it next reappears—seriously, at least—quite a few years have passed; now someone we loved so much, who was so much a part of us, is dead. My father. How different death looks! There is nothing abstract any more: the ground opened its mouth for an instant and swallowed his body. It *is* horrible. He is there, under the dirt, but he is no more, however much he may come back in dreams and conversations. And although it is not clear at first, from now on death will be no stranger. More and more drives to the cemetery, for uncles, aunts, people from work, people from the street, old friends. These drives have a cumula-tive effect. We don't like to admit it, but there is something good in them; even death can be gotten used to. So many have gone al-ready. It is no longer monstrous or horrible, just inevitable. More years pass, bringing with them fatigue and odd pains. Now, fi-nally, death has become a daily companion. It is no friend, but it is also not far away; it is just over there, in fact. It walks with us and we keep our distance, trying—sometimes hard, sometimes not very hard—to hold it at arm's length for another day.

~

THE BOOK OF ECCLESIASTES belongs to the same great body of wisdom represented in the biblical books of Proverbs and Job. Time-honored tradition says its author was King Solomon, since the book identifies its speaker as "Koheleth, the son of David, king in Jerusalem" (1:1). The only one of David's sons who was ever king in Jerusalem was Solomon, so this verse (along with 1:12, which also mentions Koheleth being "king in Jerusalem over Israel") was taken to indicate that Solomon was the book's author (and that "Koheleth," therefore, was some kind of nickname of Solomon's). But some modern scholars question this identification. The phrase "son of David" can also mean a descendant of David, a member of the Davidic line (as in, for example, 2 Chron. 13:8, 23:3), so "king in Jerusalem" might well refer to any of the subsequent kings, or even to one of the Persian-appointed rulers (governors if not quite "kings") who ruled over the Jewish province of Judah in the years following the return from Babylonian exile. Such a hypothesis has some advantages.* So perhaps Koheleth's self-identification should be taken to mean simply that he was a man of royal blood, a descendant of David's, who ruled as governor for a time in Persian-dominated Jerusalem. As for his name (or title), it probably comes from a relatively rare

---

*It would explain why Ecclesiastes contains two words that are of Persian, rather than Hebrew, origin, prds (orchard) and ptgm (royal decree). The entrance of loan words like these into a language is usually a sign of prolonged interaction between two cultures, such as that which took place between Persians and Jews only after the Babylonian exile, when Persia ruled Judah. But if so, then the reference to Koheleth's being king "over Israel" in Eccles. 1:12 must have been intended in the sense of "over the Jews," rather than over the historical Kingdom of Israel (which no longer existed).

root that means "to argue" or "to reprove." Koheleth means "the Haranguer."*

In any event, the book's place in the biblical canon (though at one time apparently contested) was ultimately won not on the basis of its Solomonic authorship but by dint of the divinely inspired wisdom found within it.** Its pungent and profound truths, such as "A name is better than scented oil, and the day of death than the day of one's birth," or "Like the sound of thorns under a pot, so is the laughter of fools" (see "Solomon's Riddles"), have guided generations of the Bible's readers. But Koheleth also has a direct, personal style that speaks to people of all kinds. He talks about the things of this world: haughty servants, fancy estates, lazy politicians, corrupt judges. He is often concerned about matters of money—loans gone bad, fortunes squandered—and even when he turns to metaphysics, it is with the brash tone of a businessman, "What'll it get you?" Though he was a sage, Koheleth did not simply transmit wisdom's timeless messages; in fact, he was openly critical of them sometimes and did not hesitate to say, "That does not make sense to me." Indeed, at times he seems to say that about life itself.

In this connection, scholars have long debated the precise significance of a word that occurs again and again in this book, the one usually translated as "vanity" (as in the book's refrain, "Vanity of vanities, all is vanity"). The Hebrew word in question does not really mean "vanity"—at least not in the usual

---

*Long ago, Jewish translators of the book into Greek misunderstood this name as if deriving from the more common root that means "gather" or "assemble." Koheleth became, in Greek, the *ekklesiastes*, "man of the assembly." Still later, when "assembly" came to mean, specifically, "church" in Greek, the *ekklesiastes* became "man of the church," which is why many Bibles still refer to Koheleth as "the preacher."

**Tosefta *Yadayim* 2:14

senses of this word in English: worthlessness or emptiness or narcissistic pride. The word *hebel* in Hebrew means a "breath" or a "vapor"; its connotation is that of something fleeting and insubstantial. Koheleth frequently uses this word to describe something in life that seems to him futile and useless (Eccles. 2:1, 11, 17, 20, 23, and frequently thereafter); at other times *hebel* seems to mean something that is just baffling (Eccles. 5:9, 7:15); at still other times it is used to mean something unfair, unjust (Eccles. 2:26; 4:7; 6:2; 8:10, 14). And when he concludes his allegorical description of old age and death with his signature phrase, he probably does not mean to say that life is as any of these things (that is, futile, baffling, or unfair), but simply to say that it is breathlike, evanescent: "So fleeting," Koheleth says, everything is so fleeting."* By this, however, he does not just mean that life is short and goes by too quickly. In order to grasp his full meaning, one has to understand another striking feature of this book, its rather unique sense of time.

~

KOHELETH SEES LIFE as a series of shifting scenes. Human beings keep passing through different phases, the book maintains, so things never look the way they did even a short while before. For the same reason, what is appropriate at one point in life is no longer proper later on. Ecclesiastes' most famous statement of this idea is that section of the book that begins, "For every thing there is a season." (Actually, there may be good reason to think that what he really meant was "for every*one* there is a season," or—a bit more

---

* Since these various meanings of *hebel* all sound very different in English, I have not tried to translate the word with a single English equivalent but have varied it according to the apparent meaning.

explicitavely—"everyone is in a season.")* That is, life is always changing, shifting its seasons, but being stuck in one season or another, people have no choice but to do the things, and *think* the things, that are appropriate to that particular time. The same verse continues, ". . . and a time of [doing] each thing under the heavens." That is, no matter what the activity, its particular time comes, and then, later, goes. So human beings are inevitably caught in an ever-shifting but preordained cycle. People's lives, of course, appear to be different, since they start at different points and unfold in different ways, but what all share is the constant rhythm of change brought about by the coming and going of certain eternally established times. Here is what he says in full:

> For everyone, a season, and a time of [*doing*] each thing under the heavens:
>
> a time of giving birth and a time of dying;
>
> a time of planting and a time of uprooting what is planted;
>
> a time of killing and a time of healing;
>
> a time of breaking down and a time of building up;
>
> a time of weeping and a time of laughing;
>
> a time of mourning and a time of dancing;
>
> a time of throwing down stones and a time of gathering up stones;
>
> a time of embracing and a time of shunning an embrace;
>
> a time of looking for and a time of losing;

---

*The word for "every" or "all" in Hebrew can, as a noun, mean either "everything" or "everyone." Elsewhere in the Bible, the noun usually means "everything," but in the Hebrew of Ecclesiastes, "everyone" is often what he means: see, for example, Eccles. 2:7, 9, 16; 3:11, 19, 20; 4:16; 5:8; 6:6; 9:2. See also Mishnah *Avot* 4:3, which may be based on Eccles. 3:1, though it explains it differently. Note that the old Aramaic translation of Ecclesiastes renders Eccles. 3:1 as "For every man there is a season."

a time of keeping and a time of throwing away;

a time of ripping and a time of sewing;

a time of keeping silent and a time of speaking;

a time of loving and a time of hating;

a time of war and a time of peace.

So what does a person gain from whatever he's working at? I considered all the activities that God has given people to occupy themselves with. He sets everyone right in his time, yet He puts in their minds a hiddenness, so that a person cannot grasp what God has created from beginning to end. Thus I realized that there is nothing better for them to do than to enjoy themselves and accumulate what is good in their lives.

ECCLES. 3:1–12

I have used the genitive "a time *of* X" throughout this catalogue, rather than the more usual translation, "a time *to* X." The difference is subtle but important. "A time to X" seems to imply that to each of us will come a time when we can do X, or are to do X, so that there is indeed a "time for everything under the sun." This is certainly a soothing message, "Don't worry, the right time will come for you to do whatever it is you may have in mind." But that is not quite what Koheleth means. Rather, he means that to each of us may come a "time of X," a time when X is done. Inevitably, like it or not, we will do X at that time. (Incidentally, this first pair of opposites is often mistranslated as "a time to be born, a time to die." But Koheleth clearly distinguishes the grammatical form "to be born," as in Ecclesiastes 7:1, from the form used here, which usually refers to a woman's giving birth, though also to a man's causing to be born. Indeed, I might have translated this more ambiguously as "a time of birth and a time of dying," save that I believe the author's intention here is to assert specifically that the opposite of dying is not merely living, existing, but causing to be born.)

Koheleth's down-to-earth question after this catalogue, "So what does a person gain from whatever he's working at?" only makes sense if one realizes the significance of the paired contraries that precede it. Everyone happens to be in one season or another, and the constant changes in life's cycles (like the agricultural ones) eventually ensure that both an action and its opposite will take place. So every act of giving birth is offset by an act of dying, every act of planting by an act of uprooting (at the harvest), and so forth. What remains in the end? There is never any "net gain" (*yitron*, one of Koheleth's favorite words). Moreover, Koheleth adds, the trouble with being in one season is that one can never see beyond it, never "grasp what God has created from beginning to end." Only having gone around one complete circuit will one begin to understand the whole from its contradictory parts.

He says something similar in the great catalogue of "vanities" that opens the book:

[*The sayings of Koheleth, a descendant of David, king in Jerusalem:*]

"So futile," says Koheleth, "everything is so futile!"

What does a person ever net from all the effort he expends under the sun?

One generation goes out and another comes in, but the earth stays the same forever.

The sun rises and the sun sets; then, rushing back to its place, it rises again.

The wind blows toward the south and then turns to the north,

it turns and turns as it goes—the wind—and goes back again by its turning.

All the rivers flow to the sea, but the sea is never full,

[*because*] to the source of the rivers' flowing, there they flow
back again.

Though all words grow wearisome, a man does not cease to speak;

the eye cannot see enough, nor can the ear be filled up with
hearing.

What has been is what will be, and what was done will be done
again, for there is nothing new under the sun.

Sometimes there is something about which people say, "Look at
this! This is new!"

Long ago it was, in the ages that existed before us.

There is no remembrance of former things, just as, with regard to
the later things that will be,

they will have no remembrance either with those who will be
after them.

ECCLES. 1 : 2 – 1 1

Here the earth, too, has its "seasons," and all the actions that take
place upon it—sunrise and sunset, the movements of the winds
or the rivers—are offset by one another. Nothing ever gets accom-
plished, no more on the personal level than on the natural. If peo-
ple are under the impression that something new has finally
occurred, something unprecedented, well, they are wrong. The
problem is that our memory, even our collective memory, does
not go back far enough; nor will it carry forward far enough to
prevent the same mistaken impression in the future.

In order to understand how shocking this view of things must
have appeared to Koheleth's contemporaries, it is necessary to
compare it to some of the basic precepts of wisdom seen else-

where. For surely in the world of wisdom, nothing is futile; good actions are rewarded and bad ones are punished. Nor is a sense of shifting seasons to be countenanced. Whatever "season" a human being is found in, he or she is required to act properly, in keeping with God's own teachings. Indeed, even Koheleth's ever-shifting "sense of time" runs counter to the view of time commonly espoused elsewhere in the Bible, where events take place once and change things forever: "The LORD freed us from Egypt with a mighty hand . . . and brought us to this place and gave us this land" (Deut. 26:8–9). Was Koheleth (as is sometimes alleged) a heretic or a cynic?

Curiously, this opening passage actually contains hidden within it its own exculpation. I do not mean to say that it is all a trick. Koheleth indeed looks out at all of existence—here, indeed, he seems to stand on some mountaintop, watching the rivers and the sea and the sun on the far horizon—and what he sees, Whitmanesque, is everything just going on, going on, going on. The view is, in a way, breathtaking. But having stated it, and without later disavowing it, he goes on to contradict it. The same pen that wrote "There is no remembrance of former things" was later to write "A name is better than scented oil" (Eccles. 7:1). If there is no remembrance of former things, then how can a name be immune to the inroads of time? What could be the point of a name at all to Koheleth? And if all activity is futile, then why is the rest of the book so full of advice about what to do?

Precisely because he believes that life is a series of seasons, what he says at any given point represents only part of the picture. It is true, and he is out to speak the truth; but he is limited to what he happens to be able to see, and say, at any one time. Koheleth's position might be compared to that of a man in a room walking around some object in the center—say, a globe—at a distance of five or ten feet. At any given moment he is able to describe *part* of the globe in great detail: now North and South America, now the Pacific Ocean, now the easternmost part of Asia, and so forth. But as he moves around, everything changes. Where once in the middle of the picture there was water there is now dry land. So in order to describe the globe he ends up presenting a series of snapshots, each one slightly different from the one before it and the one after it; in fact, from opposite points of the room they have absolutely nothing in common.

That is why, rather uniquely, this book is autobiographical, or at least marked here and there by the intrusion of an unwonted, personal "I." Ordinarily, a sage's life ought to have little to do with his wisdom. Wisdom is timeless and placeless, universal and therefore utterly impersonal. But Koheleth does not shrink from inserting himself here and there precisely because he believes that where one happens to be has everything to do with what one is able to see. And so his book is, if not quite an intellectual autobiography, at least framed by the outline of his life. When the book starts out he is still relatively young and vigorous, trying to decide whether it is better to be "wise"—that is, to tread the path of cautious self-restraint—or to be a "fool," pursuing pleasure wherever it may be found.

> I said to myself, "Let me test myself with pleasure and enjoyment," but it all turned out to be a waste. A good time, I concluded, is just stupid; and as for pleasure, what does it accomplish?

> I had resolved in my heart to lead myself on with strong drink— but my mind would always be [watching] with wisdom—and to fully embrace the life of pleasure, so that I could figure out what was the best thing for people to do on this earth in the few years of their lifetime. I increased my holdings. I built houses for

myself and planted vineyards, I made gardens and orchards in which I planted trees of different fruits. I had pools of water made and used them to water a forest blooming with trees. I bought slaves and servant girls and had household attendants. I had more herds of cattle and sheep than any who had been before me in Jerusalem. I stored up silver and gold, and the treasures of kings and governors; I gathered to myself male and female singers, and boxes and boxes of the delights of men. So I grew greater and richer than anyone who had ruled before me over Jerusalem— yet my [watching with] wisdom stayed with me. Whatever my eyes desired I did not withhold from them; I did not restrain myself from any pleasure but took enjoyment from all my labors, since this was indeed the fruit of all my labors. But when I turned to consider all the possessions that I had amassed, and all the profit that had come in from my labor, everything seemed pointless, an embrace of the wind. There is no net gain to be had on this earth.

ECCLES. 2:1–11

Interestingly, even in this apparently nihilistic summation, Koheleth upholds the basic stance of wisdom. It is better, he has found, to be "wise" and tread the straight and narrow than to surrender to one's desires. But that is, of course, not the bottom line; in fact, this book seems to revel in apparently jangling conclusions, trial balances that won't work out. So, on the one hand, "Wisdom's yield is to folly's as that of light is to darkness" (Eccles. 2:13); but on the other, "There is nothing better for a person to do than eat and drink and take pleasure from his labor" (Eccles. 2:24). And then something else always comes into view:

But I reconsidered and saw all the oppression that is done on this earth—look, there are the tears of the oppressed, who have no one on their side. Their oppressors have the power, but they have no one on their side. So I rate the dead, by the fact that they are already dead, higher than the living, since they are still alive. But better than both is one who has never been, since he has never seen the evil that is done on this earth.

ECCLES. 4:1–3

Nor, of course, will things stop there. Koheleth never denies the validity of any of these observations, but his book is constantly in motion, constantly revising things: "Then I turned to consider . . ." (Eccles. 2:11); "I realized [or "saw"] . . ." (Eccles. 2:13, 14; 3:10, 14, 16; 4:4, 15; 6:1; 9:1, 13); "I thought to myself . . ." (Eccles. 1:16; 2:1; 3:17, 18); "I returned and saw [that is, "I reconsidered"] . . ." (Eccles. 4:1, 7; 9:11); "Here is what I myself have seen . . ." (Eccles. 5:17); "Here is what I have found out . . ." (Eccles. 7:27, 29); and more. These personal references are not merely little reminders of the man behind the *mashal*, but a way of encompassing a host of different, sometimes clashing, bits of wisdom in one book. What was obvious back at the beginning no longer holds at the end. Sages and fools may meet the same end, "so why should I be wise?" (Eccles 2:15), but still, "a sage's mind is his right hand, a fool's his left" (Eccles. 10:2); a woman may be all traps and snares (Eccles. 7:26–28), but "enjoy life with the woman whom you love" (Eccles. 9:9). To Koheleth well applies the French barb, "*Il se contredit pour avoir tout dit*" ("He contradicts himself in order to have said everything").

～

MUCH OF KOHELETH'S CONTRADICTORY OUTLOOK is embodied in the "prosody" of his book. He of course knows, and loves, the well-made *mashal*.

A dream comes in amidst too much work, and the voice of a fool amidst too many words.*

ECCLES. 5:2

The more there is, the more that eats it—

so what use is it to its owner, other than just to look with his eyes? **

ECCLES. 5:10

Wisdom is as good as real estate, and it pays off right on this earth;

for whoever owns wisdom owns both the capital and its dividends—

knowing wisdom will provide its possessor a living.***

ECCLES. 7:11–12

If the snake bites without a whisper, what advantage has someone who speaks?****

ECCLES. 10:11

---

* That is, just as worries about work cause one to have [bad] dreams at night, making something bad emerge from an excess of activity, so a person's talking and talking will also make something bad emerge: excess talking inevitably causes one to say something foolish.

** This Malthusian pronouncement states that increased wealth will only produce increased people to consume it. The owner of the wealth will derive no advantage other than looking at his big balance sheet.

*** Wisdom is like a good investment, in that not only does one acquire the thing itself—wisdom—but that wisdom will also pay off dividends, that is, the activity of "knowing" wisdom will also provide one with the means of making a living.

**** Self-explanatory.

But he also often seems impatient with the neat symmetries of wisdom language, Part A, Part B. So much of his book seems to trail off from the terse, poetic *mashal* into something far more rambling and prosy:

> Everyone comes from the dust, and everyone returns to the dust.
>
> But who knows if the spirit of people goes upward and the spirit of beasts goes downward, underneath the earth? So I saw that there is nothing better than that a person should take pleasure in his possessions, since that is his lot, for no one will ever allow him to enjoy what comes after him.
>
> ECCLES. 3:20–22

> In the morning sow your seed, and in the evening do not hold back your hand,
>
> for you don't know which of these will be good, whether this one or that, or if both of them together will turn out good.
>
> ECCLES. 11:6

He can take a perfectly good *mashal* like

> Two are better than one, and a threefold cord is not quickly broken,

and instead of just quoting it, interrupt it with a long, prosy parade of illustrative examples:

> *Two are better than one*, since they will surely profit from their work. For if they should fall, one of them will pick up the other, but if there were only one and he fell, the second would not be there to pick him up. Likewise, if two people lie down together, they can keep warm, but one person alone cannot stay

warm. And if one of them is attacked, the two will be able to resist; *and a threefold cord is not quickly broken.*

ECCLES. 4:9–12

Passages like these make it seem as if Koheleth can't stand the symmetry—one might say, the poetry—of wisdom. It's just all too conclusive, too pat, for his inconclusive world; so he is constantly undoing it.

~

BUT LIFE'S INCONCLUSIVENESS cannot go on forever.

Ecclesiastes, if read from end to end in one sitting, seems much longer than its twelve chapters. By the time one reaches chapter 10 or 11, the book begins to feel like an all-night vigil, as if one had stayed up to the early hours to follow a winding, tedious argument, going over and over things, until now, just as the sky has finally started to change color and the first hint of dawn is seen, one has reached, if not one great conclusion, then at least an exhausted state of equilibrium, perhaps even some kind of peace. Meanwhile the Koheleth who was once so active and vigorous has become an older man, and now an old man. And so he turns to the little that lies ahead.

He does not say why one should "remember your Creator" before old age. Perhaps he feels the reason is obvious. His whole book, after all, has been about trying to catalogue the seasons of life in order to see beyond them, to "grasp what God has created from beginning to end." But how difficult that is! When you are young, nothing is particularly serious, I'll go Thursday or maybe I'll go early. It is only in retrospect that this chance encounter or that flippant decision, side-aways shrugged into, turns out to have been what it was, decisive. Still later, much later, and with a messy, merciless grinding that befouls the chambers of the heart, one at last also takes stock of what was never done and so was lost forever. Time is not "unforgiving," as people tend to say. It is simply time, methodically retracting its largesse, coin by coin. . . . Never, *never* to be, though so close that once! And so the mid-May sun makes its ambling, metaphorical way toward the horizon. In the season of old age, of course, the thought of the Creator comes frequently to mind, but by then life cannot be remade.

Then the light of the sun and the moon and stars—one's vision—begins to go, and the clouds—youth's vigor—return empty after the rain; the hands tremble and the legs are bent, the teeth cease their grinding and the eyes go fully dark; the ears, like twin doors in the marketplace, are shut for lack of commerce, and the voice becomes a little chirp-chirp, its former sonority now lost. Then even the day's little errands are full of terror. When at last the end comes, Koheleth says, it does not really come at once: only slowly does the body disintegrate to enrich the soil and its plant life, as the spinal cord is severed and the skull crushed in like a delicate bowl, the other inner organs likewise broken and shattered, until finally this dust and that dust are indistinguishable, one once again, for the spirit has returned to God.

Many modern scholars of Ecclesiastes have suggested that the closing lines of the book are from another, more pious hand, but this seems to me unlikely. Koheleth certainly would not have been the first, or last, author to write his own epitaph (Eccles. 12:9–11), and his final words of advice seem altogether consonant with all that precedes them.

> The end of the matter, when all has been heard: Fear God and keep his commandments, for this is all of being human.

For God will bring everyone to judgment concerning his conduct,
whether it be for good or ill.

ECCLES. 12:13–14

"For this is all of being human" means, more literally, "for this is
all of man [or: "the whole man"]," and its ambiguity is certain-
ly intentional. On the one hand, as was once said, "It's life and
life only," this is all there is to the whole going around. On the
other hand, to fear God and keep his commandments is the whole
man, the very best and fullest way of being human; to do less is
to have been less.

DATES OF IMPORTANT
FIGURES AND EVENTS

Abraham, Isaac, and Jacob, Israel's immediate ancestors; their stories are recounted in Genesis	dates uncertain
Moses and the Exodus: Israelites leave slavery in Egypt and wander the desert for forty years	13th (?) cent. B.C.E. ("Before the Common Era," that is, "B.C.")
Joshua and the entrance into the Promised Land; Deborah, Samson, and the other judges	13th (?)–11th cent. B.C.E.
Saul becomes first king of Israel	late 11th cent. B.C.E.
King David	ruled ca. 1010 to ca. 970 B.C.E.
King Solomon	ruled ca. 970 to ca. 930 B.C.E.
King Rehoboam succeeds Solomon; breakup of the United Monarchy	922 B.C.E.

Separate kingdoms of Judah (in south) and Israel (in north)

The prophets Elijah and Elisha	9th cent. B.C.E.
The prophet Amos	early to mid-8th cent. B.C.E.
Hosea, Isaiah, and Micah prophesy; Assyria threatening	latter half of 8th cent. B.C.E.
Fall of Israel (Northern Kingdom) to Assyria	722–721 B.C.E.

Henceforth only Judah (Southern Kingdom) survives

Assyria controls and intermittently threatens Judah	through mid-7th century or shortly thereafter
Josiah becomes king of Judah	640–39 B.C.E.
Jeremiah the prophet begins prophesying	627 B.C.E.
Josiah's death; Babylonians begin actively threatening Judah	609 B.C.E.
Babylonians deport King Jehoiachin and many Jerusalemites to Babylon	597 B.C.E.

Fall of Jerusalem to Babylonians; people of Judah
exiled to Babylon; Jeremiah and Ezekiel prophesy   587 B.C.E.

Half-century of Babylonian exile

Cyrus's Persian Empire conquers Babylon;
Jews may return to homeland
("Edict of Cyrus")   539 B.C.E.

Judah ruled by Persian Empire until:

Alexander the Great conquers region   332 B.C.E.

Judah ruled from Egypt until:

Seleucid (Syrian) Conquest   201–198 B.C.E.
Composition of Book of Jubilees[?]   early 2nd cent. B.C.E.
Ben Sira/Sirach, Jewish sage   ca. 180 B.C.E.
Revolt of the Maccabees   168–164 B.C.E.

A century of independent Jewish rule, then Roman domination

Dead Sea Scrolls Community founded
                                                    ca. 135 B.C.E.

NOTES ON TRANSLATIONS

The following notes are not intended as a complete reckoning with all the textual and philological problems of the texts cited; for such treatment, the reader is urged to consult the various commentaries and articles cited in this book's bibliography, many of which have served as my guide in translating. Below I simply wish to give account, as best I can, for any unusual or idiosyncratic features of my own translations.

CHAPTER 1
On Psalm 104

and covered it over with water: more literally, "roofed its top with water." These are the "upper waters" (as opposed to those of rivers and seas) from which rain descends through the sky and down to earth; they are the same as the "water loomed over the mountains" mentioned a few lines later.

The winds themselves You made messengers, and flames of fire Your servants: Ancient interpreters sometimes reversed the objects, yielding, "You made [or "make"] Your messengers (that is, the angels) into winds, and Your servants into fire," whence developed the idea of windy and fiery angels. See Kugel, *Traditions of the Bible,* 75–76.

You set loose: Throughout this section, verb tenses are unclear in Hebrew. Is this a list of God's (past-tense) acts of creation, or a present-tense recitation of His continued activity but written to follow the order of creation? I have used gerunds as well as grammatically ambiguous verbs like "set" and "let" in order to mimic, to the extent possible, this temporal vagueness.

You made the moon to mark off the seasons and You know the route of the sun: The traditional Hebrew text (Masoretic Text) understands these verbs as third-person and past-tense, "He made . . . He knew," but the participle form, "making . . . knowing," could just as well be construed by the consonantal text and would work better with the second-person verb that follows, "You bring darkness . . ."

to lie down in darkened lairs: The text has just "lairs," but their darkness was certainly the point here.

their fatness comes back: Others have "they are created." But they already were created; if the idea were that of resurrection, one would expect *yḥyw*. Perhaps the release of God's spirit (or "breath") signals a break in the drought here.

On Psalm 147

He gives food to animals, even to the crows when they caw: This verse has been explained in various ways, since the expression translated as "crows" is actually the somewhat fancier *bny ʿwrb*. This could be understood to mean either "crow-creatures" (that is, members of the "crow" class) or else "children of crows." If the latter, then one explanation has it that crows are particularly stingy with their young, who as a consequence constantly cry out for food; probably, however, merely the former is meant, and crows are being singled out for their obnoxious cawing—even *they* get fed in the divine economy.

On Psalm 139

You sift my comings and goings: The word translated as "sift" means to winnow or scatter, and the resulting image is certainly odd; it may be that there is a problem with the text here. "My comings and goings" is, more literally, "my path and my lying down." The former can refer to, specifically, traveling, and a homonymous root of the latter means "dust" in both biblical Hebrew (Num. 23:10) and Samaritan Aramaic (Tg. Gen. 18:27), but it is nonetheless difficult to put these two together with the verb in question.

In front and in back You press in on me and set Your hand upon me: On some of the history of this verse's interpretation, see Kugel, *Traditions of the Bible*, 82–84.

If I took the wings of a gull to settle at the far end of the sea: Others have "the wings of dawn." A beautiful image, but one that is somewhat troubling nonetheless: what are the "wings of dawn"? One might understand the expression spatially, that is, "If I lift [myself] up to the outskirts [another meaning of "wings" in Hebrew] of the morning..." But the next phrase, "the far end of the sea," was, for an Israelite, westward. The west was not the place of the morning or dawn —the sun rises in the east, after all— but dusk and darkness, *mʿrb*. I have not seen the suggestion elsewhere, but perhaps one should hypothesize not *šḥr* but *šḥp*, yielding, "If I took on the wings of a gull..."

nighttime will conceal me: Hebrew *ʾwr bʿdny* is a problem; translations usually follow the apparent sense.

CHAPTER 2

Psalm 42, written in an apparently Northern dialect of Hebrew somewhat different from that found in most of the Bible, presents numerous difficulties. (It is likewise to be noted that its lines are often far from the terse, two-part ideal of Hebrew's poetic style—many lines are longer than is usual elsewhere, and some clearly have three clauses instead of two.) On the language as a whole, see G. Rendsberg, *Linguistic Evidence for the Northern Origin of Selected Psalms.* Many scholars have supposed that, because of their common refrain-line, Pss. 42 and 43 were once a single composition; I am not convinced.

On Psalm 42:

as all day long I hear, "Where is your God?": more literally, "as it is said to me all day..." Note, however, that in the second-to-last verse of this psalm the text reads (or can be read) "as they say to me all day..."

But I do think of this as I pour out my soul—how I will go with a crowd, leading a throng of revelers up to the very Temple, with songs of rejoicing and praise: All com-mentators are puzzled by this verse, and all translations are speculative. The first part of the sentence might indeed be understood quite differently: "As I remember [or "make mention of"] these things, I pour out my soul; yet I will lead a throng..." It should also be noted that the Hebrew word *sk* ("throng") is otherwise unattested in the Bible, so this understanding of the verse, while common enough in translations ancient and modern, should be understood to be speculative.

So why be downcast, my soul, or murmur within me? Like other translators, I have rendered this as a question, and that is certainly a possible reading of the Hebrew words. It seems equally possible, however, that it is really a negation: "Do not be downcast, my soul..."

Trust in God, for I will yet praise Him for helping me, my God: The syntax of the Hebrew text is troubling and possibly corrupt. The traditional division into verses puts "my God" at the beginning of the next sentence.

...from Mount Mizar, and depth to watery depth—calling out above the beat of Your streams: This mountain is otherwise unknown, and some translators have tried to rearrange the letters or read *mizar* as a common noun; however, it may be that, given the apparently northern locale, this site was simply not well known elsewhere. The common translation of the next words is "Deep calls to deep," a wonderfully evocative phrase but essentially meaningless in context. (Those who wish to see in the Hebrew *thwm* a personification of watery chaos à la the Babylonian Tiamat are certainly on the wrong track.) I therefore prefer to take *qwr'* (or perhaps *qrw'*, or even *'qr'*) as quite separate from these depths, the beginning of the next line, "I call out..."

The LORD sends forth His protection by day, and at night it stays at my side: It is not often recognized that *ṣwh* sometimes has the nuance of "send forth" instead of simply "command": Lev. 25:21, Ps. 91:11, 133:3, and many others. The word *šyrh*, traditionally rendered as "song," does not work here; it is probably to be associated with *š'r* in the sense of "remain," see 1 Sam. 16:11 and cf. Arabic, Aramaic, and M. Heb. *šyr*, "remain." Once this word is no longer "song," there is no reason to consider the "prayer" mentioned next as some sort of apposed synonym: it is quite separate, a rubric that starts the last part of this psalm.

CHAPTER 3
On Psalm 29

Listen! the LORD: This phrase is usually rendered "The voice of the LORD," and both translations are equally possible: the "voice of the LORD" would presumably be a direct reference to the thunder accompanying this theophany. But if so, then the "voice of the LORD" ends up doing a lot of things that one would not normally expect voices, even divine voices, to do, such as shattering trees and shooting forth sparks. Under the circumstances, "Listen!" seems better.

and in His temple, all say, "Glory!": "...all proclaim His glory" is probably closer to the original meaning, but I have retained the common (and more literal) rendering of the traditional Hebrew text.

CHAPTER 4
On Amos 4:4–5:24

For such is your devotion: literally, "For thus do you love," but *love* in the cultic sense means to show devotion or fealty to the deity. "For so you love to do" and the like is simply not in the Hebrew and represents a misunderstanding of the text.

Beth-sorrow: There was a well-known town in the land of Benjamin called Beth-awen. When Amos says here that he will turn Bethel to *awen,* he seems to be alluding to the name of that other town while at the same time suggesting the common meaning of *awen,* "trouble" or "sorrow."

"Right-thinking" people detest a rebuker...: "at the gate they hate a rebuker" in Hebrew. The gate of the city was the place where the city's elders and judges met, the home base of the Establishment (Deut. 16:18 and frequently), indeed, the place where a woman might be proud to have her husband be found or her sons end up (Prov. 31:23, 31). Amos does not like what goes on there (Amos 5:12, 15). Others translate "people hate a rebuker at the gates," but the point is not that they hate having him *there,* nor yet that the "rebuker at the gates" is a fixture of society, but that the supposed dispensers of justice *at the gates* are particularly the sort of people who will not cotton to the rebuker. The same seems to be true of the rebuker in Isa. 29:21.

Anyone who sees what's happening...: The *mskyl* is not the "prudent one" here, but anyone with eyes to see; "for 'this is an evil time'" is Amos quoting, ironically, what people say to dismiss the evil before their very eyes.

CHAPTER 5
On 2 Sam. 1:19–27

fields of Terumoth: a long-time crux. Terumoth might be a proper name here; others have "fields of heights" or "fields of offerings" (both possible meanings of *terumoth* as a common noun), or, following the Septuagint, "fields of death" (based on the *moth* part of *Terumoth*). More recently, "upsurgings of the deep" has been proposed on the basis of an alleged Ugaritic parallel. I'm not convinced.

the shield of Saul—the chosen king—gave way: The text must be amended somehow; at present it reads, "the shield of Saul without the anointed with oil." Jerome: "as if he were not anointed with oil." Others delete the word *beli* ("without"), hence, "Saul, the anointed with oil." I prefer to think that the *beli* represents one form or another of the root *blh*, which can mean to be worn out or used up.

CHAPTER 6
Most of my translation of Job follows the excellent work of Marvin Pope, *Job*, with an occasional glance at the ingenuities of N. H. Tur-Sinai, *The Book of Job.*
On Job 28

He determines the portions of rains: Though many translators have missed it, the sense of *hq* as "portion" is clear enough, Gen. 47:22, Exod. 5:14, Prov. 8:29, 30:8, 31:15, and so forth.

On Ps. 90:10

or if mightily [doled out]: The phrase *w'm bgbwrt* is usually misunderstood as referring to the human recipients of the eighty years, that is, "if we [are] in strength" or the like. But it is God's apportioning mightily, that is, generously, that is meant here.

On Eccles. 2:11: *see below, chapter 18.*

On Prov. 10:9 and 25

I have translated these two quite literally, but some of the sense has thereby been lost. In the first instance, someone who is being pursued or is afraid of attack *doesn't* usually walk straight across a field or right through the middle of town: he seeks a more sheltered, meandering path. But with spiritual paths, the Proverbist says, it is quite the opposite: someone who walks "straight"—does nothing wrong, in other words—will have nothing to fear, whereas the one who makes his path crooked with nefarious little schemes will, precisely by doing so, eventually draw attention to himself and so will be found out. As for Prov. 10:25, the "whirlwind" actually refers to the evil that a wicked man does in his life—his wrong-doing is indeed like a cyclone, very destructive but short-lived.

On Job 30:16–27

But my sweats do not let up—strangely overlooked, "sweat" is the meaning of Arabic 'rq (not to be confused with the alcoholic beverage of the same name) and perfectly fits the context here.

But one can't be required... The word b'y is an Aramaism, the equivalent of Hebrew bqš.

I cried out mightily: This is adverbial ky ṭwb, "greatly, mightily" (cf. Aramaic ṭwb), as in Ps. 107:1 and frequently. The next phrase, "but evil came back," plays on the other sense of ṭwb, "good."

CHAPTER 7

On Judges 5

In general: Because of the apparently poor state of preservation of this text, I have been freer here than elsewhere in resorting to emendation.

revenge was sweet: this is the Aramaic pr'; see the commentary of R. David Qimhi. A more literal rendering would be "when acts of revenge were being taken." Others associate this root (wrongly, to my mind) with that meaning to let loose, as hair; hence, "when locks were long in Israel" and the like.

armies: that is, 'am.

highwaymen: that is, *perazon.* The common translation "villagers" or "peasantry" scarcely makes sense. It may be that the word is to be related to the Arabic cognate faraza, as suggested by W. F. Albright and others (yielding "warriors" or "champions"); the derived Arabic noun mafraza "[raiding] party" seems still closer to the point here. Note also the possibly related biblical Hebrew pariṣ, "violent one, robber, murderer."

were fat...were fat with spoils: a pun, the homonymous root ḥdl of the previous verse ("cease") means here to grow fat: the same phrase ḥdl 'd appears in 1 Sam. 2:5.

Until: this word, 'ad, must have been omitted by haplography after the previous phrase.

"Let God choose armed men, let the armed men of the cities come forth": Like all translations of this verse, mine is mostly speculation; as is, the verse makes no sense. Elsewhere in the song, the Deity is referred to by the name "LORD," so "God" here appears problematic; on the other hand, the translation "he will choose [or "they chose"] new gods" simply does not fit the context. My translation thus assumes the presence of some errors and improper word division in the transmission of the traditional text, amending it as: ybḥr 'lhym ḥmšym, [y]'zlw ḥmšy 'rym. Cf. Barnabas Linders, *Judges 1–5* (Edinburgh, T&T Clark, 1995), 239–40.

Deborah: as explained earlier, this might better be rendered as a common noun "soothsayer," that is a female speaker.

...and you who travel through the underbrush: Hebrew *whlky 'l drk syhym.* The whole phrase, "O you who ride the tawny donkeys, who dwell by Madon and travel through the underbrush," refers to the caravaneers who now have to travel "roundabout paths."

The sound of trumpeters...: i.e., *qwl mhṣṣrym,* cf. 1 Chr. 15:24

Then the mighty ones came down to Sarid, the army of the Lord came down for Him amongst the troops: (Hebrew: *'z yrd sryd [l] 'dyrym, 'm H' yrd lw bgbrym*). This situation (if not the words themselves) parallels that of Deborah's oracle of instruction in 4:6–7.

But Zebulon—an army scornful of death, while Naphtali climbs the heights of the plain: This line in particular seems to have suffered in transmission; all translations are speculative.

March ahead mightily, O my soul: I have reluctantly kept the common translation, but it hardly seems to fit here. Perhaps *nfš* here is, as elsewhere "neck" and not "soul," while *drk* is a transitive verb: "stomp on the mighty necks"?

that's where he stayed fallen, the oppressor: Reading *šdwd* as the active participle, "oppressor," cf. Ps. 137:8.

the spoils they've grabbed: A commonly overlooked meaning of *mṣ',* cf. Deut. 22:24, 25, 27–28; Song, 8:1, etc.

CHAPTER 8
On Psalm 51

Be generous with me: Traditionally "Have mercy on me," "Take pity on me," but the Hebrew *ḥnn* has a broad range of meanings including the more positive "show favor," "be gracious," and so forth.

You always are fair...: Heb. *m'n,* it seems to me, is sometimes the equivalent of *nṣh,* "ever, always": Deut. 33:27; Ps. 30:13; Ps. 71:3; Ps. 90:1; Prov. 2:20; Zeph. 3:7. The matter deserves further study.

But consider I was born to transgression, conceived by my mother in sinfulness: The whole of this verse was marshalled by early Christians to support the doctrine of Original Sin, indeed, the second half seemed to suggest that sexual intercourse was the means of Original Sin's transmission. But the verse appears less to be imparting doctrine here than simply pleading for forgiveness, that is, "Guilty with an excuse, sir."

I know that secretly: "Secretly" is the proper translation of *bṭḥwt,* which parallels *bstm* here; cf. Gen. 34:25.

save me from death: Literally "from bloods." The message here, as frequently in the Psalter, is that having been saved from death, the psalmist will devote himself to praising God. Perhaps, as in the expression of similar sentiments in Ps. 30:9, the original text here read not *dmym* but *dmy*, that is, "my [going down to] Silence," Sheol.

CHAPTER 9
On Prov. 26:23
Like a thick glaze: reading *kspsg*[*y*]*m* as one word, corresponding to Ugaritic *spsg* "glaze," in place of Masoretic text *ksp sgym*, "silver of dross." The latter makes little sense—one would otherwise expect "dross of silver"—and does not fit the context nearly as well.

CHAPTER 10
On Isa. 11:1–9
Yes, he shall be guided by the fear of the LORD: Many omit this phrase because of its similarity to the previous one and the absence of a parallel second half of the verse, but such factors hardly need be decisive. However, the text is problematic in another way: *whryhw* means "he will smell" or "take the scent of." This is usually reworded, without justification, as "he will delight in" by those who wish to retain this part of the verse. Perhaps the verb should be derived from *hnhh* "direct," "lead."

He will punish the arrogant: The traditional Hebrew text reads "a land" ('*rṣ*), but many have emended this to "the arrogant one," "the tyrant" ('*r*[*y*]*ṣ*).

CHAPTER 11
On Psalm 23
For thou art with me; thy rod and thy staff they comfort me: drop one letter and "comfort" becomes "guide" (*ynhwny*), as proposed by some commentators. For reasons given above, however, I still prefer the traditional text.

CHAPTER 12
On Jer. 12:1–6
No one will call us to account.: No one will see our '*aharit*, "continuation, end-time," has puzzled generations of interpreters. The Septuagint translation presupposes '*rhwtynw*, "our paths," but perhaps the word here ought to be identified with Mishnaic Hebrew '*ahrayut* (with the same consonantal spelling as here), "property to be seized in case of non-payment," hence here, the personal stake of the wicked, what they risk for their behavior.

If you topple over: is based on the Arabic *bth* ("cause to fall" and the like) rather than the usual meaning of Hebrew *bth*, "believe, trust in." Alternatively one might hypothesize a missing negation, "If you do not have trust," that is, "If you lose your nerve now."

what will you do when the Jordan floods its banks?: the phrase g'n hyrdn clearly refers to floodwaters and not (as some translators have it) the "jungle" of the Jordan.

On Job 21

Yet all that they have didn't come from themselves—the fate of the wicked is too much for me: This verse has stumped translators, despite a clearer version of the same idea in Job 22:18. As elsewhere, here 'ṣh means not "counsel" but "fate," while the verb rḥq means to be incomprehensible, as in Deut. 30:11, Eccles. 7:23, 24.

His haunches were full and plump: see on this Marvin Pope, *Job*, 161.

CHAPTER 13
On Psalm 137

where we settled: Sitting on the ground was a sign of mourning, so many translators render this "where we sat down." But "sit" and "settle" are the same verb in biblical Hebrew; it seems more reasonable to me to understand this as a straightforward reference to the fact of exile.

and our masters demanded entertainment: "Masters" corresponds to Hebrew tllnw, a verb that has puzzled commentators for centuries. It seems to be related to šll, "despoil," so its meaning here might be "those who took us as booty."

Please, O LORD, pay back the Edomites: The Hebrew idiom zkr l- means not to "remember" or even "recall to [someone]," but something like "chalk up to X's credit." It can be used sincerely, as in Jer. 2:1 (cited in "A Prophet in Israel") or, as here, ironically.

O Babylon, you destroyer!: The (rare) participial qatol-form, active in meaning.

On Lamentations 2 and 4

My eyes have no more tears and my insides are like clay: Others render the latter phrase: "my heart is in turmoil" and the like. But the opposite seems to be the point here: there is no turmoil, I have no more feelings. The root ḥmrmr may thus be connected here to ḥwmr, "clay."

at least they oozed [blood] from wounds and [not from lack of] food: the translation is speculative, the text appears to have been garbled in transmission.

On Jeremiah 26

And all the people bitterly accused: Not "assembled against" but the homonymous root qhl that means to accuse or indict: see especially Neh. 5:7 and compare Exod. 32:1, Num. 16:31, 17:7, Job 11:10, etc. Some of these were first pointed out by Edward Ullendorf (see Bibliography).

This man faces the death penalty: That is, he is to be officially tried for a capital crime; Deut. 21:22.

On Lamentations 2 and 3

He has stripped his little hut down and stopped the festival: The allusion is to the festival hut *(sukkah)* that was a central feature of the holiday of Tabernacles. Here, God's temple is like the festival hut, which, having been suddenly stripped and left bare, spells the end to all festivities. The succeeding lines continue this idea; thus, the reference to setting aside "both king and priest" focuses on them as principal figures in Temple celebration, but, of course, they have also been "set aside" in a more serious, and permanent, fashion.

Lam. 5:1–16

We are shoved around by the neck; tired out, we are given no rest: Traditional Jewish interpretation connects this line with the journey from Jerusalem through the desert into Babylonian exile, making the following lines a description of life in Babylon. See Kugel, *In Potiphar's House,* 180–183. But it need not be so; indeed, some of the following lines seem to indicate a setting in Judah/Zion among those who were allowed to remain behind after the exiles left.

Even the Egyptians gave help [*to our ancestors*], *the Assyrians supplied enough food:* This is not a description of the present (as many translators have supposed), but an allusion to previous suffering. That is, our present persecution by foreigners is even worse than those famous persecutions Israel suffered in the past. For that reason the next verse too speaks of "our ancestors." (For *ntn yd* in the sense of "help," see 1 Chr. 29:24.)

We earn our bread at our peril, in the parching desert heat: that is, *horeb* instead of *hereb*.

Boys are put to work grinding, or stagger under loads of wood: These are not jobs normally performed by boys, so to the physical abuse is added the shame. (This continues the theme of shame presented in the two previous verses.)

CHAPTER 14
On Psalm 119

to contemplate mysteries from Your teachings: Here and throughout, *npl'wt* are not merely "wonders" or "wondrous things" (as often elsewhere in the Bible), but things that are not easily understood, cryptic things; see Prov. 30:18.

My soul is drenched: The root *dlp* is certainly associated with moisture, but specifically with being "sopped with" something (rather than, as some suppose, "leaking"): this is the true sense of Eccles. 10:18.

since it enforces Your worship: The phrase *'šr lyr'tk* seems designed to evoke the same idea as that of Ps. 130:4.

All the living are Your servants: and not "all things," as found in some translations. As elsewhere in late biblical Hebrew, *hkl* is often "everyone."

I hate divisive offshoots: The precise sense (or even vocalization) of s‘pym is unclear, but this sort of "branching off" seems to be the point and well suits this speaker's mentality; see 1 Kings 18:21.

All Your precepts I hold to be right: The traditional Hebrew text appears difficult here. Perhaps one should suppose kl pqwdyk yšrty instead of kl pqwdy kl yšrty.

Your word refines and purifies: This is the rare (active) form of the participle sārôfâ.

On Ps. 22:10–11

my hope since the womb: This is the apparent sense in context, though the meaning of gḥy ("hope"; others: "benefactor") is not clear. Note gzy in apparently the same sense in Ps. 71:6. Others have "You have taken me from the womb" on the basis of a putative verb gḥḥ, "extract," connected to gyḥ, "burst forth"; the chain of hypotheses is weak.

CHAPTER 15
On the Song of Songs

Throughout this translation, the woman speaks except in those passages in quotation marks, which are spoken by her beloved.

Buds have started to sprout and pruning time is here: The root for "prune" is a homonym of that for "sing," so some have seen in this a reference to song-birds such as the "turtledove" referred to in the next line.

Not until I've brought him home, brought him to my room: Here I have flagrantly deviated from the text, which reads, "Not until I've brought him to my *mother's* house, brought him to the room *of her that bore me.*" For the non-allegorist, these words are certainly problematic: it seems unlikely that the speaker is saying that, having now at last found her lover, all she can think of doing is bringing him to where her mother resides. This problem has led to elaborate theories—the mother being referred to is dead, the speaker is referring to some time well in the future when she will indeed present her beloved to her mother, and yet others; see Pope, *Song of Songs,* 421–423. But perhaps this evocation of the mother in connection with love and marriage hints at some literary convention of whose precise nuance we are unaware; see, in this connection, v. 8:5 as well as Gen. 24:67. In any case, precisely because the reference to the speaker's mother is not understood nowadays, I thought it would be the better part of wisdom to skip it in the translation.

Who's this up from the desert? The "this" in the text is feminine; in context, one expects it to refer to the "her" of the song, all fragrant with perfumes. What a disappointment when it turns out to be Solomon's "train"—also a feminine noun—instead!

covered over with leather from Jerusalem: the word often understood as "love" seems here to be a rare homonym cognate with Arabic 'iḥāb, "skin, raw leather." The continuation reads *mbnwt yrwšlm*. Some have preferred to see these words as the beginning of the next line, "Daughters of Jerusalem, go out; and see, you daughters of Zion"; just as likely, it seems to me, the leather was "from Jerusalem," and the "daughters" migrated from the next line via a scribal error, *bnwt yrwšlm* being elsewhere a common phrase in the song. On all these see Pope, *Song of Songs*, 445.

and your mouth is so sweet: Others: "your speech." In that sense see in particular Joseph b. Judah ibn Aqnin, *The Revelation of Mysteries and the Appearance of Lights*, ed., A. S. Halkin, 176–179.

spend the night in the grass: The word *kprym* more commonly means "villages," but that could hardly be right here. (Why more than one village? And isn't going "out to the field" rather the opposite of going to a village?) For that reason, commentators have preferred to see here the name of a plant or tree, possibly connected with the *kwpr* mentioned in 1:4, which was apparently a spice bush of some sort. "Grass" may be a bit blander but in the absence of firm knowledge seems at least approximately right.

I could throw my arms around you in the street: As noted elsewhere, *mṣ'* means not only "find," but "grab," "seize." "Throw my arms around" may be a little expansive but seems right.

If a man gave all his family's wealth for love, would anybody blame him? Others: "If a man offered all the wealth of his house, it [or "he"] would be utterly scorned." But that hardly fits the context, the praise of love's great power: of course, anyone would give anything for love.

CHAPTER 16
On Exod. 34:5–7
and he [Moses] called upon the name of the LORD: Most translators understand this as "And He [God] called upon the name of the LORD," proclaiming His own nature; the verse would thus be an anticipatory statement of what follows. But elsewhere to "call on the name of the LORD" (Gen. 4:26, 12:8, 21:32, 26:25; 1 Kings 18:24; Jer. 10:25; and so forth) refers to some sort of cultic act or utterance on the part of the worshiper—here, Moses.

On Mic. 7:14
Let those who dwell alone in the forest: This sentence sounds oddly archaic in Hebrew, especially in its Masoretic vocalization, *šwkny lbdd* evoking memories of Deut. 33:16, 28; note also the apparent allusion to this verse in Jer. 50:19.

CHAPTER 17
On Isaiah 60
And I will make Peace your blueprint, with Righteousness as your foreman. Hebrew *pqwdtk* here has stumped translators, but the allusion is to the "specifications"

of the sanctuary, similar to those mentioned at the start of the verbal blueprint of the tabernacle, Exod. 38:21.

On Isa. 43:1–6

I will say to the north wind, "Come on!" and to the south wind, "Don't hold back": These are winds, not directions ("North," "South") as usually translated. Compare Song of Songs 4:16. Note also that kl' is used of the wind in Eccles. 8:8.

CHAPTER 18
On Ecclesiastes 12

Before the light of the sun goes dark: literally, "the sun and the light," a hendiadys.

and the clouds return [empty] after the rain: See Eccles. 11:3. The reference here may be to fertility, embodied everywhere in biblical Israel by rainfall.

Any height inspires fear, and a journey seems fraught with danger: This is the traditional understanding, though the word gbh ("height") is usually used of human height, that is, "tall" rather than "high." Besides, while the elderly may be reluctant to travel on long journeys, I have never heard of acrophobia being associated with the onset of old age. Perhaps the text is corrupt.

Then will the almond tree blossom, and the grasshopper drag along, and the caper bush bud: This line has always been troublesome, and credible attempts have been made to modify this or that word—"grasshopper" to the name of a plant, for example—but the problem remains to fit all these into the larger picture. Perhaps there is nothing allegorical intended here at all—certainly the words that follow are not allegory—and the point may simply be that the body, freshly buried, at once begins to disintegrate and the soil and insect life around and above it is soon enriched.

Until the silver cord is snapped and the golden bowl is crushed: Here the author reverts not to a further allegorical description of death, but a description of the corpse's degeneration: the silver cord is the spinal cord, the golden bowl is the skull. Hebrew *trwṣ* here is to be connected with the root *rṣṣ*, "shatter, crush."

and the pitcher is broken at the spring, and the jug is shattered at the well: It is impossible to be precise about what inner organs are meant here—perhaps the stomach and the spleen.

Not only was Koheleth a sage, but he also taught the people wisdom: that is, he was no closeted academic.

The words of sages are like prods, and like nails well planted are those of teachers; they were given by one Shepherd: Proverbs are proverbially sharp, so "prods" and "nails" are most appropriate images. The phrase b'ly 'spwt has been rendered as "those gathered in collections," but perhaps "teachers," that is, "masters of assemblies," is better. The last words are certainly to be emended, but any emendation is speculative.

there is no end to acquiring books: 'sh, like its brother p'l in Phoenician, means both "make" and "gather": cf. Gen. 12:5, etc. Throughout Ecclesiastes it frequently means "gather," see thus Eccles. 2:8.

On Eccles. 1:2–11

Though all words grow wearisome, a man does not cease to speak: The import of this assertion remains obscure. Many have explained it as meaning that all words are inadequate, therefore a man cannot speak [some unutterable truth]. But that does not really fit either the words themselves or their context. Besides, "a man cannot speak" without any direct object is simply false; men speak all the time. I have translated the way I have to suggest the following: *although all words grow wearisome, still, a man does not cease speaking.* Such an understanding seems better to me, though it does require amending ywkl to yykl[h] (altogether plausible in the light of late Second Temple orthography and script). In other words, just as the above phenomena of nature keep repeating and cancelling themselves out, so do people keep on talking and talking, though their words—comments, explanations—grow weary, they say one thing and then another. Speaking and speaking also fits with the two other actions that follow in this section, looking and looking and listening and listening. In all these cases, nothing definite is arrived at: the words grow wearisome, the eye cannot take it all in, and the ear cannot hear it all.

On Eccles. 2:1–11 :

I had resolved in my heart to lead myself on: literally, "to lead my flesh on," but bsr sometimes means "self" in Ecclesiastes, cf. 5:5.

and boxes and boxes of the delights of men: as in Mishnaic Hebrew šdh, "strongbox, chest." Others have seen in this phrase "servant girls" and the like, but the argument is weak.

On Eccles. 4:1–3 :

So I rate the dead, by the fact that they are already dead, higher than the living. This verse is a long-standing crux, since the verb "rate higher" has long been mistaken for its meaning in the D-form (pi'el), "praise." But it makes little sense to say that Koheleth "praises" the dead more than the living—he doesn't praise the living at all! What is more, to make this out to be the word "praise" it is necessary to assume that the form of the verb is in a totally anomalous usage in Hebrew (albeit not in Phoenician), the free-standing infinitive absolute in a finite sense. If, on the other hand, it is identified with Mishnaic Hebrew šbh in the pa'al form, "improve, augment in value"—here, "rate higher"—then it can be pointed to as a finite verb (that is, *śobēăḥ*) and all problems disappear.

On Eccles. 7:11–12:

Wisdom is as good as real estate, and it pays off right on this earth: The 'm is used in Eccles. in the sense of "as much as," cf. Eccles. 2:16. The phrase "right on this earth" means literally "those who see the sun," that is, those people down here. In general, I have translated Koheleth's frequent phrase "under the sun" or "under the sky" as "on this earth," since that is what he means.

for whoever owns wisdom owns both the capital and its dividends: This translation assumes an emendation of *bṣl* ("in the shade of") to *b'l* ("the owner of"). Not only does sense support this emendation, but the *b'l* here is quite consciously picked up by the appearance of the same word in the next line. All commentators have failed to understand that the word *ytrwn*, "net profit" (or here, loosely, "dividends") is the last part of this phrase, rather than the first word of the following phrase. Consequently, they translate the next line as "the advantage of knowing wisdom keeps alive its possessor" or the like, which is not only gobbledy-gook but ends up having a masculine noun (*ytrwn*) as the subject of a feminine verb. Koheleth's point is clear enough. Possessing wisdom is like possessing a good piece of land: not only do you have the asset itself, but it also yields up annual income to its owner, that is, the act of "knowing wisdom will provide its possessor a living." (On this: Kugel, "Qohelet and Money.")

BRIEF BIBLIOGRAPHY

Amir, Yehoshua, *Studien zum Antiken Judentum* (Frankfurt a. M.: Lang, 1985)

Anderson, A. A., *The Book of Psalms* (Grand Rapids: Eerdmans, 1972)

Anderson, Bernhard, *The Eighth Century Prophets* (Philadelphia: Fortress, 1978)

Bar Asher, M., "Rare Forms in Tannaitic Hebrew," *Leshonenu* 41 (1987), 83–102.

Beaucamp, E., *Le psautier* (Paris: Gabalda, 1976)

Bianchi, R., "The Language of Qohelet: A Bibliographical Survey," *Zeitschrift für die Alttestamentliche Wissenschaft* 115 (1993), 210–223

Bickerman, Elias, *Four Strange Books of the Bible* (New York: Schocken, 1967)

Blenkinsopp, J., "Ecclesiastes 3:1–15, Another Interpretation," *Journal for the Study of the Old Testament* 66 (1995) 55–64

Blenkinsopp, J., *Prophecy and Canon* (South Bend, Ind.: Notre Dame, 1977)

Blenkinsopp, J., *Wisdom and Law in the Old Testament* (London: Oxford, 1983)

Blommerde, J., *Northwest Semitic Grammar and Job* (Rome: Pontifical Biblical Institute, 1969)

Bottéro, Jean, *Mesopotamia: Writing, Reasoning, and the Gods* (Chicago: University of Chicago, 1992)

Buttenwieser, *The Psalms* (New York: KTAV, 1969)

Carroll, R. P., *From Chaos to Covenant: Prophecy in the Book of Jeremiah* (New York: Crossroads, 1981)

Carroll, R. P., *Jeremiah: A Commentary* (Philadelphia: Westminster, 1986)

Ceresko, A. R., "The Function of Antanaclasis (*mß*' "to find" // *mß*' "to reach, overtake, grasp") in Hebrew Poetry," *Catholic Bible Quarterly* 44 (1982) 551–569

Childs, Brevard S., *Old Testament Theology in a Canonical Context* (Philadelphia: Fortress, 1986)

Clausen, Wendell, "Virgil's Messianic Eclogue" in Kugel, *Poetry and Prophecy*, 65–74

Clements, R. E., *Jeremiah* (Atlanta: Jon Knox, 1988)

Clines, David J. A., "What Does Eve Do to Help? and Other Readerly

Questions to the Old Testament," (Sheffield: *Journal for the Study of the Old Testament* Press, 1990)

Cogan, Mordechai, *Imperialism and Religion: Judah and Israel in the Eighth and Seventh Centuries B. C. E.* (Missoula: Scholars, 1974)

Coogan, M. D., "A Structural and Literary Analysis of the Song of Deborah," *Catholic Bible Quarterly* 40 (1978), 143–66

Coote, Robert, *Amos Among the Prophets* (Philadelphia: Fortress, 1981)

Craigie, P., "Some Further Notes on the Song of Deborah" *Vetus Testamentum* 22 (1972) 349–53

Cross, Frank Moore, "Notes on a Canaanite Psalm in the Old Testament," *Bulletin of the American Society for Oriental Research* 117 (1950), 19–21

Cross, Frank Moore, *Canaanite Myth and Hebrew Epic* (Cambridge: Harvard, 1973)

Dahood, M., "The Phoenician Background of Qoheleth," *Biblica* 47 (1966) 264–82

Dahood, M., *Psalms* vol 1–3 (Anchor Bible) (Garden City: Doubleday, 1965, 1968, 1970)

Davila, J. R., "Qoheleth and Northern Hebrew" *Maarav* 5–6 (1990) 69–87

Eaton, John, *Kingship and the Psalms* (Sheffield: JSOT Press, 1985) ·

Fohrer, Georg, *Psalmen* (New York: De Gruyter, 1993)

Frankfort, Henri, *Before Philosophy: The Intellectual Adventure of Ancient Man* (Baltimore: Penguin, 1946)

Freedman, David N. and C. Frank Hyland, "Psalm 29: A Structural Analysis," *Harvard Theological Review* 66 (1973), 237–56

Gaster, T. H., "Psalm 29," *Jewish Quarterly Review* 37 (1946), 54–67

Gerstenberger, Erhard, *Psalms, Part 1* (Grand Rapids: Eerdmans, 1988)

Gilbert, M., "La déscription de la viellesse en Qohelet XII 1–7, est-elle allé-gorique?" *Vetus Testamentum* Sup. 32 (1981), 96–109.

Ginsberg, H. L., *Qohelet*, (Jerusalem and Tel Aviv: M. Neumann, 1978)

Gordis, R., *Koheleth: the Man and his World* (New York: Schocken, 1968)

Goulder, M. D., *The Psalms of David (Psalms 51–72)* (Sheffield: JSOT Press, 1990)

Goulder, M. D., *The Psalms of the Sons of Korah* (Sheffield: JSOT Press, 1982)

Gunkel, Hermann, *The Psalms: A Form-Critical Introduction* (Philadelphia: Fortress, 1967)

Hallo, W. W. et al., *The Bible in the Light of Cuneiform Literature* (Lewiston, N.Y.: Mellen, 1990)

Halpern, Baruch, *The Constitution of the Monarchy in Ancient Israel* (Chico, Cal.: Scholars, 1981)

Halpern, Baruch, *The Emergence of Israel in Canaan* (Chico, Cal.: Scholars, 1983)

Haran, Menahem, *Temples and Temple Service in Ancient Israel* (London: Oxford, 1978)

Hillers, D. R., *Micah* (Hermeneia) (Philadelphia: Fortress, 1984)

Holladay, William L., *Jeremiah* 1 (Hermeneia) (Philadelphia: Fortress, 1986)

Holladay, William L., *The Psalms Through Three Thousand Years* (Minneapolis: Fortress, 1993)

ibn Aqnin, Joseph b. Judah, *The Revelation of Mysteries and the Appearance of Lights,* ed., A. S. Halkin (Jerusalem: *Mekize Nirdamim,* 1964)

Jacobsen, Thorkild, *The Treasures of Darkness* (New Haven: Yale, 1976)

Kaiser, Otto, *Isaiah 1–12* (Philadelphia: Westminster. 1974)

Kramer, Samuel N., *The Sumerians: Their History, Culture, and Character* (Chicago: University of Chicago, 1963)

Kraus, Hans Joachim, *Psalmen* (Neukirchen: Neukirchener Verlag, 1961)

Kugel, J. L., "David the Prophet" in Kugel, ed., *Poetry and Prophecy* (Ithaca, N.Y.: Cornell, 1990), 45–55

Kugel, J. L., " 'The Bible as Literature' in Late Antiquity and the Middle Ages," *HSL: Hebrew University Studies in Literature* 11 (1983), 20–70

Kugel, J. L., "Adverbial Kî Tôb," *Journal of Biblical Literature* 99 (1980), 433–36

Kugel, J. L., "Ecclesiastes," "Poetry, Biblical" and "Psalms," *Harper's Bible Dictionary* (Harper and Row, 1985), 236–37; 804–06; 833–35.

Kugel, J. L., "On the Bible and Literary Criticism," *Prooftexts* 1 (1982), 217–36; discussion, *Prooftexts* 3 (1983), 323–32

Kugel, J. L., "Poets and Prophets," in Kugel, ed., *Poetry and Prophecy* (Ithica, N.Y.: Cornell, 1990), 1–25

Kugel, J. L., "Qohelet and Money," *Catholic Bible Quarterly* 51 (1989) 32–49.

Kugel, J. L., "The Psalms and Wisdom," *Harper Bible Commentary* (San Francisco: Harper and Row, 1989), 396–406

Kugel, J. L., "Topics in the History of the Spirituality of the Psalms," in A. Green, ed., *The History of Jewish Spirituality* (Seabury-Winston, 1986), 113–44

Kugel, J. L., *In Potiphar's House* (Cambridge: Harvard, 1994)

Kugel, J. L., *The Idea of Biblical Poetry* (New Haven: Yale, 1981; second edition, Baltimore: Johns Hopkins, 1998)

Kugel, J. L., *Traditions of the Bible: A Guide to the Bible As It Was at the Start of the Common Era* (Cambridge: Harvard, 1998)

Levenson, Jon D., *Creation and the Persistence of Evil* (San Francisco: Harper and Row, 1988)

Levenson, Jon D., *Sinai and Zion* (Minneapolis: Winston, 1985)

Lichtheim, Miriam, *Late Egyptian Wisdom Literature in the International Context* (Göttingen: Vandenhoeck und Ruprecht, 1983)

Lieberman, Saul, "Appendix," in Gershom Scholem, *Jewish Gnosticism, Merkabah Mysticism, and Talmudic Tradition* (New York: Jewish Theological Seminary, 1965)

Linders, Barnabas, *Judges 1–5* (Edinburgh: T&T Clark, 1995)

Loretz, Oswald, *Die Königspsalmen* (Muenster: Ugarit-Verlag, 1988)

Loretz, Oswald, *Kanaanische El- und Baaltraditionen in judischer Sicht* (Altenberge: CIS Verlag, 1984)

Lowth, Robert, *De Sacra Poesi Hebraeorum* (Oxford: Clarendon, 1763)

Margalit, B., "Observations on the Jael-Sisera Story," in D. P. Wright et al., *Poemgranates and Golden Bells* (Einona Lake, Ind.: Eisenbrauns, 1995), 629–641

Margulies, B., "The Canaanite Origin of Psalm 29 Reconsidered," *Biblica* 51 (1970) 332–46

Mays, James L., *Amos: A Commentary* (London: S.C.M. Press, 1969)

McCarter, P. Kyle, *II Samuel* (Anchor Bible) (Garden City: Doubleday-Anchor, 1984)

Meiri, Menahem b. Solomon, *Commentary on the Book of Psalms*, ed., Yosef b. Hayyim ha-Koihen (Jerusalem, 1936)

Mettinger, Tryggve N. D., *The Dethronement of Sabaoth: Studies in the Shem and Kabod Theologies* (Lund: Gleerup, 1982)

Mettinger, Tryggve, *No Graven Image? Israelite Aniconism in its Ancient Near Eastern Context* (Stockholm: Almqvist & Wiksell, 1995)

Miller, Patrick D., *Ancient Israelite Religion* (Philadelphia: Fortress, 1987)

Miller, Patrick D., *Interpreting the Psalms* (Philadelphia: Fortress, 1986)

Miller, Patrick D., *Sin and Judgment in the Prophets* (Chico, Cal.: Scholars, 1982)

Mowinckel, Sigmund, *The Psalms in Israel's Worship* (Sheffield, England: JSOT Press, 1992)

Nasuti, Harry, *Tradition History and the Psalms of Asaph* (Atlanta: Scholars, 1988)

Nicholson, E. W., *Preaching to the Exiles* (Oxford: Blackwell, 1970)

O'Connor, Kathleen, *The Confessions of Jeremiah* (Chico, Cal.: Scholars, 1985)

O'Connor, Michael, *Hebrew Verse Structure* (Winona Lake, Ind.: Eisenbrauns, 1980)

Oesterley, W. O. E., *The Psalms* (New York: Macmillan, 1939)

Oppenheim, A. L., *Ancient Mesopotamia: Portrait of a Dead Civilization* (Chicago: University of Chicago, 1964)

Pagis, D., *A Secret Sealed: Hebrew Baroque Emblem-Riddles from Italy and Holland*, (Jerusalem: Magnes, 1986)

Paul, Shalom, *Amos* (Minneapolis: Fortress, 1991)

Perdue, Leo G., *Wisdom and Cult* (Missoula: Scholars, 1977)

Pope, Marvin H., *Job* (AB) (Garden City, N.Y.: Doubleday-Anchor, 1973)

Pope, Marvin H., *The Song of Songs: A New Translation* (Anchor Bible), (Garden City, N.Y.: Doubleday-Anchor, 1977)

Rad, Gerhard von, *Wisdom in Israel* (New York: Abingdon, 1973)

Rendsberg, Gary, *Linguistic Evidence for the Northern Origin of Selected Psalms* (Atlanta: Scholars, 1990)

Saggs, H. W. F., *Civilization Before Greece and Rome* (London: Batsford, 1989)

Schechter, Solomon, "The Riddles of Solomon in Rabbinic Literature," *Folk-Lore I* (London, 1890) 349–358

Seybold, Klaus, *Die Psalmen* (Tübingen: Mohr, 1996)

Simon, Uriel, *Four Approaches to the Book of Psalms* (Albany: SUNY Press, 1991)

Simpson, William Kelly, *The Literature of Ancient Egypt* (New Haven: Yale, 1973)

Smith, M. S., "'Seeing God' in the Psalms: the Background to the Beatific Vision in the Hebrew Bible," *Catholic Bible Quarterly* 50 (1988), 171–183

Tur-Sinai (Torczyner), N. H., *Job* (Jerusalem: Kiryat Sefer, 1957)

Ullendorff, E., "The Meaning of QHLT," VT 12 (1962), 215

Wegner, Paul D., *An Examination of Kingship and Messianic Expectation in Isaiah 1–35* (Lewiston, N.Y.: Mellen, 1992)

Weinfeld, Moshe, *Deuteronomy and the Deuteronomic School* (Oxford: Clarendon, 1972)

Weiser, A., "Das Deborahlied," *Zeitschrift für die Alttestamentliche Wissenschaft* 71 (1959) 67–97

Weiss, Meir, "Concerning Amos' Repudiation of the Cult," in D. P. Wright et al., *Pomegranates and Golden Bells* (Winona Lake, Ind.: Eisenbrauns, 1995), 199–214

Westermann, Claus, *Praise and Lament in the Psalms* (Atlanta: John Knox, 1981)

Wildberger, Hans, *Isaiah 1–12: A Commentary* (Minneapolis: Fortress, 1991)

Würthwein, E. "Amos 5:21–27" *Theologische Literaturzeitung* 72 (1947), 150

Yee, Gale A. (ed.), *Judges and Method: New Approaches to Biblical Studies* (Minneapolis: Fortress, 1995)

SCRIPTURAL INDEX

ABOUT THE AUTHOR

JAMES L. KUGEL, Starr Professor of Hebrew at Harvard from 1982 to 2003, now lives in Jerusalem. A specialist in the Hebrew Bible and its interpretation, he is the author of *The God of Old, The Bible As It Was, On Being a Jew,* and *How to Read the Bible.* His course on the Bible was regularly one of the two most popular at Harvard, enrolling more than nine hundred students.

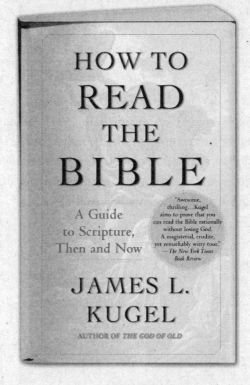